PRINCIP̶ ̶̶CY

Agency is a pervasive institution, fundamental to commercial activity, inherent to legal personality, enabling against deteriorating capacity. This new work provides a fresh, succinct examination of the principles of agency law exploring the rules of attribution, the rights and obligations arising within the agency relationship, the impact of agency in the fields of contract and tort, and the termination of an agent's authority. Throughout the book, full consideration is given to the issues arising under the Commercial Agents (Council Directive) Regulations 1993. The discussion is informed not only by common law authority that constantly nourishes the development of agency law principle, but also by international soft law instruments and the Restatement of the Law, Third: Agency.

ONE WEEK LOAN

This book is due for return on or before the last date shown below.

Principles of the Law of Agency

Howard Bennett

·H A R T·
PUBLISHING
OXFORD AND PORTLAND, OREGON
2013

Published in the United Kingdom by Hart Publishing Ltd
16C Worcester Place, Oxford, OX1 2JW
Telephone: +44 (0)1865 517530
Fax: +44 (0)1865 510710
E-mail: mail@hartpub.co.uk
Website: http://www.hartpub.co.uk

Published in North America (US and Canada) by
Hart Publishing
c/o International Specialized Book Services
920 NE 58th Avenue, Suite 300
Portland, OR 97213-3786
USA
Tel: +1 503 287 3093 or toll-free: (1) 800 944 6190
Fax: +1 503 280 8832
E-mail: orders@isbs.com
Website: http://www.isbs.com

British Library Cataloguing in Publication Data
Data Available

ISBN: 978-1-84113-885-5

Typeset by Hope Services, Abingdon
Printed and bound in Great Britain by
TJ International Ltd, Padstow, Cornwall

PREFACE

Agency is a ubiquitous and flexible institution, one that is both fundamental to commerce and socially supportive. Commercial intermediaries include lead banks in syndicated loans, insurance brokers, masters of ships, and auctioneers. Agency, moreover, supplies the lifeblood of legal personality. Socially, agency is notable in supporting a measure of individual autonomy, notwithstanding the loss of personal capacity to manage one's own affairs. This book aims to offer a fresh and accessible analysis of the principles of agency law that is succinct, yet rigorous and critical. Consideration is given throughout to both the common law and the special legislative regime governing 'commercial agents'.

I have naturally incurred a number of debts in the writing of this book. Francis Reynolds encouraged me to undertake this project, and anyone researching agency law can only benefit, in particular, from the scholarship on each side of the Atlantic accumulated through successive editions of *Bowstead and Reynolds on Agency* (currently in its 19th edition, under the editorship of Peter Watts and Francis Reynolds) and embodied in the Restatement of the Law, Third: Agency. I am also grateful to my colleagues Helen Millgate, Craig Rotherham and Sanam Saidova for comments on individual chapters. Responsibility for errors and omissions of course remains mine.

My greatest debts, inevitably, are to my family. My children, Sonia and Adam, remain puzzled as to how agency law can take precedence over far more interesting matters such as netball, cricket, cluedo, and chess. I should like to dedicate the book, however, to my wife Fouzia, who makes it all worthwhile.

I have endeavoured to state the law as on April Fool's Day, 2013.

Howard Bennett
Nottingham
April 2013

CONTENTS

TABLE OF CASES

Australia

Canada

European Court of Justice

Alphabetical order

TABLE OF LEGISLATION

International Instruments

1

Agency: A Flexible Institution

Introduction

1.1 There are several reasons why one person (the 'principal') may elect to deal with another (the 'third party') not directly but rather through an intermediary (the 'agent'). Agents may be employed for their professional expertise, for their ability to access, penetrate and develop markets, to bridge geographical remoteness between principal and third party, to enable the principal to devote time elsewhere, to conceal the principal's interest in a particular transaction, or to carry through the principal's wishes or otherwise act on behalf of the principal when the principal has lost capacity to act personally. An agent will usually be invited by the principal to intervene on the principal's behalf, but the agent may overstep the boundaries of the principal's authorisation. Occasionally, an agent may intervene without invitation by the principal. The law of agency is concerned with the legal incidents of any intervention by an agent on behalf of a principal. Potentially, three legal relationships may arise: between the principal and the agent, between the principal and the third party, and between the agent and the third party.

1.2 In the civil law tradition, a distinction is drawn, at least in legal scholarship, between the 'internal' and 'external' aspects of agency. The former corresponds to the principal–agent relationship, while the latter embraces the relationships of the third party with the principal on the one hand and the agent on the other. Although lacking formal recognition in the common law, this distinction can enhance clarity of discussion.

1.3 The focus of this book is the English law of agency. However, agency is addressed by three academic, international soft law instruments. The treatment of agency in the Principles of European Contract Law[1] and the Unidroit Principles of International Commercial Contracts (2004)[2] is confined to the external aspect, while the Principles, Definitions and Model Rules of European Private Law[3] cover

---

[1] 'European Principles', or 'PECL'.

[2] 'Unidroit Principles', or 'PICC'. The treatment of agency in the Unidroit Principles is based on the 1983 Geneva Convention on Agency in the International Sale of Goods. The Convention itself is unlikely ever to come into force, and its principal legacy is likely to be its impact on the Unidroit Principles.

[3] More commonly known, and referred to in this book, as the Draft Common Frame of Reference ('Draft CFR' or 'DCFR').

both, but distinguish between, the internal and external aspects.[4] These instruments do not constitute binding law. The drafters of soft law instruments, however, are not constrained by established concepts or principles of any national law, nor are they constrained in the manner of the common law by the accident of which issues are presented in litigation for resolution. Such instruments can, therefore, offer a coherent and comprehensive set of principles as a source of comparison for existing national law and as possible suggestions for the resolution of issues yet to be addressed. Moreover, the comparative work underpinning them serves to elucidate the values, assumptions, and techniques of existing national laws, and the resulting formulations of principle may facilitate the further development of transnational law, whether of an academic nature or formally adopted by a politically legitimate body.[5]

1.4   Reference will also be made to the Restatement of the Law Third, Agency,[6] prepared by the American Law Institute. A Restatement is a treatise or model law, designed to address uncertainty and complexity in the law in the United States of America by restating an area of the common law in the form of a series of principles. A Restatement is not a primary source of law in any of the jurisdictions within the United States, but is considered highly persuasive.[7]

Definition; a Variable Nexus of Relationships

1.5   Agency is a legal institution triggered by a manifestation on the part of the principal of willingness for its legal relations with third parties to be affected as a matter of right or power by the intervention of an intermediary (the agent), and that encompasses the relationship (characteristically fiduciary[8]) between principal and agent; the rights and obligations, whether reciprocal or unilateral, between principal and third party arising from the agent's intervention; and likewise the rights and obligations, whether reciprocal or unilateral, between agent and third party, arising from the agent's intervention.

---

[4] DCFR, Book II, ch 6: Representation, and Book IV, pt D: Mandate Contracts address, and are confined to, respectively the external and internal aspects.

[5] See generally, N Jansen and R Zimmermann, '"A European Civil Code in all but Name": Discussing the Nature and Purposes of the Draft Common Frame of Reference' (2010) 69 *Cambridge Law Journal* 98.

[6] 'Restatement'. Restatements have been prepared in three series. Agency was one of the first subjects addressed in the original Restatement of the Law, prepared between 1923 and 1944. Work on agency commenced in 1923 and was completed in 1933. A revised version was prepared for Restatement Second, appearing in 1958. Restatement of the Law Third, Agency (Professor DA DeMott acting as Reporter) was commenced in 1995 and published in 2006.

[7] For a critical commentary on the Unidroit Principles in comparison with the Restatement, see T Krebbs, 'Harmonization and How Not To Do It: Agency in the UNIDROIT Principles of International Commercial Contracts 2004' [2009] *Lloyd's Maritime and Commercial Law Quarterly* 57.

[8] Restatement, § 1.01. See further below, para 1.12.

1.6   The paradigmatic example of agency is perhaps of a principal that wishes to enter into a transaction and authorises an agent to identify a potential counter-party, conduct negotiations, and conclude the contract. All three relationships within the agency triangle are engaged. The terms within and on which the agent is to act on behalf of the principal belong to the relationship between principal and agent. In particular, the agent is authorised to effect legal relations, within certain parameters, between the principal and third party. Any resulting contract, however, will generally take effect as between principal and third party. Sometimes, the agent will also be liable and entitled to sue on the contract. Moreover, an agent that acts beyond the scope of its authority may incur liability to the third party.

1.7   Some forms of agency, however, stray far from the paradigm.[9] The role of a 'canvassing agent' is confined to identifying a potential third party and effecting an introduction to the principal. In such a case, the internal aspect of agency exists, but any contract between principal and third party is concluded by direct agreement between them and is not attributable to agency at all; any potential agency relationship between principal and third party is limited to non-contractual matters. For example, a false representation by a canvassing agent could engage the principal's liability in tort. A prime example of a canvassing agent is the estate agent.

1.8   A 'commission agent',[10] in contrast, is engaged on terms that it will conclude a contract with the third party in its own right. The sole agency relationship is again between principal and agent. The agent has no authority to act on behalf of the principal in its dealings with the third party and, therefore, no authority to create privity of contract between principal and third party. In that context, the agent acts pursuant to its authorisation, but it acts in its own right as principal, and the counterparty to the third party on the resulting contract is the agent alone.[11] For example, a confirming house may be retained as an agent for an overseas client to purchase goods in the local market on its own account.[12]

Disclosed and Undisclosed Agency

1.9   A further variant arises out of the fact that agency may be either disclosed or undisclosed. Agency is disclosed where the third party is aware that the

---

[9]   On difficulties that follow from identifying agency with what is but the paradigm, see F Reynolds, 'Agency: Theory and Practice' (1978) 94 *Law Quarterly Review* 655.

[10]   The name derives from the French 'commissionnaire': French Code de Commerce, art 94.

[11]   *Teheran-Europe Co Ltd v ST Belton (Tractors) Ltd* [1968] 2 QB 53, 60. See further below, para 9.4.

[12]   *Rusholme & Bolton & Roberts Hadfield Ltd v SG Read & Co (London) Ltd* [1955] 1 WLR 146. See also *Scottish & Newcastle International Ltd v Othon Ghalanos Ltd* [2008] UKHL 11, [2008] 1 Lloyd's Rep 462, [45] (seller contracting with carrier as agent in relation to the buyer but possibly as principal in relation to the carrier).

counterparty with which it is dealing is acting as agent for another party, even if that party is unidentified. There is, however, no requirement for the agent's role as agent to be known to the third party at the time of conclusion of any contract. The third party may contract in the belief that its counterparty is contracting on its own behalf when in truth it is acting as an agent on behalf of another entity, its principal. The legitimacy of such undisclosed agency is readily accepted by English law (but not by national civil law systems,[13] nor by the Unidroit Principles[14] or the Draft CFR[15]), and in English law an undisclosed principal may, subject to certain limitations, both sue and be sued on the contract.

Authority, Consent, and Power: Principles of Attribution

1.10   As between principal and agent, agency is generally characterised by a conferral of authority by the principal on the agent, with each party consenting to the agency relationship. Authority in this sense, known as 'actual authority', is the right to act on behalf of the principal and to affect the principal's legal position within the terms of the act of conferral.[16] For actual authority to be conferred, there must be a manifestation of the voluntary grant of authority by the principal to the agent, and the agent must manifest its consent to assume the role of agent within the terms of the grant of authority.[17] It is not, however, necessary that the principal and agent recognise or acknowledge their relationship to be one of agency: 'they will be held to have consented if they have agreed to what amounts in law to such a relationship even if they do not recognise it themselves and even if they have professed to disclaim it.'[18]

1.11   While actual authority is a product of the relationship between principal and agent, it is fully effective in the relationship between principal and third party. The power to bind the principal conferred by actual authority derives purely from the principal's consent; it does not depend upon external appearance in the eyes of the third party. Thus, an undisclosed principal is bound by acts of an agent within its actual authority.

---

[13] See DCFR, art II-6:106, Notes IV.

[14] PICC, art 2.2.4.

[15] DCFR, art II-6:106. The European Principles largely assimilate undisclosed agency to commission agency under the concept of indirect representation: see below, para 9.4.

[16] For discussion of actual authority, see below, ch 3.

[17] *Garnac Grain Co Inc v Faure (HMF) & Fairclough Ltd* [1968] AC 1130, 1137. The New York case of *Ruggles v American Central Insurance Co of St Louis* 114 NY 415 (1889) (agent acting within scope of extension of authority sent by principal but not yet received by agent) suggests that consent of the agent is unnecessary, but (a) the case was decided primarily on the scope of apparent authority and only in the alternative on the basis of actual authority, and (b) the actual authority holding is rejected by the Restatement: see § 1.01. See also § 3.01.

[18] *Garnac Grain Co Inc v Faure (HMF) & Fairclough Ltd* [1968] AC 1130, 1137 (Lord Pearson).

1.12   The agent's consent may be implicit in the agent's simply proceeding to act as authorised, but further evidence would be required were the act in question susceptible of attribution to a legitimate interest of the alleged agent acting on its own behalf.[19] Consent is also important since consent to act on behalf of the principal and acceptance of the principal's trust with respect to the authority conferred creates a relationship characterised by the law as fiduciary, resulting in the imposition on the agent of significant and strict equitable obligations ensuring that the agent acts loyally and in the best interests of the principal.[20]

1.13   Actual authority does not exhaust the agent's power to bind the principal. An agent may act without actual authority but in circumstances where the agent appears to the third party to be held out by the principal as having authority. For example, a principal may appoint an agent to a position that is widely understood as carrying certain authority but deny the agent some of the authority usually attendant upon that position. The agent may subsequently purport to exercise authority that an agent in its position usually would possess but that, unknown to the third party, has in fact been denied. In such circumstances, the agent may have acted in breach of its relationship with the principal, but that does not prevent the agent's acts from impacting upon relations as between principal and third party. The phrase 'apparent authority' denotes, therefore, not a right based on consent but a power (based in English law on estoppel) to affect the principal's legal relations with third parties.[21]

1.14   Where an agent purports to act on behalf of a principal but in truth without actual authority, the principal may subsequently ratify the unauthorised act. Ratification takes effect retrospectively so that, for most purposes at least, the agent's act is treated as if it had been genuinely authorised in advance. Thus, ratification of the unauthorised conclusion of a contract creates a contract binding on both principal and third party not from the time of ratification but from the time when the agent purported to conclude it on behalf of the principal with the third party. Where the purported act of representation is performed by someone who is not in fact an agent of the principal at all, the effect of ratification is both to validate the act as between principal and third party and to create a relationship of agency as between principal and purported agent.[22]

1.15   The estoppel basis of apparent authority in English law means that while the third party can invoke against the principal acts falling outside the agent's actual authority but within the agent's apparent authority, ratification is required for the principal to invoke such acts against the third party. Ratification, however, extends to all acts outside an agent's actual authority and not only those within the agent's apparent authority.

[19]   *Kennedy v de Trafford* [1897] AC 180.
[20]   For discussion of fiduciary obligations, see below, para 6.15 et seq.
[21]   For discussion of apparent authority, see below, ch 4.
[22]   For discussion of ratification, see below, ch 5.

1.16   Actual authority, apparent authority and ratification constitute general 'principles of attribution', whereby the principal's legal position is affected by the acts of its agent. Precisely what the consequences are is determined not by the law of agency but by the relevant area of law applicable to the agent's acts. The general attribution principles of agency law may, however, be displaced or supplemented to a greater or lesser extent. Thus, tortious liability in respect of the act of an agent depends largely upon the doctrine of vicarious liability[23] and, in appropriate circumstances, an estoppel may supplement the doctrines of apparent authority and ratification.[24]

Agency and Contract

1.17   While the conferral of actual authority imports a relationship of principal and agent that is consensual, conceptually it need not be contractual. Agency can, for example, be gratuitous.[25] It is nevertheless undeniable that, in the commercial context at least, the vast majority of principal and agent relationships are clothed in and elaborated by a contract. The existence of a contract obviously confers a contractual nature on the performance obligations undertaken by principal and agent, rendering breach amenable to sanction according to the remedies of contract law.[26] The mere existence of a contract does not, however, of itself displace the rights and obligations arising from the principal and agent relationship,[27] albeit that the contract may, by appropriate wording, modify or exclude particular rights or obligations. In *Yasuda v Orion*,[28] the authority of an underwriting agent to conclude new insurance contracts was terminated, but authority was conferred by contract to manage the run-off of matters arising under risks already written. The contract contained an obligation on the agent to maintain and make available to the principal records relating to the insurances underwritten. The authority to manage the run-off was subsequently revoked by the principal, and the contract was discharged by acceptance of repudiatory breach.[29] The issue was whether the agent remained under an obligation to disclose records to the principal. The agent argued that the obligation in respect of records was discharged

---

[23] Discussed below, para 10.9 et seq.

[24] See below, paras 4.32–4.38, 5.20.

[25] Moreover, that an agent lacks contractual capacity does not affect the validity of the agency: *Norwich & Peterborough Building Society v Steed* [1993] Ch 116, 128.

[26] As distinct from an agent's fiduciary obligations that attract different remedies for breach: see below, ch 6.

[27] *Temple Legal Protection Ltd v QBE Insurance (Europe) Ltd* [2009] EWCA Civ 453, [2009] 1 CLC 553, [26].

[28] *Yasuda Fire & Marine Insurance Co of Europe Ltd v Orion Marine Insurance Underwriting Agency Ltd* [1995] QB 174.

[29] Both principal and agent purported to accept the repudiatory breach of the other. For the purposes of the litigation, it did not matter which was correct.

along with the other primary contractual obligations. The argument failed. That an agent is entrusted with authority to affect the principal's relations with third parties engenders an obligation on the agent to provide the principal with a full and accurate account of the principal's rights and obligations arising out of the exercise by the agent of its authority. Moreover, the termination of authority to act for the future did not affect the obligation to provide an account of what had been done in the past.[30] That obligation was not subsumed into the contract, but continued as part of the agency relationship independently of the contract, the wording of which was fully consistent with its continuance.

Attribution and Legal Personality

1.18 For a natural person, the application of principles of attribution results from a choice to act through another, rather than directly in person. However demanding the realities, on a formal level at least employment of an intermediary is never compulsory. Rules of attribution are, however, inherent to legal personality. Devoid of a mind to formulate intention, make decisions, or possess knowledge and of a physical body with which to speak and act, a legal person is obliged to claim the benefit of the minds and bodies of others through rules of attribution.

1.19 With respect to corporations, as explained by Lord Hoffmann in *Meridian Global Funds Management Asia Ltd v Securities Commission*,[31] rules of attribution operate on three levels. Primary rules form part of the company's constitution, expressed in the company's articles of association (for example, empowering the board of directors to act managerially as the company) or implied by company law. Such rules, however, are too formalistic and cumbersome for the pursuit of a company's everyday activities. Accordingly, a company can employ the primary rules to appoint agents through whom it can act by virtue of the principles of general agency law, either directly through those agents' interactions with third parties or indirectly through the appointing by those agents of further agents.

1.20 Exceptionally, however, the relevant rule of law will preclude resort to general agency law. Notably, rules of criminal law may require proof of the commission of an act or possession of a state of mind by the accused personally and not vicariously. In such a case, unless the rule is simply inapplicable to legal persons or unless guilt can be engaged only through the primary attribution rules, it will be necessary to 'fashion a dedicated rule of attribution for the particular substantive

---

[30] It was also held that failure of the contractual obligation to provide records to survive discharge of the contract would frustrate the purpose of the obligation. The obligation was ancillary to the principal primary obligations under the contract and survived their discharge in the same manner as an arbitration clause.

[31] *Meridian Global Funds Management Asia Ltd v Securities Commission* [1995] 2 AC 500, 506–11.

rule'.[32] This involves interpretation of the rule in question so as to determine which person or persons should be considered as constituting the company for the purposes of the rule. In this context, such persons are not agents of the company acting on its behalf, but rather are identified with, and act as, the company.

1.21 Where the substantive rule, on its true interpretation, requires the intervention of a person with sweeping managerial authority enjoying broad, unfettered discretion and autonomy of action, it is often said that the search is for the 'directing mind and will' of the company.[33] The rule may, however, look for a more specific mandate. Thus, where the question is whether a shipowner knew of the unseaworthiness of an insured vessel when it put to sea,[34] the focus is on 'the decision-making processes required for sending the [insured vessel] to sea'.[35] Again, where for the purposes of the criminal law the issue is a company's knowledge of the age of a customer in one of its shops, the relevant knowledge is that of the person who served the customer, however junior an employee within the company's hierarchy.[36]

Attribution and Context

1.22 Context is the essence of the specific attribution rules, just referred to, that legal personality may require. Further adaptation of the extent and operation of rules of attribution may, however, be required by the transactional context. A clear example is provided by fidelity insurance, which affords employers cover against fraud and theft by employees. Application of rules of attribution ignoring the transactional context would often attribute to the employer defalcations that form the basis of claims, frustrating the purpose of the transaction: the employer's claim would be in respect of its own wilful misconduct, which is irrecoverable as a matter of public policy. The commercial context requires, therefore, that the rules of attribution must be modified as a matter of interpretation of the policy to exclude attribution of the defaulting employee's acts.

1.23 Contextual adaptation is often manifest with respect to imputation of an agent's knowledge of facts. In the commercial insurance markets, for example, insurers are asked to underwrite significant risks and are expected to make their underwriting decisions regarding whether to accept any proposed risk and, if so,

---

[32] ibid 507 (Lord Hoffmann).
[33] The phrase is that of Viscount Haldane LC in *Lennard's Carrying Co Ltd v Asiatic Petroleum Co Ltd* [1915] AC 705, 713.
[34] An insurer is not liable for loss attributable to such unseaworthiness: Marine Insurance Act 1906, s 39(5).
[35] *Manifest Shipping & Co Ltd v Uni-Polaris Insurance Co Ltd (The Star Sea)* [1997] 1 Lloyd's Rep 360, 375 (Leggatt LJ).
[36] *Tesco Stores Ltd v Brent London Borough Council* [1993] 1 WLR 1037.

on what terms and at what premium relatively quickly and without the benefit of the usual investigative process of due diligence that accompanies major acquisition and investment decisions.[37] The assured, conversely, is generally possessed of significant information regarding the risk, or is at least in a good position to access such information. In response, commercial insurance law entitles the insurer to a fair presentation of the risk,[38] including, notably, voluntary disclosure of all material circumstances about the risk known to the assured.[39] Non-disclosure of a material circumstance knowledge of which would have caused the insurer either to decline the risk entirely or to accept it on different terms renders the insurance voidable.[40] In this context, the concept of knowledge of the assured attracts particular principles of attribution and equivalent effect.[41]

1.24   First, a corporate assured requires identification, in accordance with the principles outlined above, of those natural persons among the assured's servants and agents whose knowledge constitutes the assured's knowledge for this purpose.

1.25   Secondly, the assured's disclosure obligation extends beyond the assured's actual knowledge to include a measure of constructive knowledge:[42] the assured is deemed to know all circumstances that it ought to know in the ordinary course of business, but this extends not to all circumstances that a reasonable person in the position of the assured ought to know but only to those circumstances that the assured ought to know in the ordinary course of carrying on its business in the manner in which it happens to carry on that business. The commercial context dictates that the risk of the business being run inefficiently is borne by the insurer: 'to hold otherwise would be tantamount to saying that underwriters only insure those who conduct their business prudently, whereas it is a commonplace that one of the purposes of insurance is to obtain cover against the consequences of negligence in the management of the assured's affairs'.[43] Put another way, a prospective assured owes no duty to an insurer to conduct its business in such a way as proactively to maximise its knowledge and minimise the risk assumed by the insurer.[44]

---

[37] *North Star Shipping Ltd v Sphere Drake Insurance plc (No 2)* [2005] EWHC 665 (Comm), [2005] 2 Lloyd's Rep 76, [256].

[38] *Container Transport International Inc v Oceanus Mutual Underwriting Association (Bermuda) Ltd* [1984] 1 Lloyd's Rep 476, 496–97.

[39] Marine Insurance Act 1906, s 18(1). The 1906 Act codifies for the purposes of marine insurance contracts many principles of general insurance contract law. However, the insurer's disclosure entitlement was abolished for consumer insurance contracts by the Consumer Insurance (Disclosure and Representations) Act 2012. For the definition of consumer insurance, see ibid, s 1.

[40] For the requirement of such inducement, see *Pan Atlantic Insurance Co Ltd v Pine Top Insurance Co Ltd* [1995] 1 AC 501. For the meaning of inducement, see *Assicurazioni Generali SpA v Arab Insurance Group (BSC)* [2002] EWCA Civ 1642, [2003] Lloyd's Rep IR 131, [62].

[41] *Simner v New India Assurance Co Ltd* [1995] LRLR 240, 253–55.

[42] Marine Insurance Act 1906, s 18(1).

[43] M Mustill and J Gilman (eds), *Arnould's Law of Marine Insurance and Average*, 16th edn (London, Stevens & Sons, 1981), para 640, derived from *Australia & New Zealand Bank v Colonial & Eagle Wharves Ltd* [1960] 2 Lloyd's Rep 241, 252, and cited in *Simner v New India Assurance Co Ltd* [1995] LRLR 240, 255.

[44] *Simner v New India Assurance Co Ltd* [1995] LRLR 240, 253.

In this context, constructive knowledge includes, notably, the knowledge of an agent to whom the assured has entrusted immediate managerial responsibility for and control of an insured asset (termed an 'agent to know'), such as the master of a ship, on the basis that an insurer is entitled to contract, and does contract, in reliance on the due performance by agents to know of their duty to keep the principal properly informed of all material circumstances affecting the relevant asset.[45] A failure by an agent to know to relay material information to the principal consequently places the principal in breach of its disclosure obligations.[46]

1.26   Thirdly, in the London commercial insurance market, insurance is placed through an insurance broker that acts as the assured's agent. Non-disclosure by such an 'agent to insure' of material circumstances within its knowledge again renders the insurance voidable at the insurer's option.[47] Tantamount to attribution of the agent's knowledge to the principal, the case law affirms rather a duty owed personally by the broker to the insurer.[48]

1.27   Attribution of knowledge reflecting an agent's duty to communicate information to the principal, whether in the insurance context or otherwise, does not extend to matters that the agent in reality would seek to conceal from the principal, notably the commission of a fraud against the principal.[49] Sometimes analysed as a discrete principle of non-attribution,[50] it is better considered as an extrapolation from the particular context and an implicit restriction on the applicable scope of attribution.[51]

Remuneration

1.28   Agents are typically remunerated by commission, namely a sum of money that varies according to the volume and the value of the transactions attributable to the agent's fulfilment of its contractual duties. It is, nevertheless, an exaggeration to

---

[45] *Proudfoot v Montefiore* (1867) LR 2 QB 511, 521–22; *Blackburn, Low & Co v Vigors* (1887) LR 12 App Cas 531, 540; *Simner v New India Assurance Co Ltd* [1995] LRLR 240, 254–55. Although rejected in *El Ajou v Dollar Land Holdings plc* [1994] BCC 143, 157, a duty to inform as a basis of attribution of knowledge retains the support of a significant body of case law, and a proposed alternative (ibid, 156–57) has attracted criticism: P Watts and F Reynolds, *Bowstead & Reynolds on Agency,* 19th edn (London, Sweet & Maxwell, 2010), para 8-211.

[46] *Gladstone v King* (1813) 1 M & S 35; *Proudfoot v Montefiore* (1867) LR 2 QB 511.

[47] Marine Insurance Act 1906, s 19(a).

[48] *Blackburn, Low & Co v Vigors* (1886) 17 QBD 553, 559, (1887) LR 12 App Cas 531, 541, 542–43; *Société Anonyme d'Intermediaries Luxembourgeois v Farex Gie* [1994] CLC 1094, 1101–02; *PCW Syndicates v PCW Reinsurers* [1996] 1 Lloyd's Rep 241, 255.

[49] *PCW Syndicates v PCW Reinsurers* [1996] 1 Lloyd's Rep 241; *Group Josi Re v Walbrook Insurance Co Ltd* [1996] 1 Lloyd's Rep 345. It is not, however, confined to fraud: *Kingscroft v Nissan Fire & Marine Insurance Co* (Comm Ct, 4 March 1996).

[50] Often referred to as the rule in *Re Hampshire Land Co Ltd* [1891] 2 Ch 743.

[51] As in *PCW Syndicates v PCW Reinsurers* [1996] 1 Lloyd's Rep 241, 254–55.

describe commission as 'one of the fundamental indicia of agency'.[52] Agents may instead be remunerated in other ways. Some will charge professional fees on a time basis or as a lump sum for specified work. Alternatively, an agent may be retained to sell goods on a mark-up basis. The agent negotiates a contract of sale between the principal and a third party and receives whatever price the agent can negotiate in excess of an agreed figure,[53] although, in the absence of documentary evidence to the contrary, the freedom so to negotiate price with third parties to the advantage of the intermediary constitutes cogent evidence of the absence of agency.[54] In a not dissimilar vein, insurance brokers in the London market act for their clients, the assureds, on the basis that they receive such commission[55] as they can negotiate with the insurers in the form of a percentage of the premium to be paid under the insurance placed by the brokers. Finally, remuneration on a profit-sharing basis is not inconsistent with a principal–agent relationship.[56]

Intermediaries as Agents or Principals: Optional Relationship Structures

1.29 The use of an intermediary may present a choice between different relationship structures, not all of which will necessarily involve agency. In the context of the supply of goods, any one of four legal analyses of the ensuing transaction(s) is possible depending on the arrangement between intermediary and client.[57] Assume the client is a purchaser. First, the intermediary may purchase and re-sell, acting in each contract on its own account and remunerated in the form of a mark-up: the client stipulates the price it is prepared to pay and the intermediary retains the difference between that figure and the price at which it procures the goods from the supplier. No agency relationship arises.[58] Secondly, the intermediary may act purely as a purchasing agent for its client without undertaking any liability on its own account to the seller, the resulting contract taking effect in the normal way between seller and client.[59] The intermediary is remunerated either through a traditional agent's commission or by mark-up quantified as the

---

[52] *Customs & Excise Commissioners v Paget* [1989] STC 773, 782 (Otton J).

[53] *Mercantile International Group plc v Chuan Soon Huat Industrial Group Ltd* [2002] EWCA Civ 288, [2002] 1 All ER (Comm) 788. See also *Re Smith, ex p Bright* (1879) 10 Ch D 566.

[54] *Re Nevill, ex p White* (1871) LR 6 Ch App 397; *AMB Imballaggi Plastici SRL v Pacflex Ltd* [1999] 2 All ER (Comm) 249; *Sagal v Atelier Bunz GmbH* [2009] EWCA Civ 700.

[55] Known as 'brokerage'.

[56] *Pole v Leask* (1860) 28 Beav 562; *Associated Portland Cement Manufacturers (1910) Ltd v Ashton* [1915] 2 KB 1.

[57] D Hill, 'Confirming House Transactions in Commonwealth Countries' (1971–72) 3 *Journal of Maritime Law and Commerce* 307, 316–29.

[58] *Ireland v Livingston* (1872) LR 5 HL 395, 407; *Potter v Customs & Excise Commissioners* [1985] STC 45; *Customs & Excise Commissioners v Paget* [1989] STC 773; *AMB Imballaggi Plastici SRL v Pacflex Ltd* [1999] 2 All ER (Comm) 249.

[59] See below, para 9.6

difference between a stipulated figure and the contract price negotiated by the intermediary. In either case, the intermediary is an agent.[60] Thirdly, the intermediary may act as a purchasing agent in concluding a contract of sale on behalf of its client, while on its own account confirming the contract to the seller.[61] Fourthly, the intermediary may act as a commission agent, acting on its own account towards the seller but as agent towards its client.[62]

1.30 Various analyses are again available in the context of the supply of services.[63] The client's counterparty may undertake responsibility for their supply, even though it is not infrequently understood that the actual service supplier may be either the counterparty or a subcontractor.[64] In either case, the counterparty undertakes contractual responsibility that the services will be provided with due diligence. Consequently, if performance is subcontracted, the counterparty will incur liability for any loss occasioned by negligence on the part of the subcontractor in delivering the services.[65] Alternatively, the counterparty may intervene as the client's agent, procuring a contract for the provision of services between its client as principal and a third party service provider. In such a case, the agent's liability is confined to exercising reasonable care in selecting the third party; liability in respect of the services themselves lies solely with the third party.

1.31 An example is provided by freight forwarders, who act as procurers or providers of services in connection with the transportation of goods. Where, for example, goods are to be exported, a freight forwarder may, inter alia, arrange for the carriage of goods possibly involving different modes of transport, consolidate the goods with other consignments in order to obtain better terms of carriage, arrange for any necessary storage and handling of the goods, and obtain customs clearance. A freight forwarder may procure services from a third party as agent for its client or provide services to its client on its own account, often delivered through one or more subcontractors. Indeed, it may, within the same contract, adopt a different status for different services.[66] There is also no theoretical reason why a freight forwarder may not act as a commission agent.[67]

[60] *Mercantile International Group plc v Chuan Soon Huat Industrial Group Ltd* [2002] EWCA Civ 288, [2002] 1 All ER (Comm) 788. On the form of agents' remuneration, see above. An agreement between client and intermediary may contemplate individual transactions taking effect on different bases: *Angove Pty Ltd v Bailey* [2013] EWHC 215 (Ch), [12] (sale and purchase, or agency).

[61] In the absence of contrary intention, in this context 'confirmation' means to guarantee performance of the contract: *Sobell Industries Ltd v Cory Bros & Co Ltd* [1955] 2 Lloyd's Rep 82, 89.

[62] *Ireland v Livingston* (1874) LR 5 HL 395, 408–09, 416; *Cassaboglou v Gibb* (1883) 11 QBD 793.

[63] *Wong Mee Wan v Kwan Kin Travel Services Ltd* [1996] 1 WLR 38.

[64] On delegation generally, see below, para 3.12 et seq.

[65] *Riverstone Meat Co Pty Ltd v Lancashire Shipping Co Ltd (The Muncaster Castle)* [1961] AC 807; *Dow Europe v Novoklav* [1998] 1 Lloyd's Rep 306; Package Travel, Package Holidays and Package Tours Regulations 1992, reg 15.

[66] British International Freight Association Standard Trading Terms (2005 edition), cl 4(A) permits the forwarder, subject to certain exceptions, 'to procure any or all of the services as an agent or to provide those services as a principal.'

[67] For detailed discussion of the status of freight forwarders, see D Glass, *Freight Forwarding and Multimodal Transport Contracts,* 2nd edn (London, Informa, 2012), paras 2.45–2.94.

1.32 Again, in the context of certain services, often with something of a personal nature, a business may provide a structure for suppliers to contract with customers on their own account, albeit perhaps subject to controls on terms[68] (including the possibility that the business will collect payment from the client as agent for the suppliers[69]), or the suppliers may contract to provide to the business services that, contractually, the business supplies to the customers through the suppliers acting as its agents.[70]

1.33 In cases such as those just outlined, there is a choice of commercially realistic business structures. The issue is simply which structure has been chosen: there is no basis for a presumption in favour of any particular structure, and the courts will give effect to the intention of the parties in the light of relevant documentation and other relevant circumstances.[71] However, where the commercial reality is that an intermediary acts on its own account, courts will look behind agency language and give effect to the reality. In a number of cases, sellers of goods on title retention terms have sought to extend their security to the proceeds of resale by the buyer of the goods supplied or to products made by the buyer from the goods supplied, and have sought to do so without relying on a charge created by the buyer that would require registration to be enforceable in the buyer's insolvency.[72] This requires the buyer to resell or create a new product in a fiduciary capacity on behalf of the seller. Where, however, a trading company purchases goods on title retention terms for resale or for transformation into a new product that will in turn be sold, the natural inference is that it deploys its commercial acumen in reselling or manufacturing on its own account, not as agent for the seller.[73] If the buyer resold as agent for the seller, the proceeds of resale would belong to the seller. The buyer would have a claim against the seller for its agent's remuneration, but this claim would be unsecured, leaving the buyer exposed in the seller's insolvency. It is one thing to contract on terms designed to protect the seller against the buyer's insolvency, another thing entirely to agree to terms that create an insolvency risk for the buyer.[74] Reflecting the commercial implausibility

---

[68] *Kieran Mullin Ltd v Customs & Excise Commissioners* [2003] EWHC 4 (Ch), [2003] STC 274 (stylists in hairdressing salons); *Spearmint Rhino Ventures (UK) Ltd v Commissioners for HM Revenue & Customs* [2007] EWHC 613 (Ch), [2007] STC 1252; *Stringfellow Restaurants Ltd v Quashie* [2012] EWCA Civ 1735, [2013] IRLR 99 (dancers in clubs).

[69] *Yuen v Royal Hong Kong Golf Club* [1998] ICR 131; *Stringfellow Restaurants Ltd v Quashie* [2012] EWCA Civ 1735, [2013] IRLR 99.

[70] *Cronin v Commissioners of Customs & Excise* [1991] STC 333 (driving instructors).

[71] In some instances, however, legislation overrides common law contractual analysis: eg, Consumer Credit Act 1974, s 56 (deeming an independent contractor to act as an agent contrary to the common law, as to which see *Branwhite v Worcester Works Finance Ltd* [1969] 1 AC 552).

[72] Companies Act 2006, s 860(1). Registration must be effected within a period of 21 days beginning with the day after the day of creation of the charge (s 870(1)), failing which the charge is void against a liquidator, administrator or creditor of the charger company.

[73] *Pfeiffer (E) Weinkellerei-Weineinkauf GmbH v Arbuthnot Factors Ltd* [1988] 1 WLR 150, 159. See also *Ian Chisholm Textiles Ltd v Griffiths* [1994] BCC 96, 101.

[74] See also the discussion by Michael Hart QC of possible financial analyses in *Modelboard Ltd v Outer Box Ltd* [1992] BCC 945, 949–50, concluding that the only analysis that 'meets the requirements

of such an agreement, a transferred security clause has always been construed as creating a charge.[75]

Simultaneously Agent and Principal

1.34 No legal principle precludes a party from acting simultaneously within the same relationship as both agent and principal. A carrier of goods by sea may interact with a shipper both as principal in respect of the contract of carriage and as agent on behalf of another party that will perform some of the transportation services, generating contractual privity between the shipper and that party. Accordingly, the carrier as agent of stevedores may accept on their behalf the benefit of terms in the contract of carriage.[76] Alternatively, the principal carrier under a contract for the carriage of goods may have the authority of the goods owner to agree that certain transportation services will be rendered by other parties under certain conditions, binding the goods owner by the relevant terms in the agreement between the principal carrier and such other parties.[77]

of commercial reality and does not involve the implication of an elaborate system of implied contractual obligations' imports a charge.

[75] With the exception of the proceeds clause in *Aluminium Industrie Vaassen BV v Romalpa Aluminium Ltd* [1976] 1 WLR 676, a decision that generated much excitement but that has never been followed in the English courts and has, indeed, been questioned: *Tatung (UK) Ltd v Galex Telesure Ltd* (1989) 5 BCC 325, 337.

[76] *New Zealand Shipping Co Ltd v AM Satterthwaite & Co Ltd (The Eurymedon)* [1975] AC 154.

[77] *The Pioneer Container* [1994] 2 AC 324 (broad express actual authority regarding terms on which carriers could subcontract actual carriage, binding the goods owner through the doctrine of subbailment on terms); *Norfolk Southern Railway Co v Kirby*, 543 US 14 (2004) (limited implied actual authority of freight forwarder to agree actual carriage of goods subject to limitation rules).

2

Commercial Agency

2.1 January 1, 1994 saw the entry into force of the Commercial Agents (Council Directive) Regulations 1993.[1] Commercial agency, within the meaning of these regulations, is concerned with market penetration and business development.

Commercial Background

2.2 A supplier of goods or services that wishes to penetrate a new market or enhance its position within an existing market has three possible strategies. In-house initiatives may founder on a lack of expertise or understanding of the relevant market, especially in the case of a foreign market. They may also require an investment in permanent staff that is uneconomic, or involve media advertising that is simply ineffective.[2] The choice then lies between engaging a representative on an agency basis, or, if the supplier trades in goods, using a distributor. From a commercial perspective, the choice is about control over and responsibility for marketing and promotion, choice of customer, terms of supply including price, contract performance, importing and distribution logistics, and after-sales service, and about incidence of the risk of customer default. A distributor purchases goods from the supplier on its own account and resells on a mark-up, consequently enjoying considerable autonomy with respect to market development and exploitation[3] but carrying any credit risk on the resales. Agency permits the supplier to grant the agent such authority and discretion as it wishes; the supplier may retain the right to decide whether to enter into any particular contract.[4] Any resulting contracts are between the supplier and the customer, with the supplier clearly liable for performance and carrying any credit risk.

---

[1] Commercial Agents (Council Directive) Regulations 1993, SI 1993/3053, as amended by the Commercial Agents (Council Directive) Amendment Regulations 1993, SI 1993/3173 and the Commercial Agents (Council Directive) Amendment Regulations 1998, SI 1998/2868.

[2] See *Tamarind International Ltd v Eastern Natural Gas (Retail) Ltd* [2000] CLC 1397, [31].

[3] Indeed, any restrictions that the supplier sought to impose would be subject to competition law.

[4] Even in the case of commission agency, the principal may circumscribe the range of eligible third parties with whom the agent may contract.

2.3   One feature of commercial agency is that it will not only generate transactions during the currency of the agency but also create an asset in the form of the
enhanced business of enduring benefit to the principal beyond the termination of
the agency. Moreover, the increased profile of the business may result in additional
customers approaching the principal directly, rather than through the agent. On
the traditional view of the common law, however, commercial agents do not merit
special treatment. In particular, the financial rights of the agent both during and
on termination of the agency are a matter for contract. Consequently, transactions
only indirectly attributable to the agent's efforts may not qualify for remuneration.[5] On termination of the agency, moreover, the agent has no claim in respect of
ongoing enhanced business goodwill, except to the extent that the agent was able to
negotiate such a right as part of the original contract. The only legal protection
afforded a commercial agent at common law is restricted to unlawful conduct of
the principal and lies in the usual sanctions for breach of contract.

2.4   Civil law jurisdictions have adopted a different approach. A commercial
agent and its principal are considered in effect as engaged in a form of partnership
or joint venture so that the agent is entitled to a fair share of both the profits during the lifetime of their cooperation and the value of the ongoing business that
will endure beyond the termination of the cooperation. However, recognition
that commercial agents merit legal protection does not necessarily involve con-
currence in the protection to be offered. Until the 1990s, therefore, across the
European Union commercial agents received either significant, but variable,
favourable treatment in civil law jurisdictions, or no specific recognition at all in
the common law jurisdictions.

The European Directive

2.5   The disparity in treatment of commercial agents led, after an extended
drafting and consultation process,[6] to the adoption in 1986 of a Council Directive
'on the coordination of the laws of the Member States relating to self-employed
commercial agents'.[7] It is founded by way of legal basis on the right of establishment, specifically the coordination of the domestic laws of Member States in
order to facilitate self-employed persons pursuing activities throughout the
European Union, and competition law, specifically the approximation of domestic laws of Member States to advance the operation of the single market.[8]

---

[5] Because of the 'effective cause' principle: see below, para 8.6.
[6] The first proposal for a directive was submitted to the Council of Ministers by the European
Commission on 17 December 1976.
[7] Council Directive 86/653/EEC.
[8] The preamble to the Directive refers to the Treaty Establishing the European Economic Community,
arts 57 and 100. See now the Treaty on the Functioning of the European Union, Title IV, ch 2, and Title
VII.

2.6 The Directive is designed to harmonise law across the Member States. It does not, however, contemplate complete harmonisation of law. In certain important respects, the Directive affords individual Member States a choice when implementing the Directive, notably with respect to the definition of the term 'commercial agent' and with respect to the financial rights of a commercial agent on termination of the agency.[9] In other respects, the Directive is silent, so that national law must then apply.[10]

2.7 The substance of the Directive is derived largely from French and German law. However, that a concept in the Directive is inspired by national law does not mean that the Directive and implementing legislation must be interpreted and applied in accordance with the body of rules attaching to that concept in the relevant national law unless that body of rules is inconsistent with the terms of the Directive. Rather, the Directive is to be interpreted in its own right as a piece of European Union legislation.[11]

2.8 For most Member States, implementation of the Directive was required by 1 January 1990. However, on the questionable basis of the novelty of the concept of commercial agency for common law jurisdictions, the United Kingdom and Ireland were granted an extended period for implementation until 1 January 1994.[12] On that date, the Commercial Agents (Council Directive) Regulations 1993 entered into force, implementing the Directive for the territory of Great Britain.[13] They do not apply to Northern Ireland,[14] but similar implementing legislation does.[15]

2.9 Outside of the European Union, the Directive applies also to the parties to the European Economic Area.[16] Consequently, in the context of the 1993 Regulations, the phrase 'Member State' denotes not only Member States of the European Union but also the non-EC Member States that are contracting parties to the Agreement on the European Economic Area.[17]

---

[9] Directive, arts 2(2), 17(1). See also arts 6(1), 7(2), 13(2), 15(3), 17(2)(a). Accordingly, differences in implementation of the Directive maintain the potential for applicable law disputes as between the laws of different Member States of the European Union: see, eg, *Lawlor v Sandvik Mining & Construction Mobile Crushers & Screens Ltd* [2013] EWCA 365.

[10] For example, with respect to remedies for breach of obligations imposed on the agent under art 3 and on the principal under art 4.

[11] *Lonsdale v Howard & Hallam Ltd* [2006] EWCA Civ 63, [2006] 1 WLR 1281, [25], [2007] UKHL 32, [2007] 1 WLR 2055, [16]–[21].

[12] Italy was also granted an extension until 1 January 1993 to implement one aspect of the Directive.

[13] Commercial Agents (Council Directive) Regulations 1993, reg 1(1), (2). 'Great Britain' means the territory of the United Kingdom except for Northern Ireland: Interpretation Act 1978, s 5, Sch 1 ('United Kingdom').

[14] ibid, reg 2(5).

[15] Commercial Agents (Council Directive) Regulations (Northern Ireland) 1993, SR 1993/483, as amended by SR 1999/201.

[16] Agreement on the European Economic Area, art 30, Annex VII para 30.

[17] Commercial Agents (Council Directive) Regulations 1993, reg 2(1). The remaining non-European Union Member States within the EEA are Iceland, Liechtenstein, and Norway.

2.10   Most, but not all, of the Directive's terms are mandatory, in that the parties are not permitted to derogate either at all or to the detriment of the agent. This includes articles 17–19, which address financial reparation on termination of the agency. In *Ingmar GB Ltd v Eaton Leonard Technologies Ltd*,[18] the European Court of Justice held that the Directive's objectives of freedom of establishment and undistorted competition for commercial agents could not be achieved unless all commercial agency within the territory of Member States was subject to the harmonisation prescribed by the Directive. Consequently, the termination rules in articles 17–19 were mandatory for the purposes of private international law,[19] so that they could not be avoided by a choice of law clause in favour of a non-Member State even though the principal was a company incorporated in a non-Member State and the parties had chosen the law of that state. While the judgment on its terms is confined to articles 17–19, there can be no doubt that the reasoning applies equally to all other articles in the Directive that forbid derogation.[20]

2.11   *Ingmar* concerned a choice of law clause. It is, however, clear also that a jurisdiction or arbitration clause providing for a forum outside the European Union coupled with a choice of law clause in favour of a law that would not give effect to the Directive would be invalid to the extent that such clauses had the effect of requiring issues falling within mandatory provisions of the Directive to be resolved otherwise than in accordance with the Directive.[21]

2.12   The judgment in *Ingmar* addresses only a choice of law clause in favour of a non-Member State. It does not preclude the choice by the parties of the law of a Member State other than that in which the commercial agent will act on behalf of the principal. Thus, the Directive contemplates two alternative methods of financial reparation of an agent on termination of the agency: indemnity and compensation. Assuming that the agent is to act in a Member State that has adopted the indemnity method in its implementing legislation, there is nothing in the Directive to preclude a choice of law in favour of the law of another Member State that has adopted the compensation method in its implementing legislation.[22]

2.13   Moreover, the Directive's objectives have legitimacy with respect only to the territory of the Members States. In so far as a commercial agent is to act in a non-Member State, nothing in the Directive precludes the parties from choosing the law of that or another non-Member State to govern their relationship.[23] It

---

[18]   Case C-381/98 *Ingmar GB Ltd v Eaton Leonard Technologies Ltd* [2001] CMLR 9.

[19]   See now Rome I Regulation on Law Applicable to Contractual Obligations (EU 593/2008), art 9.

[20]   For criticism of this as an overly expansive concept of mandatory rules in the context of European Union law, see H Verhagen, 'The Tension between Party Autonomy and European Union Law: Some Observations on *Ingmar GB Ltd v Eaton Leonard Technologies Inc*' (2002) 51 *International & Comparative Law Quarterly* 135.

[21]   *Accentuate Ltd v Asigra Inc* [2009] EWHC 2655, [2010] 2 All ER (Comm) 738.

[22]   For the position under the Regulations, see below, para 2.62 et seq.

[23]   Subject, of course, to any mandatory rules of any relevant non-Member State.

follows that where a commercial agent acts for the same principal under the same contract in part within and in part outside the territory of the Member States, a choice of the law of a non-Member State as the governing law will be effective with respect to the activities of the agent outside the territory of the Member States but ineffective to the extent of the Directive's mandatory provisions with respect to those activities that apply to the territory of the Member States. Instead, the governing law for the activities of the agent within any Member State will be determined in accordance with the normal rules of private international law for determining a governing law in the absence of an express choice of law, subject to any mandatory rules or rules of territorial applicability in the implementing legislation of that Member State.[24] Any undesirable resulting complexity in determining the governing law can be avoided either by acceptance by the parties of legislation implementing the Directive in the relevant Member State for the full scope of the agency or by expressly adopting different governing laws for activities within and activities outside the territories of Member States.[25]

The Commercial Agents (Council Directive) Regulations 1993

2.14   As already stated, the European Directive is implemented into English (and Scottish) law by the Commercial Agents (Council Directive) Regulations 1993.[26] Consistent with the general approach to implementation of directives adopted by the United Kingdom, the Regulations largely adopt the language of the Directive and make no attempt to translate the Directive's terms into the language and concepts of national law. This approach is calculated to minimise the United Kingdom government's exposure to liability for improper implementation but has two adverse consequences for parties to agreements governed by the Regulations. First, where the terms of the Directive are unclear, so are the Regulations; no attempt has been made to clarify meaning. Secondly, where the approach of the Directive sits awkwardly with the approach of English law to complementary issues, it is left for the courts to work out how to match the two together. Thus, in English law an agent engaged by contract owes the principal two types of obligation, namely contractual and fiduciary. The different types of obligations attract different remedies for breach. The characterisation of any particular breach of obligation is, therefore, essential. The Regulations follow the Directive in articulating certain obligations owed by the agent to the principal but do not address remedies for their breach

---

[24] Thus, for activities as a commercial agent within Great Britain, issues of governing law are addressed by mandatory rules of territorial applicability in the Regulations: see below, paras 2.63–2.67.
[25] See further the discussion of the territorial applicability of the 1993 Regulations, below, para 2.62 et seq.
[26] Delegated legislation promulgated pursuant to the power granted by the European Communities Act 1972, s 2(2).

either in terms or indirectly through the characterisation of the obligations as a matter of English law.[27]

2.15   The remainder of this chapter will be devoted to the scope of the Regulations, addressing, first, the definition of 'commercial agent' and, secondly, the territorial applicability of the Regulations.

The Definition of 'Commercial Agent'

2.16   The definition of commercial agent in both the Directive and the Regulations has four elements. First, a basic definition, in the Regulations found in regulation 2(1), contains a number of elements requiring analysis. Secondly, a number of types of agent are specifically excluded from the scope of the legislation. Thirdly, sub-agents may satisfy the basic definition, but they are excluded by the general tenor of the Regulations. Fourthly, the Directive affords each Member State 'the right to provide that the Directive shall not apply to those persons whose activities as commercial agents are considered secondary by the law of that Member State'.[28] The United Kingdom elected to exercise that right, so that persons who satisfy the basic definition and so qualify as commercial agents within the meaning of the legislation and who are not specially excluded will nevertheless be denied the benefit of the legislation if their activities as a commercial agent are considered 'secondary'.

The Basic Definition

2.17   By virtue of regulation 2(1), the term 'commercial agent'

> means a self-employed intermediary who has continuing authority to negotiate the sale or purchase of goods on behalf of another person ('the principal'), or to negotiate and conclude the sale or purchase of goods on behalf of and in the name of that principal.

Several elements of this definition require discussion.

'Self-employed'

2.18   The distinction between an employee under a contract of service and a self-employed person acting under a contract for services (often termed an independent contractor) cannot be formulated by reference to one critical feature. In *Ready Mixed Concrete (South East) Ltd v Minister of Pensions & National Insurance*,[29]

---

[27] See further, below, para 7.2.
[28] Directive, art 2(2).
[29] *Ready Mixed Concrete (South East) Ltd v Minister of Pensions & National Insurance* [1968] 2 QB 497.

MacKenna J suggested that, as a general proposition, there is a contract of service if three conditions are fulfilled:

(i) The servant agrees that, in consideration of a wage or other remunerations, he will provide his own work and skill in the performance of some service for his master.

(ii) He agrees expressly or impliedly that in the performance of that service he will be subject to the other's control in a sufficient degree to make that other master.

(iii) The other provisions of the contract are consistent with it being a contract of service.[30]

2.19 In considering these criteria, determining the true agreement between the parties is critical. Unless the contract is to be rejected as a sham, the substance of the agreement on its true interpretation will determine status as employed or self-employed.[31] Thus, the relevant degree of control is that for which the contract provides rather than that which is in fact exercised.[32] Any characterisation by the parties themselves of the agreement is highly relevant but not decisive.[33]

2.20 The third condition identified by MacKenna J was decisive in *Smith v Reliance Water Controls Ltd.*[34] The defendant sales representative requested to continue working in a changed capacity as self-employed rather than employed.[35] The claimant employer agreed and a new agreement was concluded. Subsequently, the claimant wrongly terminated the new agreement, and the question was whether the defendant was indeed self-employed and entitled to the termination rights of a commercial agent or still employed and confined to damages for wrongful dismissal. The Court of Appeal held in favour of the defendant. It was not contended that the new agreement was a sham, and several terms of the new agreement were held to be inconsistent with employment. In particular, under the new agreement: first, the defendant was remunerated on a commission basis, ceased to be treated as employed for the purposes of income tax and national insurance, and lost financial benefits of being an employee, such as holiday pay and eligibility for the claimant's company pension scheme; secondly, subject to

---

[30] ibid, 515.

[31] In the context of the applicability of employee protection legislation, courts are aware of the possibility that a party offering work might abuse a dominant bargaining position by requiring signature to a contract containing terms that, at face value, are inconsistent with employee status, and are astute to recognise and give effect to the reality of the relationship: *Autoclenz Ltd v Belcher* [2011] UKSC 41, [2011] ICR 1157. In the context of commercial agency, however, the party that has provided the services will generally be arguing for non-employee status so as to benefit from the commercial agency legislation. Consequently, whether an agreement can be disregarded as a sham falls more readily to be determined according to whether the evidence establishes a common intention of the parties that a document is not to create the legal rights and obligations it appears to create: *Snook v London & West Riding Investments Ltd* [1967] 2 QB 786, 802.

[32] *Smith v Reliance Water Controls Ltd* [2003] EWCA Civ 1153, [2004] ECC 38, [26].

[33] *Massey v Crown Life Insurance Co* [1978] 1 WLR 676.

[34] [2003] EWCA Civ 1153, [2004] ECC 38.

[35] The request was motivated by the fact that the defendant was separated from his partner and wish to preclude any attempt to enforce an assessment for maintenance of their child by an order for deduction from earnings. See also *Nigel Fryer Joinery Services Ltd v Ian Firth Hardware Ltd* [2008] 2 Lloyd's Rep 108, [2].

achieving 80 per cent of his sales targets, the defendant was entitled to represent other manufacturers, provided they were not in competition with the claimant, and was not required to devote any particular proportion of his time to representing the claimant; thirdly, the defendant was liable for all promotional expenses unless and to the extent that the claimant agreed to the contrary and was responsible for providing the main tools required to fulfil his obligations, namely a car, fuel to run it, and a mobile telephone.

2.21   As a matter of English language, the terminology of 'employed' or 'self-employed' is suggestive of natural persons. In the context of the 1993 Regulations, however, it is derived from the provisions of the European Union Treaty dealing with freedom of establishment and freedom to provide services and clearly includes legal persons as well.[36]

2.22   It should be noted that, while an employee cannot be a commercial agent, whether a commercial agent may benefit from 'employment' legislation depends on the precise terms and true interpretation of the legislation in question.[37]

'Continuing Authority'

2.23   The requirement that the authority granted by a principal to a commercial agent be 'continuing' has been interpreted broadly. That the Regulations explicitly contemplate fixed term agency contracts[38] clearly imports that 'continuing' is not synonymous with indefinite. Moreover, although the agent's authority will most commonly be limited in some way by time and, therefore, within that time will extend to all authorised activities, and notwithstanding that the Directive refers on several occasions to 'customers' and 'transactions', the European Court of Justice has held that authority to conclude even a single contract with a single customer will suffice, provided that authority is conferred to negotiate 'successive extensions' to the contract.[39] Similarly, authority that is confined to a specified series of transactions will also suffice.[40] Moreover, on the basis that it is difficult to see any significance in a particular number of transactions, it is difficult to see why two transactions should not constitute a series for these purposes. Conversely, authority that is confined to the initial conclusion of a single contract cannot suffice; otherwise the reference to 'continuing' would be deprived of all meaning.[41]

---

[36]   *Bell Electric Ltd v Aweco Appliance Systems GmbH & Co* [2002] EWHC 872 (QB), [2002] CLC 1246, [50].
[37]   *Giannelli v Edmund Bell & Co Ltd* (EAT, 6 September 2005): whether commercial agent a 'worker' as defined by the Employment Rights Act 1996, s 230(3).
[38]   See below, para 11.6.
[39]   *Poseidon Chartering BV v Marianne Zeeschip VOF* [2006] 2 Lloyd's Rep 105 (ECJ).
[40]   ibid, [23].
[41]   Opinion of AG Geelhoed in *Poseidon Chartering* [2006] ECR I-2505, [23].

2.24 More difficult is the case of authority to conclude one contract and only one extension to that contract.[42] However, if authority to conclude two contracts with different counterparties is sufficient, it is difficult to see why status as a commercial agent should depend on whether authority is confined to renewal with the same counterparty or extends to negotiation with a different possible counterparty.[43] On that basis, authority is continuing whenever it extends beyond the initial conclusion of a single contract to either one or more other contracts or one or more renewals of the same contract.

2.25 An agent may receive more than one grant of authority, each limited to the conclusion of one solitary contract. In such a case, it will be a question of fact whether a literal interpretation of the grants reflects or masks the reality. The more numerous and the more frequent the grants, the more likely the reality to be continuing authority.[44]

'Sale or Purchase of Goods'

2.26 For the purposes of the Directive, commercial agency is confined to transactions involving goods; services are excluded. Nevertheless, nothing in the Directive forbids Member States from affording national legislation implementing the Directive a wider scope than commercial agency as defined in the Directive, and some Member States have taken advantage of that freedom to include services within their concept of commercial agency.[45] The 1993 Regulations, however, follow the Directive, so that an agent who acts in relation to contracts for the provision of services cannot be a commercial agent in English law. Consequently, for example, self-employed agents retained to solicit applications for insurance and financial services products fall outside the scope of the Directive and the 1993 Regulations.[46] Agency for a combination of goods and services raises the issue of 'secondary activities', discussed below.[47]

2.27 Neither the Directive nor the Regulations elaborate upon the meaning of 'goods'. For the purposes of English sale of goods law, 'goods' are defined by the Sale of Goods Act 1979 as including 'all personal chattels other than things in action and money'.[48] However, national law concepts cannot dictate the interpretation of

---

[42] Such authority was not before the Court in *Poseidon Chartering*.

[43] [2006] ECR I-2505, [25].

[44] *cf* below, para 11.35.

[45] Thus, in *Poseidon Chartering*, the agent negotiated a charterparty, which is a contract for the provision of services involving a ship. The agency contract was, however, subject to Dutch law, which extends commercial agency to services. And see DCFR, art IV.E-3:101, which adopts a definition of commercial agency that makes no reference to the subject-matter of the contract, and, therefore, automatically includes both goods and services.

[46] Case C-449/01 *Abbey Life Assurance Co Ltd v Kok Theam Yeap* [2003] OJ C146, 13.

[47] See para 2.42 et seq, esp paras 2.51–2.52.

[48] Sale of Goods Act 1979, s 61(1). The definition goes on to clarify that 'in particular "goods" includes emblements, industrial growing crops, and things attached to or forming part of the land which are agreed to be severed before sale or under the contract of sale; and includes an undivided share in goods'.

European Union legislation or national implementing legislation. One possibility is to construe the term 'goods' in accordance with the Treaty on the Functioning of the European Union, which requires a distinction to be drawn between 'goods' and 'services' for the purposes of different rules governing freedom of movement within the European single market. While the Treaty does not define the term 'goods', the European Court of Justice regards the concept as embracing essentially any tangible product susceptible of forming the subject matter of a commercial transaction. Thus, waste that is non-recyclable and therefore has no intrinsic commercial value qualifies as goods given the commercial waste disposal industry,[49] while a grant of fishing rights constitutes a service.[50]

2.28   Three particular areas may be addressed.[51] First, it is likely that the exclusion of money in the Sale of Goods Act 1979 refers to a medium of payment, so that banknotes and coins sold as commodities, for example by weight or as curios, would be considered goods even if those notes or coins were still legal tender. Conversely, a contract to supply foreign currency for use as a medium of exchange may be described as a 'sale and purchase',[52] but the subject matter of such a contract is not goods. The essential question is whether in the context of the particular transaction the notes or coins are being supplied as an object of exchange or as a medium of exchange.[53] The European Court of Justice has drawn a similar distinction,[54] but not by reference to the relevant contract. Notes or coins that qualify as legal tender in a Member State and possibly anywhere in the world 'are, by their very nature, to be regarded as means of payment'[55] and, therefore, are not goods, irrespective of whether in the context of the particular transaction the notes or coins were being traded as a commodity. The failure to relate the enquiry to the transaction in question has been criticised[56] and, it is suggested, should not be followed for the purposes of the Regulations.

2.29   Secondly, an energy contract for the supply of electricity or unpackaged gas may be described as a contract of sale,[57] but whether it is correctly characterised as a sale of goods for the purposes of the Sale of Goods Act 1979 is unclear. In contrast, in a departure from its general requirement that goods be tangible, the

---

[49] Case C-2/90 *Commission v Belgium* [1992] ECR I-4431.

[50] Case C-97/98 *Jägerskiöld v Gustafsson* [1999] ECR I-7319.

[51] On English law, see generally M Bridge et al, *Benjamin's Sale of Goods*, 8th edn (London, Sweet & Maxwell, 2010), paras 1-084–1-087.

[52] *Re British & American Continental Bank Ltd, Goldzieher & Penso's Claim* [1922] 2 Ch 575, 586 (Warrington LJ).

[53] C Proctor (ed), *Mann on the Legal Aspect of Money* 7th edn (Oxford, Oxford University Press, 2012), paras 1.61–1.66.

[54] *R v Thompson* [1980] QB 229 (ECJ); Case C-358/93 *Bordessa* [1995] ECR I-361.

[55] *R v Thompson* [1980] QB 229, 272.

[56] See C Proctor (ed), *Mann on the Legal Aspect of Money* 7th edn (Oxford, Oxford University Press, 2012), para 1.62.

[57] And, as such, may attract the quality implications recognised in the context of a true sale of goods: *Bentley Bros v Metcalfe & Co* [1906] 2 KB 548.

European Court of Justice has held that electricity constitutes goods,[58] and contracts for the mains supply of gas to domestic households have been assumed to be contracts for the sale of goods within the meaning of the Regulations.[59]

2.30 Thirdly, computer software is not goods: 'software is intellectual property, not a chattel, but hardware is a chattel.'[60] A computer disk, therefore, constitutes goods but a computer program in itself, 'being instructions or commands telling the computer hardware what to do', is not. Nevertheless, if a program is supplied impressed on to a disk or other hardware carrying it (as opposed to being downloaded directly from the internet), the program constitutes an integral part of the composite product, which falls within the statutory definition of goods and is susceptible of attracting the application of sale of goods law even if any subsequent problem is attributable solely to the program.[61]

2.31 A similar distinction may be drawn with respect to visual entertainment products. Broadcasting as a supply of television signals, however transmitted, is a service,[62] and satellite programming has been treated as a service under the Regulations,[63] while a tangible recording device carrying a film or other visual programme constitutes goods.[64] By analogy with computer software, the same films and programmes made available for downloading directly from the internet would be considered an entertainment service.

2.32 Assuming that the subject matter of the contract falls within the concept of goods as correctly understood, the contract must be one of 'sale or purchase'. Thus, even if software could in itself constitute goods, developing a market for software to be made available on licence rather than sold could not constitute commercial agency.[65] Likewise, a contract for the bailment of goods on hire is clearly not a contract of sale. It is, however, less clear whether the Directive, and therefore the Regulations, should be construed as following English law in regarding a contractual commitment to the passing of ownership in goods as a defining

---

[58] Case C-393/92 *Almelo v Energiebedrijf Ijsselmij* [1994] ECR I-1477; Case C-158/94 *Commission v Italian Republic* [1997] ECR I-05789. See also Public Contracts Regulations 2006 (implementing Directive 2004/18/EC), reg 2(1).

[59] *Tamarind International Ltd v Eastern Natural Gas (Retail) Ltd* [2000] CLC 1397.

[60] *Accentuate Ltd v Asigra Inc* [2009] EWHC 2655, [2010] 2 All ER (Comm) 738 [56] (Tugendhat J). In Case C-3/88 *Commission v Italy* [1989] ECR 4035, the development and supply of software was treated by the European Court of Justice as a service, albeit without discussion.

[61] *St Albans City & District Council v International Computers Ltd* [1996] 4 All ER 481, 493 (Sir Iain Glidewell). *Cf London Borough of Southwark v IBM UK Ltd* [2011] EWHC 549 (TCC), (2011) 135 Con LR 136, [96]–[97]. But the goods must still be sold: see below, para 2.32.

[62] Case C-155/73 *Italy v Sacchi* [1974] ECR 409; Case C-52/79 *Procureur du Roi v Debauve* [1980] ECR 833.

[63] *Crane v Sky In-Home Service Ltd* [2007] EWHC 66 (Ch), [2007] 1 CLC 389, [11].

[64] Case C-60/84 *Cinéthèque SA v Fédération Nationale des Cinémas Français* [1985] ECR 2605.

[65] *London Borough of Southwark v IBM UK Ltd* [2011] EWHC 549 (TCC), (2011) 135 Con LR 136, [95] (licence agreement does not involve a transfer of property as required to constitute a sale of goods contract under the Sale of Goods Act 1979).

hallmark of a sale of goods,[66] generating a distinction between an agreement to sell, under which there is a commitment to the passing of ownership on the fulfilment of a future condition,[67] and a hire-purchase agreement, under which the passing of ownership is dependent on the exercise of an option.[68]

2.33 Services and goods may be combined in a contract for work and materials, Thus, assume a contract for the supply of a complex bespoke system where the essence of the product resides not in the inherent functionality of individual parts but rather the design of the system as a whole in terms of the selection of suitable parts and their combination in an effective manner. Where the system malfunctions by reason of a shortcoming in design, liability must be pursued on the basis of a failure to exercise reasonable care in the supply of services rather than strict liability for defective goods.[69] Nevertheless, ownership in goods is transferred in return for monetary consideration, and the supply of goods element of the contract attracts a number of rules identical to those applicable to sale of goods contracts. It is unclear whether such contracts would be considered a sale of goods for the purposes of the Regulations.[70]

'Negotiate' or 'Negotiate and Conclude'

2.34 Negotiation represents the authorised threshold of involvement in the generating of contracts for the principal that is required for commercial agency. In *PJ Pipe & Valve Co Ltd v Audco India Ltd*,[71] Fulford J construed the term 'negotiate' in the light of the purpose of the Directive: since the Directive was designed to ensure fair treatment of agents who developed the goodwill of a business, 'the courts should avoid a limited or restricted interpretation of the word "negotiate" that would exclude agents who have been engaged to develop the principal's business'.[72] The case concerned an agent (PJV) in the petrochemicals industry acting on behalf of an Indian manufacturing company (AIL). According to Fulford J:

> PJV's role was to deal with and conduct (and, in part, manage) the relevant discussions and transactions at the time when the manufacturers were being selected by the contractor; in particular, they effected the crucial introductions and they played a significant role in persuading the contractor to be interested in AIL's products, not least because of their own real standing in this industry. Thereafter, they assisted in ensuring that their client was placed on the approved list of vendors and received the invitations to tender, in part

---

[66] Sale of Goods Act 1979, s 2(1).

[67] Sale of Goods Act 1979, s 2(5).

[68] *Helby v Matthews* [1895] AC 471; *Forthright Finance Ltd v Carlyle Finance Ltd* [1997] 4 All ER 90; *Close Asset Finance Ltd v Care Graphics Machinery Ltd* [2000] CCLR 43.

[69] *Trebor Bassett Holdings Ltd v ADT Fire & Security plc* [2012] EWCA Civ 1158, [2012] BLR 441, [42]–[49].

[70] Even if they were, so that an agency agreement would satisfy the definition under reg 2(1), the benefit of the Regulations might, nevertheless, be denied by the secondary activities restriction: below, para 2.42 et seq, esp 2.53.

[71] *PJ Pipe & Valve Co Ltd v Audco India Ltd* [2005] EWHC 1904 (QB), [2006] Eu LR 368.

[72] ibid, [155]. See also at [149].

by putting in an appropriate bid; they assisted with quotations and queries; and they provided feedback and advised on how the quotation could be improved. In both the short and the long term they are retained, inter alia, to develop goodwill on the part of AIL.[73]

2.35 Consequently, that PJV lacked authority to agree prices or commercial terms did not deny it status as a commercial agent.[74] Indeed, it may be sufficient that the agent is authorised merely to locate and introduce potential purchasers but not to take any further involvement in the contracting process (sometimes known as 'canvassing'). The attendant raising of the profile of the principal and its products will inevitably contribute to developing the goodwill of the principal's business.

2.36 In contrast, an agent operating a customer self-service business selling exclusively the principal's goods at prices set by the principal and doing so in accordance with rules laid down by the principal, and whose only discretion is confined to payment methods themselves specified by the principal, cannot be said to negotiate.[75] The mere placing of goods before potential customers for them to select and then administering payment of the amount required by the principal does not involve the agent in making any personal contribution to developing the goodwill of the business.[76] Similarly, retention of an independent consultant to create a vehicle whereby the principal will market its goods, such as a website, does not involve the conferral of authority to negotiate contracts.

'On Behalf of Another Person ("The Principal"), or . . . on Behalf of and in the Name of that Principal'

2.37 The fundamental idea that commercial agents merit protection because they develop a potentially enduring asset in the form of enhanced business goodwill that will benefit the principal is reflected also in the requirement that the agent negotiates contracts 'on behalf of' the principal or negotiates and concludes contracts 'on behalf of and in the name of' the principal. It is clear from the second limb that a commercial agent cannot negotiate on behalf of the principal but

---

[73] ibid, [155].

[74] See also *Nigel Fryer Joinery Services Ltd v Ian Firth Hardware Ltd* [2008] 2 Lloyd's Rep 108: agent retained to generate interest in principal's products with authority to give an indicative price, and then to complete a quotation form and transmit it to the principal, held to have authority to negotiate the sale of goods for the purposes of reg 2(1).

[75] *Parks v Esso Petroleum Co Ltd* [2000] ECC 45 (petrol service station).

[76] In addition, the Directive permits Member States to exclude from its benefit commercial agents whose activities as such are 'secondary'. Under English law, that 'customers normally select the goods for themselves and merely place their orders through the agent' is an indication that the agent's activities are secondary: Commercial Agents Regulations, Sch, para 4(c). For discussion of secondary activities, see below, para 2.42 et seq. Para 4(c) was relied upon in *Parks* as showing 'beyond doubt' that the benefit of the Regulations was not available in that case: ibid, [33]. In the Irish case of *Kenny v Ireland ROC Ltd* [2005] IEHC 241, in contrast, an independent contractor operating a petrol service station was held to be a commercial agent. It appears that the contractor in *Kenny* enjoyed greater autonomy and discretion than his counterpart in *Parks*, but it is also noteworthy that Ireland elected not to have a secondary activities limitation on the benefit of the commercial agents regime.

contract on its own behalf and/or in its own name.[77] A commission agent will negotiate on the instructions and, in that sense, on behalf of its principal but will conclude any resulting contract in its own name, such contract taking effect between the agent and the third party. Any ensuing customer goodwill will accrue primarily to the agent, not to the business of the principal, and the European Court of Justice has duly held that a commission agent cannot be a commercial agent within the terms of the Directive.[78] Similarly, an agent for an undisclosed principal is authorised to act for the principal and to create privity of contract between principal and third party but covertly and therefore, as regards the third party, acts in its own name. The third party being wholly unaware it is dealing with any entity other than the agent, the rationale for protection of the agent is absent.[79] A fortiori, an intermediary that contracts to purchase from the supplier and resell in its own name for its own benefit at a mark-up determined by itself is unlikely to be characterised as an agent at all but, in any event, will not qualify as a commercial agent.[80]

2.38   In certain circumstances, an agent acting for a disclosed principal undertakes liability on the contract so that the third party can enforce liability against either principal or agent.[81] Such an agent, it is submitted, falls within the statutory definition. The agent does act on behalf of the principal and in the principal's name. That is all the definition requires; it does not require that the agent exclusively so acts. From a commercial perspective, moreover, any enhanced business goodwill will still accrue to the benefit of the principal. It is, therefore, suggested that an agent that acts on behalf of and in the name of its principal is not precluded from commercial agent status simply because it also to some extent acts on its own behalf.[82]

No Further Requirement Imposed or Permitted

2.39   Provided the definition in regulation 2(1) is satisfied, the agreement is one of commercial agency, subject to the exclusions discussed below. The rights and obligations articulated elsewhere in the Regulations are not to be interpreted as

---

[77]   *Sagal v Atelier Bunz GmbH* [2009] EWCA Civ 700, [2009] 2 CLC 1, [12].

[78]   Case C-85/03 *Mavrona & Sie OE v Delta Etaireia Symmetochon AE* [2004] ECR I-1573, although there is nothing to prevent a Member State from extending the protective regime of commercial agency to commission agents as a matter of national law: ibid, [20]. And see DCFR, art IV.E-3:101, which adopts a definition of commercial agency that makes no reference to acting 'in the name of' the principal, and, therefore, accommodates commission agents.

[79]   Although not where the existence and identity of the principal is generally subsequently revealed.

[80]   *AMB Imballaggi Plastici SRL v Pacflex Ltd* [1999] 2 All ER (Comm) 249; *Sagal v Atelier Bunz GmbH* [2009] EWCA Civ 700, [2009] 2 CLC 1. See also above, para 1.28.

[81]   See below, paras 9.10–9.12.

[82]   For a contrary view, see P Watts and F Reynolds (eds), *Bowstead & Reynolds on Agency,* 19th edn (London, Sweet & Maxwell, 2010), para 11-019. If, however, the agent's activities as a commercial agent are secondary, it will be denied the benefit of the Regulations: see below.

creating further pre-conditions to commercial agency status.[83] Moreover, Member States are not permitted to make the applicability of the Directive's provisions depend upon anything other than satisfaction of the Directive's test for commercial agency. They are, however, free to subject commercial agency to additional regulatory requirements, such as registration, provided that satisfaction of any such requirement is not connected to the applicability of the Directive's provisions, as implemented by the relevant national legislation, to the agency.[84]

Agents Specifically Excluded from Commercial Agency

2.40   Six categories of agent are specifically excluded from the Regulations. Having given the basic definition of commercial agent, regulation 2(1) itself further provides that the concept does not embrace: first, officers of a company or association;[85] secondly, partners; and, thirdly, insolvency practitioners. Moreover, regulation 2(2) provides that the Regulations do not apply to: first, unpaid commercial agents; secondly, commercial agents operating on commodity exchanges or in the commodity market; and, thirdly, Crown Agents for Overseas Governments and Administrations.

Sub-agents

2.41   Nothing in the basic definition of commercial agent in regulation 2(1) precludes a sub-agent from status as a commercial agent. Nevertheless, in *Light v Ty Europe Ltd*,[86] the Court of Appeal held that the general tenor of the substantive provisions of the Regulations contemplated a direct legal, usually contractual, relationship between commercial agent and the principal. Moreover, the contrary view was a recipe for 'chaos and confusion' with uncertainty over the multiplication of financial rights or their apportionment between the agent and any sub-agents together with a problem for the principal in knowing the range of people to whom it might incur liability under the Regulations.[87] However, the interposition of an intermediary between the principal and a representative that otherwise qualifies for commercial agent status will be disregarded as a sham if it is a charade that masks the commercial reality and is designed purely to render the representative nominally a sub-agent in an attempt to avoid the Regulations.[88]

---

[83]   *Rossetti Marketing Ltd v Diamond Sofa Co Ltd* [2011] EWHC 2482 (QB), [2012] 1 All ER (Comm) 18, [49] (cannot derive an argument from the obligation of good faith under reg 3(1) (discussed in ch 7) that an agency for multiple, competing principals otherwise compliant with reg 2(1) falls outside the Regulations).

[84]   Case C-215/97 *Bellone v Yokohama SpA* [1998] 3 CMLR 975; Case C-485/01 *Caprini v CCIA* [2003] ECR I-2371.

[85]   Many of whom will be employees and, therefore, ineligible to be commercial agents in any event.

[86]   *Light v Ty Europe Ltd* [2003] EWCA Civ 1238, [2004] 1 Lloyd's Rep 693.

[87]   ibid, [25] (Tuckey LJ). See also ibid, [45].

[88]   ibid, [27].

Secondary Activities

2.42 Article 2(2) of the Directive provides that each Member State has the right to provide that the Directive does not apply to 'those persons whose activities as commercial agents are considered secondary by the law of that Member State'. A two-layered discretion is thereby introduced, diluting the extent of the harmonisation achieved by the Directive. First, each Member State has the right to decide for itself whether to adopt a secondary activity restriction on the scope of its implementing legislation. Secondly, in the event of adoption of such a restriction, the concept of 'secondary activity' is not defined by the Directive but is remitted to the national law of the Member State in question.

2.43 The United Kingdom elected to narrow the scope of the commercial agents regime by adopting a secondary activities limitation. The criteria for determining whether the activities of a commercial agent are to be considered secondary are found in the Schedule to the Regulations.[89] Any person so determined to act as a commercial agent on a secondary basis is then denied the benefit of the Regulations.[90] The Schedule is complex, but it should be emphasised that the secondary activity limitation in no way detracts from the basic definition in regulation 2(1). Nor, indeed, does it technically retract commercial agency status from an agent that otherwise satisfies the definition. Rather, the effect of the secondary activity limitation is to deny status as a commercial agent pursuant to regulation 2(1) of any relevance by withholding the benefit of the regulations.

'Secondary': The Essential Enquiry

2.44 Paragraphs 1 and 2 of the Schedule provide as follows:

(1) The activities of a person as a commercial agent are to be considered secondary where it may reasonably be taken that the primary purpose of the arrangement with his principal is other than as set out in paragraph 2 below.

(2) An arrangement falls within this paragraph if-

    (a) the business of the principal is the sale, or as the case may be purchase, of goods of a particular kind; and

    (b) the goods concerned are such that-

        (i) transactions are normally individually negotiated and concluded on a commercial basis, and

        (ii) procuring a transaction on one occasion is likely to lead to further transactions in those goods with that customer on future occasions, or to transactions in those goods with other customers in the same geographical area or among the same group of customers, and

---

[89] Commercial Agents Regulations, reg 2(3).
[90] ibid, reg 2(4).

that accordingly it is in the commercial interests of the principal in developing the market in those goods to appoint a representative to such customers with a view to the representative devoting effort, skill and expenditure from his own resources to that end.

2.45 In determining whether an agent's activities as commercial agent are to be considered as secondary, the context of the enquiry is vital. A so-called 'horizontal' approach embraces the full range of a person's working activities, both as agent for the principal in question and also as agent for any other principal or indeed independently on the person's own account. On this approach, the Regulations will benefit only those persons whose entire working activity consists predominantly in acting as a commercial agent for one or more principals. In contrast, a 'vertical' approach relates the enquiry to a particular relationship between the agent and one principal and asks what, within the context of their arrangement alone, was the primary focus. The nature and extent of the agent's working activities outside the relationship with that principal are irrelevant. The view has been expressed obiter that Article 2(2) of the Directive appears to contemplate a horizontal approach.[91] There is, however, little to commend it. The applicability of the Regulations as between an agent and a particular principal cannot sensibly depend on the extent and nature of any working activities that the agent may happen to pursue outside of the relationship with that principal. Happily, the Court of Appeal has since considered that a natural reading of paragraph 1 favours the vertical approach and that this should be followed.[92]

2.46 Adopting a vertical approach, paragraph 1 of the Schedule directs a comparison of the 'primary purpose' of the commercial agent's arrangement with the principal with that as set out in paragraph 2. If it may 'reasonably be taken' that the primary purpose falls outside paragraph 2, then the commercial agent's activities as such are secondary and the commercial agent is denied the benefit of the Regulations.[93] Paragraphs 3 and 4 then identify a number of indicators of whether the test formulated by paragraph 2 is satisfied. It follows from this focus on the purpose of the arrangement that the test for secondary activity status falls to be applied definitively by reference to the time of conclusion of the contract between agent and principal,[94] and how the agency is in fact performed has no direct

---

[91] *AMB Imballagi Plastici SRL v Pacflex Ltd* [1999] 2 All ER (Comm) 249, 254. Waller LJ also noted that Guidance Notes on the Regulations issued by the then Department of Trade and Industry stated clearly that a horizontal approach was to be adopted, indicating that the vertical approach contemplated by the Schedule was 'probably unintentional'. It may be, however, that the Guidance Notes are simply wrong on this matter, as they have been proved to be on others.

[92] *Edwards v International Connection (UK) Ltd* [2006] EWCA (Civ) 662.

[93] In the event of an arrangement having two equal purposes, one within para 2 and one outside, neither of which can be described as 'primary', para 1 cannot apply, secondary status cannot be established, and the commercial agent will retain the benefit of the Regulations: *Crane v Sky In-Home Service Ltd* [2007] EWHC 66 (Ch), [2007] 1 CLC 389, [54].

[94] *Crane v Sky In-Home Service Ltd* [2007] EWHC 66 (Ch), [2007] 1 CLC 389, [77]; *McAdam v Boxpak Ltd* [2006] Eu LR 901, [17], [20].

relevance to the question of whether the primary purpose test is satisfied.[95] Accordingly, whether (as stipulated in paragraph 2(b)) transactions are indeed generally negotiated on an individual basis and whether they in fact lead to further transactions are not in point.[96]

2.47　The language of paragraph 2 has occasioned some difficulty since it appears to describe features of a principal's business rather than a possible purpose of an arrangement with an agent.[97] The Court of Appeal, however, has highlighted the final lines of paragraph 2, so that paragraph 2 needs to be read as prescribing the purpose of furthering the principal's commercial interests in the manner stated in those final lines of the paragraph by reference to the goods and transactions stipulated in sub-paragraphs (a) and (b).[98]

2.48　This focus on the final lines of paragraph 2 is reinforced by the indicators in paragraphs 3 and 4, some of which do not relate to the subject matter of sub-paragraphs (a) and (b) but only to the general, albeit central, question of furthering the principal's commercial interests by developing a market for the principal's goods through the industry and contacts of the agent.[99] It would, therefore, be wrong to suggest that sub-paragraphs (a) and (b) are determinative of whether the primary purpose test is satisfied.[100] On the contrary, the final lines encapsulate an independent and 'essential' criterion of the primary purpose test.[101]

2.49　Paragraph 2 identifies key aspects of commercial agency. Sub-paragraph (b)(ii) speaks to enduring product reputation and business goodwill, which sub-paragraph (b)(i) and the concluding lines of paragraph 2 contemplate will be developed or enhanced as a result of the agent's abilities, efforts, and resources. Slightly curious is the requirement in sub-paragraph (a) that the goods be 'of a particular kind'. It may be that a distinct type of product will more readily acquire a reputation that will engender further transactions. Alternatively, it may be that the term 'particular' links to sub-paragraph (b), which highlights whether the goods are specifically identified with the principal in the relevant market as opposed to being readily available from several sources of supply with-

---

[95] Although post-formation conduct is admissible as part of the factual matrix to evidence the purpose of a contract: *Dunlop Tyres Ltd v Blows* [2001] EWCA Civ 1032, [2001] IRLR 629.

[96] *Edwards v International Connection (UK) Ltd* [2006] EWCA (Civ) 662. Clearly there has to be a moment at which the applicability of the Regulations is determined. The only logical moments would appear to be those of the conclusion and termination of the agency agreement. The latter was favoured at first instance in *McAdam v Boxpak Ltd* 2005 SLT (Sh Ct) 47, arguably supported by the language of paras 2–4. This would produce the possibility of the commercial agent drifting in and out of the benefit of the Regulations during the course of the agency and of strategic calculations as to the timing of termination. That is avoided by the clear view of the English courts, as stated in the text.

[97] *AMB Imballaggi Plastici SRL v Pacflex Ltd* [1999] 2 All ER (Comm) 249, 254.

[98] *Edwards v International Connection (UK) Ltd* [2006] EWCA (Civ) 662, [17]. See also at [19].

[99] Notably para 3(c), but the same argument can be made in respect of paras 3(e), 4(b).

[100] This argument was advanced in *McAdam v Boxpak Ltd*, but it proved unnecessary for the court to express a view: [2006] Eu LR 901, [26]–[27].

[101] *Edwards v International Connection (UK) Ltd* [2006] EWCA (Civ) 662, [17] (Moore-Bick LJ). See also *Gailey v Environmental Waste Controls* [2004] Eu LR 708, [34].

out differentiation.[102] This has been described as an indicator 'clearly of critical importance' such that in its absence there is a 'strong likelihood' that the requirement in the final lines of paragraph 2 will not be satisfied, although, as but one among a number of indicators, the weight to be attributed to its absence must ultimately be a question of fact.[103]

2.50 Regardless of the meaning to be attached to the term 'particular', a reputation for quality, reliability, and value may also attach to a supplier, which will then benefit any products that that supplier decides to market. While it may be unlikely that principals employing commercial agents will supply a wholly diverse range of goods, it is difficult to see why the agent should be denied the benefit of the Regulations in circumstances where business goodwill has been generated for the supplier, and thereby but only indirectly its goods, merely because those goods lack particularity or identifiability. As noted, however, paragraph 1 does not ask whether the purpose of the arrangement between principal and commercial agent falls outside paragraph 2 on a strict reading, but rather whether 'it may reasonably be taken' that it falls outside. It is, accordingly, suggested that strict or full compliance with all aspects of paragraph 2 is not essential for it not to be reasonable to take the purpose of the arrangement as outside paragraph 2.[104]

2.51 An application of paragraph 2 may result in a conclusion that activities as a commercial agent are secondary in either of two ways. First, the arrangement between principal and agent may provide for the agent to operate in part as a commercial agent and in part in some other capacity. For example, the agent may be engaged to represent the principal in respect of both goods and services. In such a case, the question is whether the activities as a commercial agent constitute the predominant part of the activities authorised under the agreement.

2.52 In *Crane v Sky In-Home Service Ltd*,[105] the claimant sales agent for the Sky group had separate contracts with two members of the group. A 'Sky Digital Sales Agency Agreement' (SDSA) governed the sale of subscriptions to satellite broadcasts on behalf of British Sky Broadcasting (BSB), while a 'Customer Offer Purchase and Agency Agreement' (COPA) governed sales of a 'Box Package', consisting of a set top decoder, satellite dish aerial, and block converter, together with installation on behalf of Sky In-Home Service Ltd (SHS). The former could not constitute commercial agency because satellite programming is a service, not

---

[102] See, eg, *Tamarind International Ltd v Eastern Natural Gas (Retail) Ltd* [2000] CLC 1397 (marketing campaign to create identification between gas devoid of any distinguishing characteristic as gas and a particular supplier in the general gas supply industry: 'the essential characteristic of the goods was gas supplied by a cheaper and reliable supplier': ibid, [33] (Morison J)).

[103] *Gailey v Environmental Waste Controls* [2004] Eu LR 708, [36] (Lord Drummond Young); *McAdam v Boxpak Ltd* [2006] Eu LR 901, [29]. There is no requirement that the sale or purchase of goods be the principal's sole or dominant business: *Crane v Sky In-Home Service Ltd* [2007] EWHC 66 (Ch), [2007] 1 CLC 389, [58].

[104] A strict approach is advocated in *Crane v Sky In-Home Service Ltd* [2007] EWHC 66 (Ch), [2007] 1 CLC 389, [55]–[57], but the wording of para 1 appears to have been overlooked.

[105] [2007] EWHC 66 (Ch), [2007] 1 CLC 389.

goods. Moreover, the COPA was held to fall outside paragraph 2 for two reasons. First, under sub-paragraph 2(b)(ii) the goods must generate goodwill so as to lead to future orders, but on the facts the goodwill attached to the programmes, not to the hardware. 'The Box Package is like the key which unlocks the attractive new car.'[106] There was no market in the hardware, but rather in satellite programming. The position might, however, have been different had the hardware possessed features additional to being a decoder that were capable of constituting a market attraction in their own right.[107] Secondly, turning to the final lines of paragraph 2, the claimant's efforts, skill and expenditure as an agent were devoted rather to generating extra subscriptions to satellite programming services. While they may indirectly have promoted sales of the Box Packages, they arose under the SDSA and were, therefore, irrelevant to the COPA.[108]

2.53   Similarly, in the case of contracts for work and materials, where the subject matter of the contract lies fundamentally in the service element, the incidental supply of goods will be secondary.[109]

2.54   Activities as a commercial agent may be considered secondary in another way. The arrangement between principal and agent may contemplate the agent acting exclusively, or at least predominantly, as a commercial agent as defined in regulation 2(1), but the activities of the commercial agent may not fall within the spirit of the legislation. The Directive is aimed at the agent that has been engaged to develop enduring goodwill attaching to the principal's business, with the agent consequently meriting a share in that goodwill, to which it cannot be assumed that the agent is able to negotiate a right. The Schedule reflects that underlying mischief so that agents who fall within the technical definition in regulation 2(1) are nevertheless denied the benefit of the Regulations where they fall outside the spirit of the legislation as reflected in the Schedule, again underlining the significance of the final lines of paragraph 2.[110] Where, for example, the agent does have continuing authority to negotiate and conclude sales of goods on behalf of and in the name of the principal, but the same, or undifferentiated, goods are available from several sources so that customers place orders on the basis of price alone, the agent may satisfy the definition of a commercial agent but the agent's activities as a commercial agent will not generate enduring goodwill accruing to the benefit of the principal's business and in which the agent ought to have a share.[111]

---

[106]   ibid, [67] (Briggs J).

[107]   ibid, [69].

[108]   ibid, [73]. That the Box Packages were sold at a loss to enable BSB to profit from subscriptions to programming did not, however, deny that the COPA was in the commercial interests of the principal (SHS) since it was perfectly legitimate for one member of a corporate group to act so as to benefit another group member: ibid, [72].

[109]   It is unclear whether promoting such contracts would be precluded in any event from commercial agency as not constituting contracts for the sale of goods: above, para 2.33.

[110]   *Tamarind International Ltd v Eastern Natural Gas (Retail) Ltd* [2000] CLC 1397, [28]; *Gailey v Environmental Waste Controls* [2004] Eu LR 708, [26].

[111]   *McAdam v Boxpak Ltd* [2006] Eu LR 901, [7] (quoting para 11 of the Sheriff's judgment).

Indicators of a Paragraph 2 Purpose

2.55 Paragraphs 3 and 4 of the Schedule list eight indicators of whether the test posed by paragraph 2 is satisfied. Evidence that the paragraph 2 test is satisfied is provided by the presence of the five indicators listed in paragraph 3, while the absence of those indicators and the presence of the three indicators listed in paragraph 4 evidences that the test is not satisfied. The absence of the indicators listed in paragraph 4 is not said to evidence that the test is satisfied, but that must be the case.

2.56 The paragraph 3 indicators are as follows:

(a) the principal is the manufacturer, importer or distributor of the goods;
(b) the goods are specifically identified with the principal in the market in question rather than, or to a greater extent than, with any other person;
(c) the agent devotes substantially the whole of his time to representative activities (whether for one principal or for a number of principals whose interests are not conflicting);
(d) the goods are not normally available in the market in question other than by means of the agent;
(e) the arrangement is described as one of commercial agency.

2.57 The paragraph 4 indicators are as follows:

(a) promotional material is supplied direct to potential customers;
(b) persons are granted agencies without reference to existing agents in a particular area or in relation to a particular group;
(c) customers normally select the goods for themselves and merely place their orders through the agent.

2.58 Since, as already noted, paragraph 2 is to be read as describing a purpose of an arrangement in accordance with paragraph 1, how the arrangement is in fact performed is irrelevant. The indicators in paragraphs 3 and 4 must be read in that context as describing general market conditions as at the time of conclusion of the arrangement between principal and agent and probative of its primary purpose, rather than what may or may not have occurred pursuant to that arrangement.[112]

2.59 The function of the indicators is to inform and assist the court in reaching a decision as to the status of the commercial agency activities. On the facts, a number of indicators may point towards a purpose within the Regulations, while others may indicate that the commercial agency activities are secondary. The court will take an overall view; the status of the activities is not resolved according to a simple

---

[112] *Edwards v International Connection (UK) Ltd* [2006] EWCA (Civ) 662, [19]. Even para 3(c) is to be read as informing the background against which the arrangement was concluded and therefore its primary purpose: ibid, [20].

majority of the indications. The significance of any particular indicator will vary according to the facts.[113]

Commercial Agents Presumed to Act as such in a Secondary Capacity

2.60   By virtue of paragraph 5 of the Schedule, the primary purpose of the arrangement with two types of agent is rebuttably presumed not to satisfy the paragraph 2 test. The agents in question are mail order catalogue agents for consumer goods and consumer credit agents. This paragraph is based on views expressed by the European Economic and Social Committee and the European Parliament in commenting on an initial proposal in 1976 of the European Commission for a directive concerning commercial agency.

Burden of Proof

2.61   It is clear that an agent wishing to claim the benefit of the Regulations carries the burden of proving that the basic definition in regulation 2(1) is satisfied. On ordinary principles, the burden of proving the applicability of a specific exception generally falls on the principal. As already seen however, in the context of commercial agency activities considered to be secondary, the Schedule in effect endeavours to elaborate on the fundamental idea behind commercial agency of goodwill development. From that perspective, the definition in regulation 2(1) is purely mechanical while the Schedule seeks to address the spirit of the legislation. The view has accordingly been adopted that the claimant should prove not only that that it falls within the letter of regulation 2(1) but also that it falls within the true mischief addressed by the legislation as illuminated by the Schedule,[114] although the point has been stated to be arguable.[115]

Territorial Applicability

2.62   As already seen, the Directive constitutes mandatory law throughout the territory of the Member States in the sense that effect will not be given to a provision within a commercial agency agreement relating to jurisdiction, alternative dispute resolution, or choice of law that has the effect that the non-derogable provisions of the Directive will not be applied to commercial agency activities within the territory of a Member State.[116] Within the territory of the Member States,

---

[113]   *Edwards v International Connection (UK) Ltd* [2006] EWCA (Civ) 662, [14]; *Crane v Sky In-Home Service Ltd* [2007] EWHC 66 (Ch), [2007] 1 CLC 389, [59].
[114]   *Gailey v Environmental Waste Controls* [2004] Eu LR 708, [40]; *Crane v Sky In-Home Service Ltd* [2007] EWHC 66 (Ch), [2007] 1 CLC 389, [54].
[115]   *Edwards v International Connection (UK) Ltd* [2006] EWCA (Civ) 662, [15], [27]–[28].
[116]   See above, paras 2.10–2.11.

however, it is not the Directive as such that applies to commercial agency agreements, but rather the relevant national implementing legislation. As already noted, the Directive harmonises only certain aspects of the internal relationship between principal and commercial agent, albeit many of the more important aspects, and even within its scope offers options to national legislators on certain matters. Consequently, it may be important to identify which implementing instrument applies and also the governing law for issues on which the Directive is silent. It is, however, beyond the scope of this book to consider the governing law for agency generally,[117] or even for all matters within the internal aspect of agency. The focus here is the applicability of the 1993 Regulations.

The General Rule

2.63   Regulation 1(2) provides a general rule of applicability of the Regulations 'in relation to activities of commercial agents in Great Britain'. The rule of applicability requires therefore the localisation of the commercial agency activity, raising uncertainty where for example promotional, marketing or selling tools are established outside but reach into Great Britain, for example a website hosted on a server outside Great Britain but aimed at buyers inside Great Britain and accessible by such buyers from within Great Britain. It is suggested that provided the activity achieves market penetration in Great Britain in terms of access by potential buyers from within Great Britain, it should be regarded as occurring 'in' Great Britain for the purposes of regulation 1(2).

The Exceptions

2.64   Regulation 1(3) provides for two exceptions to the general territorial rule in regulation 1(2), giving effect, subject to certain conditions and limits, to party autonomy.

Commercial Agency in Great Britain but Choice of Law of Another Member State

2.65   By virtue of regulation 1(3)(a), regulation 1(2) is displaced in respect of commercial agency activities in Great Britain where the principal and agent have agreed that the implementing legislation of another Member State will apply instead. In such a case, regulations 3–22 will not apply and instead the corresponding provisions of the implementing legislation of the designated law will apply to the issues addressed by regulations 3–22 and the designated law will of course apply to issues not addressed by the 1993 Regulations at all. However, the

---

[117] See generally P Watts and F Reynolds (eds), *Bowstead & Reynolds on Agency,* 19th edn (London, Sweet & Maxwell, 2010), ch 12.

remainder of the 1993 Regulations continue to apply. In consequence, first, any provisions of the designated implementing legislation relating to territorial applicability will not apply. An English court will, therefore, apply the designated law even if that law's own terms decline any extra-territorial applicability.[118] Secondly, for an English court the range of persons entitled to invoke the benefit of legislation implementing the Directive remains governed by the 1993 Regulations. A person whose activities as a commercial agent are secondary in accordance with the criteria in the Schedule will not be able to invoke the designated legislation even if that legislation contains no secondary activity restriction. The Regulations, however, are silent with respect to jurisdiction. Suppose that the ordinary private international law rules on jurisdiction award jurisdiction to the courts of the Member State that has implemented the law designated by the parties, which law contains no secondary activities restriction. There is no reason for the courts of that state to give effect to the secondary activities rules of English law.

2.66   As already seen, a choice of law clause in favour of the law of a non-Member State is ineffective as contrary to the overriding mandatory nature of the Regulations. In consequence, by virtue of regulation 1(2), an English court will then apply the Regulations to commercial agency activities within Great Britain.

2.67   Where a person's activities as a commercial agent extend to more than one Member State, an English court will apply the Regulations in the absence of a choice of law clause satisfying regulations 1(3)(a), but only to those activities within Great Britain.

Commercial Agency Outside Great Britain but Choice of English Law

2.68   By virtue of regulation 1(3)(b), the Regulations may apply to commercial agency activities outside Great Britain but within the territory of another Member State. The Regulations apply provided the parties designate English law as the governing law and if and to the extent that its application is permitted by the implementing legislation of the relevant Member State.

---

[118]   This is consistent with the general rejection of the doctrine of renvoi in the 'Rome I' Regulation on the law applicable to contractual obligations (EC 593/2008), art 20.

3

Actual Authority

3.1   In the vast majority of cases, agency is based on consent by the principal to the agent's acting in some way on the principal's behalf.[1] The authority enjoyed by the agent in so acting has genuinely been conferred and, so, is termed 'actual'. Such authority is a full authority in the sense that the principal is not only bound by acts of the agent within the scope of actual authority, but is also entitled to the benefit of any rights against third parties created by the agent's authorised acts. However, while the conferral of actual authority renders the principal's legal relationship with third parties susceptible to alteration, actual authority belongs to the internal aspect of agency: it derives from an agreement between principal and agent to which the third party is a stranger and of which the third party may be unaware.[2]

Scope of Actual Authority

3.2   The scope of actual authority is determined by the interpretation of the principal's manifestation of consent as reasonably understood by the agent in the light of all the surrounding circumstances,[3] including any knowledge of the principal's intentions. Where the manifestation is unclear, ambiguous or uncertain, the agent is entitled to act in accordance with its own reasonable interpretation, and the principal will be bound accordingly. Thus, a principal that instructed its agent to procure and ship goods in the quantity of '500 tons . . . 50 tons more or less', with the unspecified intention that there be a single shipment of that quantity, was held bound by the agent's shipment of an initial quantity of 400 tons with the intention of procuring a supplementary shipment to make up the shortfall.[4] Where, however, the lack of clarity is perceived by the agent or is reasonably apparent, the agent should revert to the principal for clarification where this is

---

[1] For the exception, see below, paras 4.1–4.3 Further on consent, see above, paras 1.10–1.12.
[2] *Freeman & Lockyer v Buckhurst Park Properties (Mangal) Ltd* [1964] 2 QB 480, 502.
[3] *Ashford Shire Council v Dependable Motors Pty Ltd* [1961] AC 336, 348–50.
[4] *Ireland v Livingston* (1872) LR 5 HL 395. See also *Midland Bank Ltd v Seymour* [1955] 2 Lloyd's Rep 147, 153.

practicable.[5] In default of supplementary instructions, the agent is entitled to formulate and follow its own interpretation of the original instructions.[6]

3.3   Similarly, a situation may arise that calls for a decision in furtherance of its authorised mandate that the agent is not authorised to take unless it is impractical for the agent to refer to the principal for instructions. In such a case, a principal that fails to respond to a request for instructions will have to take the consequences of any opportunity foregone or any ensuing paralysis unless its conduct can be construed as conferring authority on the agent to take such decision as appears reasonable in all the circumstances and the agent duly exercises that additional authority.[7]

3.4   Just as the conferral of actual authority depends upon a manifestation of consent, so its continuance depends upon the absence of any manifestation of revocation of that consent. Except in narrowly prescribed circumstances, authority is revocable by the principal at any time.[8] Even if the agent has a contractual entitlement to enjoy the authority for a specified period, the principal retains the power to revoke the authority, albeit no right to revoke so that revocation falls to be sanctioned as a breach of contract.[9] It follows that the question of whether an agent enjoys actual authority falls to be determined at the time of the relevant act. It follows also that, where agency is created by contract, the question of the scope of the actual authority to be conferred pursuant to the contract is distinct from the question of whether any particular act of the agent was in fact authorised. The former question is determined as a matter of contractual interpretation in accordance with the normal principles of contract law.[10] However, post-formation statements or conduct inadmissible as to the interpretation of the original agreement[11] will be admissible to prove an exercise by the principal of its power to vary at any time the scope of the agent's actual authority.

3.5   Actual authority may be said to be 'express' where conferred by explicit stipulation, or 'implied' where inferred from the express terms or circumstances of the conferral. An agent expressly charged to accomplish a task or fulfil a role has, subject to contrary intention, implied actual authority to undertake all matters necessary to that accomplishment[12] or that would ordinarily be undertaken by

---

[5] *Woodhouse AC Israel Cocoa Ltd SA v Nigerian Produce Marketing Co Ltd* [1972] AC 741, 772; *European Asian Bank AG v Punjab & Sind Bank* [1983] 1 WLR 642, 656. In the analogous case of *Credit Agricole Indosuez v Muslim Commercial Bank Ltd* [2000] Lloyd's Rep 275, the timeframe rendered the seeking of clarification commercially unrealistic.

[6] See also below, paras 3.8, 3.10.

[7] *cf* DCFR, which similarly requires the agent to seek directions if practical (art IV.D-4:102, 4:104), but always entitles the agent to exercise its discretion in default of any response (art IV.D-4:103).

[8] For the exception of irrevocable authority, see below, paras 11.21–11.25.

[9] See below, para 11.13.

[10] *Freeman & Lockyer v Buckhurst Park Properties (Mangal) Ltd* [1964] 2 QB 480, 502.

[11] *James Miller & Partners Ltd v Whitworth Street Estates (Manchester) Ltd* [1970] AC 572, 603.

[12] *Howard v Baillie* (1796) 2 H Bl 618, 619 (Eyre CJ): an express authority 'necessarily includes medium powers, which are not expressed. By medium powers, I mean all the means necessary to be used, in order to attain the accomplishment of the object of the principal power'. Also *Pole v Leask* (1860) 28 Beav 562, 574.

someone so charged. Consequently, appointment to a position that ordinarily carries with it a range of powers, such as the managing director or chief executive officer of a company or the master of a ship, confers implied actual authority to exercise all such powers, although always subject to contrary intention.[13] Similarly, appointment of a professional agent to act on behalf of the principal in certain matters falling within the trade, business or profession of that agent impliedly authorises the agent to act in all respects and in all matters as is normal for such a person so appointed.

3.6 The principal may also be considered impliedly to consent to the agent acting in accordance with the customs of a particular market, namely practices that are not merely generally followed but to which all participants in that market are considered obliged to adhere.[14] A market practice will not, however, be considered a market custom to which the principal impliedly consents unless:[15] first, it is clear and certain; secondly, it attracts universal acquiescence within the market as 'in effect the common law within that place to which it extends although contrary to the general law of the realm';[16] and, thirdly, it is reasonable. Thus, the mere fact of appointment of an agent will not found implied consent to a practice that requires the agent to act against the principal's interests or to deny its status as fiduciary of the principal by acting also on behalf of the third party. For example, in the London insurance market, the broker acts as agent for the assured, and the courts accordingly declared unreasonable a practice whereby the broker would act on behalf of the insurer in the investigation and handling of a claim by obtaining for the insurer a confidential assessor's report and maintaining confidentiality as against the assured.[17] A principal will be bound only on proof of knowledge of the unreasonable practice demonstrating adoption of the custom by the principal.[18] Knowledge

[13] *Hely-Hutchinson v Brayhead Ltd* [1968] 1 QB 549 (company chairman who also acted as de facto managing director and chief executive had implied actual authority in the latter capacity, albeit not in the former to give letters of indemnity and guarantee on behalf of the company); *Smith v Butler* [2012] EWCA Civ 314, [2012] BCC 645 (no implied actual authority for a company's managing director to dismiss the executive chairman of the board of directors). Note that the scope of ordinary powers may change over time, requiring the application of principle to a particular office to be reassessed: *Panorama Developments (Guildford) Ltd v Fidelis Furnishing Fabrics Ltd* [1971] 2 QB 711 (position of company secretary carries more extensive powers than in the nineteenth century).

[14] On this distinction between practices commonly followed and legal customs, see *Drexel Burnham Lambert International NV v El Nasr* [1986] 1 Lloyd's Rep 356, 365.

[15] *Oricon Waren-Handels GmbH v Intergraan NV* [1967] 2 Lloyd's Rep 82, 96; *Cunliffe-Owen v Teather & Greenwood* [1967] 1 WLR 1421, 1438.

[16] *Oricon*, 96 (Roskill J), citing W McNair et al, *Scrutton on Charterparties*, 17th edn (London, Sweet & Maxwell, 1964), p 23.

[17] *Anglo-African Merchants Ltd v Bayley* [1970] 1 QB 311; *North & South Trust Co v Berkeley* [1971] 1 WLR 470 .

[18] In the absence of proof of the requisite knowledge and acquiescence, therefore, an assured will not be bound by a London insurance market custom of discharging claims liabilities through a system of general accounts between insurers and brokers in which premium rights and claims liabilities under all policies placed by the broker are pooled and set off: *Bartlett v Pentland* (1830) 10 B & Cr 760; *Sweeting v Pearce* (1861) 30 LJCP 109. Such a custom produces the result that, in the event of the broker becoming insolvent between set-off and payment over to the assured, the proceeds of the assured's

will not, however, save a custom that is not merely unreasonable but unlawful where enforcement of the custom would frustrate the rule of illegality.[19]

3.7   Expressions of apparent consent to wide-ranging authority must be construed with care so that they are not read as conferring more extensive authority than a proper interpretation of the wording can fairly justify. Where the wording refers to specific purposes and also includes general powers, a proper interpretation of the instrument as a whole may confine the general powers to that which is necessary to accomplish the specific purposes. Where the instrument takes the form of a deed, such a restrictive interpretation will be adopted.[20] If it is indeed desired to confer actual authority in the widest terms, namely unfettered power to do anything that the principal can itself lawfully do through an agent, subsequent disputes about interpretation can be avoided by executing a power of attorney in a prescribed form.[21]

Necessity

3.8   An agent confronted by an emergency not expressly contemplated by the terms of its actual authority, and unable realistically to seek further instructions, may respond either by entering into a contract with a third party for the provision of assistance purportedly on behalf of the principal, or by procuring assistance in its own name and thereby incurring expenditure. In such a case, the traditional analysis has been an extension of authority by virtue of 'agency of necessity', importing an exercise of authority endowed by the circumstances of emergency, rather than by consent. It is suggested, however, that any authority lends itself to analysis as an aspect of implied actual authority as reflecting, in the circumstances, the natural response of any reasonable person in the position of the principal.[22] Where, moreover, the agent's response does not affect the principal's legal relations with any third party, the better analysis does not involve agency at all.

3.9   Respect for the autonomy of the principal over its own affairs militates against a wide extension of an agent's mandate, resulting in a narrow concept of necessity. There is indeed only one clearly recognised contemporary example of extended authority to engage the principal in legal relations with a third party, and that is confined to the distinctive domain of maritime law. The master of a

---

claim are applied in discharge of premium payments owed by other assureds and the assured is left an unsecured creditor in the broker's insolvency.

[19] That the effect of illegality depends on the purpose behind the particular rule of illegality, see *St John Shipping Corp v Joseph Rank Ltd* [1957] 1 QB 267, 283; *Archbold's (Freightage) Ltd v S Spanglett Ltd* [1961] 1 QB 374.

[20] *Midland Bank Ltd v Reckitt* [1933] AC 1.

[21] Powers of Attorney Act 1971, s 10(1). This does not preclude challenges based on vitiated intent.

[22] Restatement, § 2.02 Comment (b).

vessel as agent of the shipowner enjoys actual authority to take all reasonable measures in the safe prosecution of the maritime adventure upon which the vessel is engaged.[23] Consequently, a contract of salvage concluded in appropriate circumstances of danger binds the shipowner.[24] However, at common law, the master and the shipowner also have the power to bind cargo-owners to such a contract where it is impractical to communicate with them to obtain express instructions,[25] because of the imminence of the emergency or the number of parties involved. Such authority, however, while triggered in its operation by circumstances of necessity, may be analysed as an implied incident of the contract of carriage, and thus as a form of implied actual authority.[26] The matter is now addressed by international convention, which provides not only that the master of a vessel has authority to conclude salvage contracts on behalf of the shipowner, but that the shipowner and the master have authority to do so on behalf of the owner of any property on board.[27] Were, however, similar circumstances of necessity to arise outside the maritime context, for example in the course of the carriage or storage of goods on land, it would remain necessary to appeal to common law principle.[28]

3.10   On termination of authority, a need may arise for the agent still to intervene on the principal's behalf. For example, where an agent makes an authorised purchase of perishable goods but the agency is then terminated, the circumstances may be such that only intervention by the former agent of its own motion (it being, crucially, impractical to seek instructions from the principal[29]) to sell or store the goods will preserve the value they represent.[30] The international instruments all provide that, notwithstanding termination of authority, the agent continues to have

---

[23]   *The Unique Mariner (No 1)* [1978] 1 Lloyd's Rep 438, 449 (Brandon J): 'the implied actual authority of a master, unless restricted by . . . instructions lawfully given, extends to doing whatever is incidental to, or necessary for, the successful prosecution of the voyage and the safety and preservation of the ship.'

[24]   *The Renpor* (1883) LR 8 PD 115, 118.

[25]   *Industrie Chimiche Italia Centrale & Cerealfin SA v Alexander G Tsavliris & Sons Maritime Co (The Choko Star)* [1990] 1 Lloyd's Rep 516.

[26]   Even conclusion of a contract of salvage reasonable in the circumstances but contrary to instructions sought and obtained should be considered as falling within actual authority. The requirement for cargo-owners' consent if practical to be obtained should be read as subject to the limitation that consent is not to be unreasonably withheld. Otherwise, any cargo-owner could veto the conclusion of an *ex hypothesi* appropriate response to a threat to not just its own cargo but also the vessel and other cargoes on board. Indeed, such subordination of the autonomy of individual interests to the maritime adventure as a whole is the basis of the maritime law doctrine of general average.

[27]   International Convention on Salvage 1989, art 6(2), incorporated into English law as Sch 11, Merchant Shipping Act 1995. The concept of salvage imports a response to danger (see art 1(a)) that may be equated with the circumstances of emergency required to trigger authority of necessity: *Tsavliris Salvage (International) Ltd v Guangdong Shantou Overseas Chinese Materials Marketing Co (The Pa Mar)* [1999] 1 Lloyd's Rep 338, 342.

[28]   It has been stated obiter that delay in land transit of perishable goods could generate an authority to sell (*Sims & Co v Midland Railway Co* [1913] 1 KB 103, 112), but the land context reduces the likelihood of inability to communicate with the principal.

[29]   *China Pacific SA v Food Corp of India (The Winson)* [1982] AC 939, 961–62; *ENE Kos 1 Ltd v Petroleo Brasileiro SA (No 2)* [2012] UKSC 17, [2012] 2 WLR 976, [26].

[30]   The example is taken from PICC, art 2.2.10(2), Comment 3.

authority to take such measures as are necessary to prevent harm to the principal's interests.[31] It is unclear whether English law would adopt a similar position or consider that a principal that terminates the authority of an agent previously authorised to deal in perishable goods without making provision for goods in the agent's possession takes the risk of any ensuing loss. However, any recognition of continuing authority need not be based on a separate concept of agency of necessity. Authority could be analysed as operating, in the manner of contractual obligations, on primary and secondary levels,[32] with a secondary level of authority reflecting the assumed intention of the principal and encompassing necessary interventions upon termination of the primary level of actual authority. So analysed, the secondary level of authority would fall within implied actual authority.[33]

3.11   Where an agent does not purport to bind its principal to a third party but merely seeks recovery of expenditure incurred, the matter falls to be analysed not as one of implied actual authority leading to reimbursement under the agent's indemnity, but rather as a claim not dependent upon agency at all but arising in the law of unjust enrichment by reason of necessitous intervention. Such a claim arises notably where a contract giving rise to a bailment is terminated, but the bailee remains in possession without instructions for the disposition of the goods. The bailee having a continuing duty to care for the goods, a claim for restitution of expenses reasonably and necessarily incurred in their preservation will arise even if instructions can be and are sought of the bailor but none are forthcoming.[34]

Delegation

Whether Delegation Authorised

3.12   Agency involves an election by the principal of the person who is to act on the principal's behalf, in whose judgement and skill the principal is content to trust, and by whom the principal is content to be represented in dealings with third parties. An agent is not entitled to substitute its own judgement on such

---

[31] PECL, art 3:209(3); PICC, art 2.2.10(2); DCFR, art II-6:112(4).

[32] See *Photo Productions Ltd v Securicor Transport Ltd* [1980] AC 827.

[33] An analysis based upon implied actual authority would, it is admitted, be strained where there was no pre-existing relationship so that necessity was the basis not just of authority but of agency itself. Even in such a case, however, agency would be relevant only if the principal's relationship with a third party were in issue rather than indemnification in respect of liabilities incurred (see next paragraph).

[34] *China Pacific SA v Food Corp of India (The Winson)* [1982] AC 939; *ENE Kos 1 Ltd v Petroleo Brasileiro SA (No 2)* [2012] UKSC 17, [2012] 2 WLR 976, [18]–[29]. The cases analyse recovery as based on bailment rather than unjust enrichment, but the principle of necessitous intervention in the law of unjust enrichment is sufficiently broad to embrace interventions whether originating in bailment or otherwise: C Mitchell, P Mitchell and S Watterson (eds), *Goff & Jones, The Law of Unjust Enrichment*, 8th edn (London, Sweet & Maxwell, 2011), ch 18; G Virgo, *The Principles of the Law of Restitution*, 2nd edn (Oxford, Oxford University Press, 2006), ch 11.

election for that of the principal; consequently, appointment by an agent of its own motion of a delegate to fulfil the function allocated to it by the principal is not permitted[35] and, indeed, is considered a breach of fiduciary duty.[36] Delegation is legitimate, in consequence, only when the true interpretation of the agent's actual authority so permits. Thus, where the agent lacks necessary expertise or market access to perform a requested act, the agent will have implied actual authority to employ an appropriate delegate.[37] More broadly, it may be asked whether it would be reasonable to expect personal performance by the agent, since a principal must be taken impliedly to consent to delegation of acts that it would be unreasonable to expect the agent to perform personally.[38]

3.13 The prohibition on delegation does not extend to ministerial acts, namely acts that do not involve any exercise of skill and judgement, or any personal representation. It is assumed that agents will not necessarily perform purely mechanical acts personally. Accordingly, an advertising contractor authorised to terminate licences to advertise on certain sites was entitled to employ solicitors to perform the ministerial act of issuing termination notices. The solicitors did not exercise any judgement as to whether or when to terminate, but acted entirely on the contractor's instructions, in effect as the contractor's amanuensis.[39] The agent will, of course, incur liability to the principal should a ministerial act not be performed properly.

Consequences of Authorised Delegation

3.14 In English law, there is generally no direct contractual relationship between a principal and an agent's delegate. Authority to delegate is not of itself considered to import authority to generate contractual privity between the principal and the delegate.[40] Consequently, in exercising the authority to delegate, the agent contracts on its own account with the delegate, acting in this respect as a commission agent. The delegation generates a sub-agency, with contractual liabilities operating strictly in string: in the event of default, the delegate sub-agent is liable to the

---

[35] *McCann (John) & Co v Pow* [1974] 1 WLR 1643. The point is often expressed by means of the Latin maxim *delegatus non delegare potest*.

[36] See below, para 6.28.

[37] For example, only Lloyd's registered brokers have direct access to all insurers operating in the Lloyd's insurance market. Where a risk is to be placed at Lloyd's and the broker engaged by the assured lacks Lloyd's registration, the assured's agent (known as a 'producing broker') will in turn engage a Lloyd's broker as sub-agent to act as a 'placing broker'. Similarly, where an agent is engaged to sell goods in parts of the world where it has no presence: *De Bussche v Alt* (1878) 8 Ch D 286.

[38] See PECL, art 3:206; PICC, art 2.2.8; DCFR, art II-6:104(3). The European Principles explicitly prohibit delegation in respect of acts 'of a personal character', but this adds nothing, since it would by definition be reasonable to expect personal performance of such acts by the agent.

[39] *Allam & Co v Europa Poster Services Ltd* [1968] 1 WLR 638. See also *Burial Board of the Parish of St Margaret, Rochester v Thompson* (1871) LR 6 CP 445, 457–58 (digging a grave and ringing a bell).

[40] *Calico Printers Association v Barclays Bank Ltd* (1930) 36 Com Cas 71.

agent, and the agent is liable to the principal.[41] The agent's liability for the default of the delegate reflects not only the absence of liability of the delegate to the principal but also the fact that authority to obtain assistance in performing cannot be construed as a licence to the agent by delegation to absolve itself of liability for non-performance or malperformance.[42]

3.15 It may be clear from the terms of the contracts that a chain of discrete contractual relationships, with rights and obligations operating strictly in string, is the deliberate choice of the parties.[43] Otherwise, however, the rationale for the denial of a direct contractual relationship between principal and sub-agent delegate is elusive. Why should privity between principal and the agent's counterparty be the norm when the agent is procuring a contract with a third party[44] but the exception when the counterparty is a sub-agent? Absence of a direct relationship is said to reflect the normal desire of the agent to maintain a position between its client principal and the sub-agent,[45] but unless the identity of the principal is kept secret, the agent's commercial position as intermediary is unavoidably vulnerable. It may also reflect a difference in nature between the relationship between the agent and sub-agent as two professionals in the same market or profession and that between the agent and the market-outsider principal.[46] However, any difference in market status would be accommodated when considering whether the sub-agent had discharged its obligations in communicating with the agent and does not require, in the event of a finding of liability, immunity from suit at the hands of the principal. It is notable that the contrary position is adopted by the Restatement and international soft law instruments, all of which provide for a direct relationship between principal and sub-agent (without prejudice to that between principal and appointing agent).[47]

3.16 English law does acknowledge the possibility of an alternative analysis of the agent being authorised to introduce a second (co-)agent with a direct rela-

---

[41] *Trading & General Investment Corp v Gault Armstrong & Keble Ltd (The Okeanis)* [1986] 1 Lloyd's Rep 195, 201.

[42] And see above, para 1.30.

[43] *Grosvenor Casinos Ltd v National Bank of Abu Dhabi* [2008] EWHC511 (Comm), [2008] 1 CLC 399 (Uniform Rules for Collections (URC 522)).

[44] See below, para 9.6.

[45] *Prentis Donegan & Partners Ltd v Leeds & Leeds Co Inc* [1998] 2 Lloyd's Rep 326, 334.

[46] *Pangood Ltd v Barclay Brown & Co Ltd* [1999] Lloyd's Rep IR 405, 408 (the suggestion in the judgment is directed towards refuting tortious liability, but is equally apposite with respect to contractual liability).

[47] Restatement, § 3.15(1) (the provision speaks of principal and sub-agent having a 'relationship of agency', which accommodates the possibility of the sub-agent being engaged on a non-contractual basis). See also PECL, art 3:206, including Comment C; PICC, art 2.2.8. The Draft CFR distinguishes delegation of authority from delegation of performance. Delegation of authority by the agent is authorised when personal performance by the agent cannot reasonably be expected; it takes effect as if effected by the principal, generating direct relations between principal and delegate: DCFR, art II-6:104(3), II-6:105. In contrast, the agent is permitted to delegate performance of any obligation in whole or in part unless the agency agreement requires personal performance, but the agent remains responsible for due performance of the delegated acts: DCFR, art IV.D-3:302.

tionship with the principal.[48] The appointing agent is responsible only for the exercise of appropriate care in selecting the co-agent and not for any subsequent default by the co-agent. Such an analysis has, however, been said to be 'indeed an exception, and a narrow one' requiring proof of 'special factors' to support its applicability.[49] Possible factors indicative of co-agency include evidence either of direct communications between the principal and second agent or that the appointing agent had authority to introduce a second agent but not itself to accomplish the principal object of the agency.[50]

3.17 It is noteworthy that in the leading example of co-agency, a finding of contractual privity was the basis for holding a delegate liable as a fiduciary to account to the principal for secret profits.[51] It is, however, unclear that fiduciary remedies are dependent on a direct relationship.[52] Were they indeed exercisable by a principal against a delegate one or more links removed in a relationship chain, a co-agency analysis would lose attractiveness and utility as an instrumental device.[53]

3.18 Reverting to the traditional and dominant English law analysis, of sub-agency with no direct relationship between principal and sub-agent, the principal may nevertheless hold the sub-agent liable in the case of a contractual sub-agency attracting the operation of the Contracts (Rights of Third Parties) Act 1999. Two conditions must be satisfied. First, either the sub-agency must provide that it is enforceable by the principal, or the term the principal wishes to enforce must purport to confer a benefit on the principal and, in this latter case, the contract as a whole must not rebut a resulting presumption that the principal is intended to be able to enforce the term.[54] Secondly, the principal must be 'expressly identified in the contract by name, as a member of a class or as answering a particular description'.[55]

3.19 Assuming, however, that the 1999 Act does not apply and that recourse against the agent is frustrated by insolvency or barred by exemption from liability,

---

[48] *De Bussche v Alt* (1878) 8 Ch D 286.
[49] *Prentis Donegan & Partners Ltd v Leeds & Leeds Co Inc* [1998] 2 Lloyd's Rep 326, 332 (Rix J).
[50] ibid.
[51] *De Bussche v Alt* (1878) 8 Ch D 286.
[52] See P Watts and F Reynolds (eds), *Bowstead & Reynolds on Agency*, 19th edn (London, Sweet & Maxwell, 2010) para 5-012. And see A Tettenborn, 'Principals, Sub-Agents and Accountability' (1999) 115 *Law Quarterly Review* 655.
[53] Modern jurisprudence demonstrates judicial resistance to be compelled to allow a wrongdoer to escape liability through the separation of cause of action from incidence of loss: *Offer-Hoar v Larkstore Ltd* [2006] EWCA Civ 1079, [2006] 1 WLR 2926, [85].
[54] Contracts (Rights of Third Parties) Act 1999, s 1(1), (2). If the remainder of the contract is neutral on enforcement by the principal, the presumption is not rebutted: *Nisshin Shipping Co Ltd v Cleaves & Co Ltd* [2003] EWHC 2602 (Comm), [2003] 2 CLC 1097, [23]. It is not, however, sufficient that the term will, in its performance, benefit the principal; rather it must, on its interpretation, be intended to confer a benefit.
[55] Contracts (Rights of Third Parties) Act 1999, s 1(3).

resort may be had to the *Albazero* exception to the privity rule,[56] whereby the appointing agent may recover damages in respect of the principal's loss, which it will then hold on trust for the principal, but the agent cannot be compelled to act and some uncertainty attends the precise circumstances in which the exception is available.[57] Exceptionally, the relationship between principal and agent may generate an interest on the part of the agent in performance of the delegated act,[58] but this is unlikely in the case of agent insolvency, and in any event the damages will compensate for a loss to the agent. They may not meet the loss sustained by the principal: where, for example, substitute performance is not possible and the agent is protected from liability against the principal, the agent's loss lies purely in possible prejudice to its prospects of future represention of the principal as a result of the sub-agent's default, whereas the principal may have sustained significant immediate loss. Moreover, the damages are received by the agent for its own account: if substitute performance is available, the agent's interest in performance that justifies their award may ensure their allocation towards procuring substitute performance; otherwise, however, they will swell the agent's bank account, leaving the principal devoid of benefit.

3.20   The discussion above concentrates on liability in contract. A sub-agent, in no direct relationship with the principal, may owe the principal a duty of care in the tort of negligence. Thus, the managing agent of a syndicate participating in the Lloyd's insurance market (sub-agent) owes a duty of care to an individual (principal) accepted on the syndicate under its management, albeit that the individual is represented by a members' agent which contracts with the managing agent. The latter professes special expertise regarding insurance business on which the individuals, to the knowledge of the managing agent, place absolute reliance.[59] Conversely, a placing Lloyd's broker (sub-agent) engaged by a producing broker (agent)[60] does not ordinarily owe a duty of care to draw the attention of the assured (principal) to particular terms in the contract of insurance obtained. The mere accepting of instructions from the producing broker to obtain a quotation and, subsequently, to procure cover on the terms of the quotation do not import an assumption of responsibility to the assured to explain the terms of the policy. The placing broker is entitled to assume that the assured will rely on the producing broker for any appropriate advice on the policy terms. The placing broker's only obligation is to ensure that the producing broker is properly advised of the terms of cover.[61]

---

[56] So known after *The Albazero* [1977] AC 774. See also *Alfred McAlpine Construction Ltd v Panatown Ltd* [2001] 1 AC 518.

[57] For discussion, see H Bennett, 'Bank Collections, Privity of Contract, and Third Party Losses' (2008) 124 *Law Quarterly Review* 532.

[58] The agent must be 'seeking compensation for a genuine loss and not merely using a technical breach to secure an uncovenanted profit': *Radford v de Froberville* [1977] 1 WLR 1262, 1270 (Oliver J).

[59] *Henderson v Merrett Syndicates Ltd* [1995] 2 AC 145.

[60] On producing and placing brokers, see above, n 37.

[61] *Pangood Ltd v Barclay Brown & Co Ltd* [1999] Lloyd's Rep IR 405.

Formalities

3.21   In general, the conferral of authority does not require compliance with any particular formalities. Even where the validity or enforceability of the authorised act is subject to compliance with a formality, there is no principle of complementarity whereby the conferral of authority to undertake such an act is subjected to the same formality requirement. Accordingly, authority may be conferred orally to purchase land, even though the authorised purchase must be formalised in writing.[62]

3.22   By way of exception, authority to execute a deed must be conferred by deed,[63] and, by virtue of statute, written authority is required for the creation or disposal of an interest in land[64] (but not for the creation of a contract for the disposition of an interest in land[65]) or for the disposition of an equitable interest or trust subsisting at the time of the disposition.[66]

---

[62] *Heard v Pilley* (1869) 4 Ch App 548. See also *McLaughlin v Duffill* [2008] EWCA Civ 1627, [2010] Ch 1.

[63] *Berkeley v Hardy* (1826) 5 B & C 355.

[64] Law of Property Act 1925, s 53(1)(a).

[65] *McLaughlin v Duffill* [2008] EWCA Civ 1627, [2010] Ch 1.

[66] Law of Property Act 1925, s 53(1)(c).

4

Apparent Authority

4.1   Actual authority gives effect to the intentions of the parties to the agency relationship. However, whether through innocent oversight or otherwise, an agent may overstep the boundaries stipulated by the principal, while appearing to remain within its mandate. The utility of agency would be significantly diminished if third parties could not repose confidence in the external appearance of authority, but needed, on the occasion of any interaction with an intermediary known to be an agent, to seek verification of the authorised nature of the agent's actions.[1] This is the rationale for 'apparent authority' (also known as 'ostensible authority'), whereby the principal is bound by an act that is not in fact authorised. Most commonly, it arises where a genuine agent exceeds the scope of its actual authority, but it may also arise where the legal recognition of agency itself reflects appearance rather than true consent.

Juridical Nature of Apparent Authority

4.2   Some difficulty surrounds the theoretical underpinning of apparent authority. One explanation is that apparent authority is a manifestation of the same objective approach to consent that operates in the law of contract.[2] That an objective appearance of agreement belies the true intentions of one party does not deny an agreement effective in law to found an enforceable contract.[3] Accordingly, an offer remains available for acceptance notwithstanding that the offeror has changed its mind but has not communicated that change of mind to the offeree.[4] Likewise, where an agent is ostensibly authorised to make an offer on behalf of the principal, any offer the agent subsequently makes that does not appear to trans-

---

[1]   W Seavey, 'The Rationale of Agency' (1920) 29 *Yale Law Journal* 859, 885 (drawing an analogy in the commercial context with the need for third party confidence that underpins the concept of a negotiable instrument).

[2]   W Cook, 'Agency by Estoppel' (1905) 5 *Columbia Law Review* 36; Conant, 'The Objective Theory of Agency: Apparent Authority and the Estoppel of Apparent Ownership' (1968) 47 *Nebraska Law Review* 678; G McMeel, 'Philosophical Foundations of the Law of Agency' (2000) 116 *Law Quarterly Review* 387.

[3]   *Smith v Hughes* (1871) LR 6 QB 597; *Paal Wilson & Co A/S v Partenreederei Hannah Blumenthal (The Hannah Blumenthal)* [1983] AC 854, 915–16.

[4]   *Byrne & Co v Van Tienhoven* (1880) 5 CPD 344.

gress the scope of the authority conferred indicates, viewed objectively, the willingness of the principal to contract on the terms stated. That the offer in truth transgresses a restriction on the agent's authority unknown to the third party offeree is no more effective than a decision by the principal not communicated to the third party not to contract after all. The alternative analysis invokes a form of estoppel. On this approach, apparent authority is based on a misrepresentation by the principal of the existence or scope of the agent's authority that induces a change of position by the third party.

4.3 The Restatement comprehends apparent authority in terms of objective consent.[5] The English courts, in contrast, have consistently espoused an estoppel analysis.[6] It is arguable that some dilution of the traditional requirements for estoppel is required in order to accommodate the scope of apparent authority as established in the cases.[7] However, the doctrine of estoppel has been described as 'powerful and flexible',[8] and leading treatises on the doctrine accommodate apparent authority with no hesitation.[9] And indeed, estoppel by representation and apparent authority share a common underlying policy, namely to preclude an 'unconscionable' and 'prejudicial inconsistency of conduct' on the part of the principal in first holding out and subsequently denying certain conduct as authorised.[10] The substantive concern is whether the need to channel apparent authority through the requirements for estoppel impacts adversely upon the protection offered by agency law against injurious reliance by the third party upon misleading appearances of authority facilitated or permitted by the principal.

4.4 The difference in analysis also affects the position of the principal. Analysed as giving rise to fully effective consent, apparent authority is a form of full authority that generates a contract binding on both principal and third party.[11] In contrast, an estoppel confers no rights on the party estopped as against the party in whose favour the estoppel arises. Consequently, an estoppel analysis of apparent authority prevents the principal from denying the agent's authority, entitling the third party to hold the principal to the agent's act, but affords the principal no rights against the third party. This one-sided approach is adopted also by the

---

[5] Restatement, § 2.03, Comment (c).

[6] *Rama Corp Ltd v Proved Tin & General Investments Ltd* [1952] 2 QB 147, 149–50; *Freeman & Lockyer v Buckhurst Park Properties (Mangal) Ltd* [1964] 2 QB 480, 494, 498, 504–05; *Armagas Ltd v Mundogas SA (The Ocean Frost)* [1986] AC 717, 777.

[7] P Watts and F Reynolds (eds), *Bowstead and Reynolds on Agency*, 19th edn (London, Sweet & Maxwell, 2010) para 8-029.

[8] *Canada & Dominion Sugar Co Ltd v Canadian National (West Indies) Steam Ships Ltd* [1947] AC 46, 55 (Lord Wright), quoting Sir Frederick Pollock.

[9] Spencer Bower, *The Law Relating to Estoppel by Representation*, 4th edn, (P Feltham, D Hochberg and T Leech eds, London, LexisNexis UK, 2004) ch IX; K Handley, *Estoppel by Conduct and Election* (London, Sweet & Maxwell, 2006) ch 9. *Cf* S Wilken and K Ghaly, *The Law of Waiver, Variation and Estoppel*, 3rd edn (Oxford, Oxford University Press, 2012), paras 16.11–16.16.

[10] *Homburg Houtimport BV v Agrosin Pte Ltd (The Starsin)* [1999] CLC 1769, 1781 (Colman J).

[11] Restatement, § 2.03, Comment (e) (but note that the Restatement preserves estoppel as a distinct rule of attribution: § 2.05). See also PECL, art 3:201(3), 3:202; DCFR, art II-6:103(3).

Unidroit Principles.[12] The practical significance of this difference is diminished by the possibility for the principal to generate enforceable rights against the third party by ratifying the agent's unauthorised act, although there are circumstances where ratification is unavailable.[13]

Apparent Authority Within the External Aspect of Agency

4.5   While actual authority is created by a manifestation of consent from the principal to the agent that the latter should act on the principal's behalf, apparent authority constitutes a relationship between the principal and the third party based upon the principal's holding out of the agent as authorised to act on the principal's behalf.[14] Actual authority, therefore, belongs to the internal aspect of agency, apparent authority to the external aspect. The two forms of authority may coexist, but are independent of each other.[15] Where there is actual authority for the agent's act, the coexistence of apparent authority is of no practical significance. Where the agent's act lacks actual authority, apparent authority will entitle the third party to hold the principal to the agent's act, but will not protect the agent from suit by the principal.[16]

The Basic Requirements for Apparent Authority

4.6   According to English law's estoppel analysis, apparent authority has two requirements: first, a representation by the principal to the third party that the agent is clothed with certain authority, and, secondly, reliance on the representation by the third party. These will be considered in order to establish the general picture before returning to more difficult questions concerning the making of the requisite representation.

---

[12] PICC, art 2.2.5(2). This is regarded as an application of the principle of good faith in art 1.7 and of the prohibition on inconsistent behaviour in art 1.8, drafted in terms redolent of estoppel.

[13] For discussion of ratification, see below, ch 5.

[14] *Freeman & Lockyer v Buckhurst Park Properties (Mangal) Ltd* [1964] 2 QB 480, 503.

[15] ibid, 502.

[16] Whether and to what extent the agent may be held liable even where the principal ratifies is more difficult: see below, paras 5.26–5.32.

A Representation of Authority

4.7 Consistent with the general approach to contract formation, whether the principal has made to the third party a representation of authority in respect of a certain person and, if so, the extent of authority represented, is determined objectively in the light of all relevant circumstances by reference to a reasonable person in the position of the third party, tempered by any contrary knowledge the actual third party possesses.[17]

4.8 A principal may state expressly, in terms, and directly to the third party that the agent enjoys authority that in truth the agent does not. Generally, however, the representation arises impliedly by conduct. The appointment of an agent to a position generally associated with the exercise of certain powers, such as managing director of a company or master of a vessel, amounts to a representation that the person so appointed is authorised to exercise the usual powers of a person so appointed (or is 'clothed with the trappings of authority' usually attendant upon such a position). Assuming nothing has been agreed to the contrary between principal and agent, the agent will have actual authority to that extent. Where, however, a limitation upon the usual range of powers has been agreed, the agent's actual authority will be so limited, but the agent will have apparent authority to the full extent of the usual range of powers when dealing with any third party unaware of the agreed limitation.[18] Accordingly, where a company director is authorised to sign certain contracts of a type a director would normally be authorised to sign but subject to inclusion of certain terms, and signs a contract of the authorised type but omitting the required terms, the company will still be bound because of the representation made by the company to the third party by appointment to a directorial position:

> The representation in such a case is not that the director is acting with the approval of the company in respect of each detail of the contract but that the transaction is one of a kind to which the director has authority to bind the company and that his conduct in relation to the entering into of transactions of that kind may be relied upon as conduct authorised by the company and as giving rise to obligations by which the company will treat itself as bound. Notwithstanding that the director may not have had actual authority to agree to the details of the transaction and that the third party may have appreciated that the director would ordinarily need such authority, the company will still be bound under the ostensible authority principle unless the third party knew that the director did not have the requisite authority.[19]

---

[17] *MCI WorldCom International Inc v Primus Telecommunications Inc* [2004] EWCA Civ 957; [2004] 2 All ER (Comm) 833, [30]; [2003] EWHC 2182 (Comm); [2004] 1 All ER (Comm) 138; *ING Re (UK) Ltd v R & V Versicherung AG* [2006] EWHC 1544 (Comm), [2006] 2 All ER (Comm) 870, [128].

[18] *Re Henley* (1876) 4 Ch D 133; *Hely-Hutchinson v Brayhead Ltd* [1968] 1 QB 549, 583.

[19] *Homburg Houtimport BV v Agrosin Pte Ltd (The Starsin)* [1999] CLC 1769, 1781 (Colman J).

4.9   Again, a principal that honours an unauthorised act without qualification and continues to employ the same agent in further dealings with the same third party thereby represents to that third party that the agent has authority in respect of the act and will be bound by repeat examples of that act by the agent.[20] Conversely, a statement that denies authority and of which the third party knows or ought reasonably to know negates any representation that might otherwise exist.[21]

4.10   Where an agent enjoys both actual and apparent authority, termination of actual authority will not affect the third party unless the termination is effected in such a manner as also to negate the representation on which the apparent authority is based.[22]

Reliance

4.11   As an orthodox example of a traditional form of estoppel, namely common law estoppel by representation, apparent authority should require reliance upon the representation in the form of an alteration of position such that the third party would incur a detriment if the principal were now permitted to deny the authority represented.[23] However, formulations adopted by the English courts generally refer simply to reliance with no mention of detriment,[24] reliance often being envisaged as consisting of no more than entering into the proposed transaction with the principal on the faith of the representation.[25] There can, accordingly, be no reliance if the third party is unaware of any representation or is aware of but not actuated by it,[26] although the fact of entering the proposed transaction is generally sufficient, in the absence of contrary factors, to prove a causal link between the representation and the transaction.[27] No consideration, however, is given to

---

[20]   See, by analogy, *Rockland Industries Inc v Amerada Minerals Corp of Canada Ltd* (1980) 108 DLR (3d) 513, below para 11.26.

[21]   *Overbrooke Estates Ltd v Glencombe Properties Ltd* [1974] 1 WLR 1335.

[22]   See below, paras 11.26–11.27.

[23]   *Grundt v Great Boulder Pty Gold Mines Ltd* (1937) 59 CLR 641, 674–75.

[24]   *Rama Corp Ltd v Proved Tin & General Investments Ltd* [1952] 2 QB 147, 149–50.

[25]   *Freeman & Lockyer v Buckhurst Park Properties (Mangal) Ltd* [1964] 2 QB 480, 505–06; *Arctic Shipping Co Ltd v Mobilia AB (The Tatra)* [1990] 2 Lloyd's Rep 51, 59; *Armagas Ltd v Mundogas SA (The Ocean Frost)* [1986] AC 717, 777. Even this is an exaggeration: since under English law the liability of the third party is not engaged by the agent's unauthorised purported conclusion of a contract, technically the third party forsakes the opportunity to seek a more advantageous alternative under the mistaken belief of incurral of obligation and usually exposes itself to the possibility of engagement of liability through ratification by the principal.

[26]   *Polish Steamship Co v AJ Williams Fuels (Overseas Sales) Ltd (The Suwalki)* [1989] 1 Lloyd's Rep 511, 515; *Acute Property Developments Ltd v Apostolou* [2013] EWHC 200 (Ch), [25] (third party induced to act not by position to which agent appointed but by the close personal relationship between them).

[27]   *Thanakharn Kasikorn Thai Chamkat (Mahachon) v Akai Holdings Ltd* [2010] HKFCA 64, [2011] 1 HKC 357, [74]–[75].

the consequences to the third party of loss of the transaction were the principal permitted to resile from the representation of authority. Even a suggestion that detriment flowing from resiling from the representation is presumed is open to the objection that an example of a principal seeking to adduce evidence in rebuttal of such a presumption is elusive. It is probable, therefore, that apparent authority is based upon an attenuated form of estoppel that does not require any detrimental aspect to reliance.

4.12   There can be no reliance where the third party is possessed of actual knowledge of the lack of authority, including subjective awareness of the possibility that the agent may lack authority and recklessly proceeding without obtaining verification.[28] Reliance, however, need not be objectively reasonable: the mere fact that a reasonable person in the position of the third party would not have relied on the representation at all, or in the way the third party did rely, affords no defence to a claim of apparent authority. People are entitled to rely on what they are told, and a principal that misleadingly represents an agent as having authority cannot complain if a third party believes the principal's representation. The third party owes the principal no obligation to consider the reliability of the representation with due diligence.[29] This is consistent with the general law of misrepresentation.[30] The latter, however, requires that a misstatement must both be objectively material in the sense of relevant in the mind of a hypothetical representee,[31] as well as subjectively affect the response of the actual representee. This, it is suggested, explains a concession that third party reliance must not be 'irrational', importing a seemingly objective limitation;[32] apparent authority is precluded where reliance would be not merely unreasonable by the third party in question but perverse, in that no reasonable third party would have placed reliance on the representation.[33]

---

[28] Reference is sometimes made to 'blind-eye knowledge' that arises where the third party is aware the agent in all probability lacks authority and declines formal confirmation. This may be regarded as actual knowledge in the strict sense of that phrase or a form of recklessness.

[29] *Thanakharn Kasikorn Thai Chamkat (Mahachon) v Akai Holdings Ltd* [2010] HKFCA 64, [2011] 1 HKC 357, [49]–[62]; *Quinn v CC Automotive Group Ltd* [2010] EWCA Civ 1412, [23], [27]; [2011] 2 All ER (Comm) 584 *Acute Property Developments Ltd v Apostolou* [2013] EWHC 200 (Ch), [39]. Contrary dicta in *Egyptian International Foreign Trade Co v Soplex Wholesale Supplies Ltd (The Raffaella)* [1985] 2 Lloyd's Rep 36, 41 must be considered as not good law.

[30] *Redgrave v Hurd* (1881) 20 Ch D 1. A contrary position is adopted by the European and Unidroit Principles and the Draft CFR, which require that reliance on which apparent authority is based must be reasonable (PECL, art 3:201(3); PICC, art 2.2.5(2); DCFR II-6:103(3)), and appear not to draw a direct parallel with the general law of misrepresentation in which reliance is denied only if the induced mistake is 'inexcusable' or 'grossly negligent' or reflects an assumed allocation of risk (PECL, art 4:103; PICC, art 3.5; DCFR, art II-7:201(2)).

[31] *Pan Atlantic Insurance Co Ltd v Pine Top Insurance Co Ltd* [1995] 2 AC 501. The author of a fraudulent misrepresentation is, however, denied any immateriality defence: *Gordon v Street* [1899] 2 QB 641.

[32] *Thanakharn Kasikorn Thai Chamkat (Mahachon) v Akai Holdings Ltd* [2010] HKFCA 64, [2011] 1 HKC 357, [49]–[50].

[33] Compare the limitation upon contractual discretions: below, para 6.11.

4.13 In a Singaporean case,[34] the finance manager of a trading company fraudulently induced a commercial bank into believing that the company had accepted credit facilities and misappropriated funds subsequently advanced. The trading company was held not to have represented the finance manager to have authority either to accept the facilities or to communicate the company's decision to accept them. However, even had such a representation been made, the requisite reliance was absent. The bank had failed to exercise due diligence according to its own internal verification procedures to ensure that the facilities had indeed been accepted by the purported borrower in circumstances where it could easily have communicated with the company's senior management.[35] Moreover, the importance of banks to the proper functioning of the economy justified requiring of banks a higher standard of financial prudence and responsibility, and vigilance against fraud, than that expected of trading companies.[36]

4.14 The case was decided on the basis that a third party's reliance must be reasonable, and the bank had behaved unreasonably.[37] On that basis, it does not represent English law. Nevertheless, as a commercial lender, the bank was aware of the possibility of fraudulent appearances of authority and had designed verification procedures accordingly. On the facts, the bank knowingly failed to follow those procedures. The bank could not, therefore, plausibly be said to have been unaware of the possibility that any representation of authority was unreliable and was, therefore, not merely negligent but reckless in proceeding without obtaining verification. And, indeed, it was held at first instance that the bank 'willingly assumed the risk' of fraud on the part of the agent and hence of a lack of authority.[38]

4.15 Reliance cannot be placed on a representation where the third party knows or cannot reasonably believe that it numbers among the intended representees.[39] Accordingly, a statement overheard by one who was not reasonably contemplated as a party to the conversation cannot give rise to apparent authority.[40] Where the representation is made to the world – typically where the representation takes the form of appointment to a position associated with certain authority – this issue necessarily does not arise.

---

[34] *Skandinaviska Enskilda Banken AB v Asia Pacific Breweries (Singapore) Pte Ltd* [2009] SGHC 197, [2009] 4 SLR (R) 788, affd [2011] SGCA 22, [2011] 3 SLR 540.

[35] [2009] SGHC 197, [125]–[127], [137]–[139], [173]–[191], [2011] SGCA 22, [22]

[36] [2011] SGCA 22, [94] (comments addressed to the issue of vicarious liability, but the policy concern is equally applicable to apparent authority).

[37] [2009] SGHC 197, [173]–[174], [177], [189]–[190].

[38] ibid, [173] (Belinda Ang J).

[39] *ING Re (UK) Ltd v R&V Versicherung AG* [2006] EWHC 1544 (Comm), [2006] 2 All ER (Comm) 870, [104]. An objective standard on this point is appropriate since the issue relates to the correct interpretation of the representation. Formulations later in the judgment that appear to adopt a subjective test of whether the third party knew or believed it was not an intended representee (ibid, [118]–[119]) reflect the defendant's submissions in the case rather than depart from the objective approach clearly espoused earlier.

[40] ibid, [118].

Fraud and Forgeries

4.16 The doctrine of apparent authority applies as normal in respect of an agent's acts that not only fall outside the agent's actual authority but also consti-tute a fraud on the principal,[41] reflecting the impracticality of challenging an agent's motives for acting in accordance with its apparent authority.[42] Suggestions, moreover, that an exception arises in respect of forged instruments, on the basis that a forgery is not merely a fraud but a total nullity so that in law there is no act that can be the subject of any form of authority, have been rejected. If the forgery appears to be a duly authorised instrument and the requirements of apparent authority are present, the third party is entitled to hold the principal bound.[43]

Representation by or on Behalf of the Principal

4.17 To bind the principal, the representation of the agent's authority must be made by the principal or be traceable to the principal in terms of actual or apparent authority to make a representation as to the agent's authority. Thus, where A1 has actual or apparent authority to make a representation on behalf of the principal ('representor authority') concerning the scope of the authority enjoyed by A2 to act on behalf of the principal ('actor authority'), the principal will be bound by any misrepresentation by A1 as to A2's actor authority. And where A1 has actual or apparent representor authority concerning the scope of A2's representor authority as to the scope of A3's actor authority, the principal will be bound by any mis-representation by A2 as to A3's actor authority that falls within A2's apparent representor authority, as itself created within A1's representor authority.[44]

---

[41] *Lloyd v Grace, Smith & Co* [1912] AC 716 (solicitors held liable for the acts of their managing clerk who fraudulently persuaded a client to sign documents transferring her entire estate to him); *Reckitt v Barnett, Pembroke & Slater Ltd* [1928] 2 KB 244, 257–58; *Briess v Woolley* [1954] AC 333. Unless, of course, the third party is aware the agent is acting against the principal's interests.

[42] *Hambro v Burnand* [1904] 2 KB 10, 26.

[43] *Uxbridge Permanent Building Society v Pickard* [1939] 1 KB 248, 256; *Lovett v Carson Country Homes Ltd* [2009] EWHC 1143 (Ch), [2009] 2 BCLC 196, [81]–[95].

[44] *Egyptian International Foreign Trade Co v Soplex Wholesale Supplies Ltd (The Raffaella)* [1985] 2 Lloyd's Rep 36, 43 (Browne-Wilkinson LJ). The seminal discussion of apparent authority by Diplock LJ in *Freeman & Lockyer v Buckhurst Park Properties (Mangal) Ltd* [1964] 2 QB 480, 505–06 appears to suggest that the representation must be traceable to the principal in terms of actual authority (see, eg, Kerr LJ in *The Raffaella*, 43), but there is no reason of logic or policy to deny the possibility of apparent authority to make representations as to authority, and other cases acknowledge apparent representor authority: *British Bank of the Middle East v Sun Life Assurance Co of Canada (UK) Ltd* [1983] 2 Lloyd's Rep 9, 16; *ING Re (UK) Ltd v R&V Versicherung AG* [2006] EWHC 1544 (Comm), [2006] 2 All ER (Comm) 870, [100]–[101].

4.18   Actual actor authority, whether express or implied through appointment
to a position that is associated with concluding certain transactions, imports
authority to make representations relating to matters within that actor authority.[45] Such actor authority, however, can neither sustain actual representor authority regarding extraneous matters nor constitute a representation that the agent
has representor authority regarding extraneous matters.[46] That does not, of
course, preclude an agent from otherwise having actual or apparent representor
authority to make representations regarding other matters, including the extent
of its own actor authority.[47] Commonly, apparent representor authority arises
through appointment to an appropriate position, the extent of such authority
being measured by what is usual for the holder of that position. In the absence of
representor authority, however, an agent without actual actor authority is incapable of generating apparent actor authority by itself making a representation as
to its own authority,[48] and apparent representor authority that extends to the
scope of the agent's own authority requires a most specific and unequivocal representation.[49] In the sense of this principle against self-authorisation, an agent
cannot pull himself up by his own bootstraps.[50]

4.19   Accordingly, where the only representation of authority takes the form of a
written instrument issued by the principal, the third party may not rely on a statement by the agent as to the content of the instrument;[51] reliance can be based only
upon knowledge of the content obtained by direct reading of the instrument or by
representation of the principal or another agent of the principal with authority,
actual or apparent, to speak to the content.

4.20   A principal may find itself precluded from disputing the validity of an
unauthorised act by virtue of apparent representor authority to represent that a
requisite precondition to actor authority is present. The prime example of this is
provided by solicitors' financial undertakings. It is part of the normal range of a
solicitor's professional services to provide financial undertakings on behalf of a
client, but only where the solicitor holds or expects to hold an appropriate sum of
the client's money, and only in connection with an underlying commercial transaction in respect of which the solicitor is acting for that client. Solicitors are not in
the business of extending financial undertakings for clients out of their own funds

---

[45] Such consequential authority will generally be actual, but to the extent of any restriction imposed
by the principal there will be apparent consequential representor authority.

[46] *Armagas Ltd v Mundogas SA (The Ocean Frost)* [1986] AC 717, 732 (Robert Goff LJ).

[47] *Egyptian International Foreign Trade Co v Soplex Wholesale Supplies Ltd (The Raffaella)* [1985]
2 Lloyd's Rep 36, 43 (Browne-Wilkinson LJ).

[48] *A-G for Ceylon v Silva* [1953] AC 461; *Freeman & Lockyer v Buckhurst Park Properties (Mangal)
Ltd* [1964] 2 QB 480, 504–05.

[49] See generally *Armagas Ltd v Mundogas SA (The Ocean Frost)* [1986] AC 717, discussed below,
para 4.24 et seq.

[50] *Egyptian International Foreign Trade Co v Soplex Wholesale Supplies Ltd (The Raffaella)* [1985]
2 Lloyd's Rep 36, 46.

[51] *Jacobs v Morris* [1902] 1 Ch 816.

or in respect of a matter to which they have no connection. Solicitors, in short, are not bankers. Suppose, however, that a culpable solicitor extends a financial undertaking on behalf of his firm in the absence of an appropriate underlying transaction. The firm will be bound through the doctrine of apparent authority where the third party reasonably believes, on the basis of information provided by the firm, that there is such a transaction. Importantly, the information on which the third party may formulate that view may be provided by the culpable solicitor.[52] A distinction must, however, be drawn. If the third party asks merely whether the solicitor is authorised to extend the undertaking, an affirmative answer constitutes illegitimate self-authorisation. The third party must instead receive information relating to the supposed transaction permitting the third party reasonably to formulate a judgement on the existence and nature of the described matter.[53]

4.21 Solicitors, therefore, have actual actor authority to provide financial undertakings binding on their firm in the ordinary course of their business as solicitors and actual representor authority to provide information relating to the underlying transaction. Where in truth but unknown to the third party there is no underlying transaction, there is apparent but not actual representor authority to provide information relevant to the existence of an underlying transaction and apparent but not actual actor authority to extend the undertaking. Solicitors do not, therefore, have the power to extend the scope of their actor authority beyond financial undertakings in the ordinary course of solicitorial business but do have apparent representor authority regarding whether the undertaking in question falls within the scope of such business and therefore, indirectly, whether the solicitor is in fact acting within the scope of actual authority.[54]

4.22 In some circumstances, it may be clear that the agent does not have authority to act in a particular matter without obtaining prior approval. The principal may, nevertheless, represent that the agent has authority to communicate the granting of approval or can be relied upon to proceed only after obtaining the requisite approval (in which case, the agent in effect has representor authority to intimate through the fact of proceeding that approval has been obtained). This may arise where, for example, the principal has disclaimed any voice in respect of the relevant matter other than the agent. In *Lovett v Carson Country Homes Ltd*,[55] a company contested the validity of a debenture granted to a bank and ostensibly carrying the signatures of the company's two directors, Carter and Jewson. In fact,

---

[52] *United Bank of Kuwait v Hammoud* [1988] 1 WLR 1051; *Hirst v Etherington* [1999] Lloyd's Rep PN 938.
[53] *Hirst v Etherington* [1999] Lloyd's Rep PN 938.
[54] See also *Acute Property Developments Ltd v Apostolou* [2013] EWHC 200 (Ch), [38] (manager of a business carried on by a limited company has implied actual authority to ask a customer to pay to a third party money owed to the company, but only if there is a good reason and has apparent representor authority to provide the third party with what is ostensibly a good reason even where in truth it does not exist).
[55] *Lovett v Carson Country Homes Ltd* [2009] EWHC 1143 (Ch), [2009] 2 BCLC 196.

Jewson had forged the signature of Carter, who knew nothing of the instrument, but the forgery was held binding on the company. Since the company's inception, Carter had concentrated exclusively on operational matters and left all financial matters to Jewson. The latter carried the title of finance director and undertook all interaction with the bank. Carter even declined to attend meetings with the bank to which he was invited. Under these circumstances, the company was held to have represented to the bank that in matters financial it acted exclusively through Jewson and that Jewson could be relied upon to procure the proper execution of all financial instruments. Jewson, accordingly, had apparent authority impliedly to represent the genuineness of the signature, and the company was bound by the debenture.

4.23 Greater difficulty arises where the sole basis for the alleged representation of authority to communicate approval by superior management for a transaction in respect of which the agent is known to lack actor authority is the position held by the agent. Two cases require discussion.

4.24 In *The Ocean Frost*,[56] A was prepared to buy M's ship, but only if M agreed to charter the ship back for three years. M was willing to charter it for only one year, but a three-year contract was signed purportedly on behalf of M by one Magelssen, who held the position of M's 'vice-president (transportation) and chartering manager'. A knew that Magelssen lacked authority to conclude this type of charter, but argued that, by appointing Magelssen to his position, M had represented Magelssen as having authority to communicate that he had obtained specific approval from M for transactions not falling within his pre-existing authority to conclude, and that he had so communicated by the act of signing the contract. A contended also that it would have been impractical to seek confirmation from M of this approval. The House of Lords rejected this argument.

4.25 As a matter of principle, the House of Lords acknowledged that it would be possible for a principal to represent that a third party might rely on an agent to obtain specific approval from the principal before entering into a transaction known not to fall within the agent's existing authority, but such a case 'must be very rare and unusual'.[57] The requisite representation must be directed specifically at authority to communicate the principal's decision regarding a transaction outside the agent's authority.[58] Fundamentally, the House of Lords rejected the proposition, central to A's argument, that apparent representor authority to communicate consent to a transaction as a usual adjunct to the actor authority derived from the agent's appointment is conceptually different from apparent actor

---

[56] *Armagas Ltd v Mundogas SA (The Ocean Frost)* [1986] AC 717.

[57] ibid, 777 (Lord Keith). See also ibid, 779: 'most unusual and peculiar'.

[58] The fact that in previous dealings a principal chose to employ a particular agent to communicate decisions to enter into transactions outside the agent's authority to conclude does not by itself amount to a representation that the agent has authority to communicate approval in the context of future transactions: ibid, 732.

authority so derived.[59] Consequently, the fact that Magelssen's appointment as chartering manager was known not to carry authority for the particular charter negated any suggestion of apparent representor authority to communicate specific approval for it derived from that appointment. And the difficulty of obtaining confirmation from M of its approval was simply irrelevant.[60]

4.26   To be contrasted with *The Ocean Frost* is *First Energy (UK) Ltd v Hungarian International Bank Ltd.*[61] The defendant in this case was a merchant bank operating in the United Kingdom through a head office in London and a further office in Manchester. The head of the Manchester office, Mr Jamison, held the title of 'senior manager'. The claimant approached the Manchester office to seek finance for its business of installing heating systems in buildings. Throughout the ensuing negotiations, the defendant bank was represented predominantly by Jamison. As the claimant knew, however, Jamison did not have authority to agree funding. During the negotiations, ad hoc funding was provided, authorised by a letter signed by two senior executives in London, for an initial heating installation project. Subsequently, further ad hoc funding was sought for a further three projects. The claimant received a letter signed by Jamison offering such funding in terms corresponding to those on which the initial ad hoc funding had been provided. This it accepted. Shortly afterwards, the decision was taken by the defendant bank in London to break off negotiations for a continuing facility. The question arose as to whether the bank was bound by the offer of funding for the three projects, which had in fact been made by Jamison without the requisite approval from London.

4.27   The parallels with *The Ocean Frost* are clear. In each case, an office-holder purports to enter a transaction on behalf of his principal for which he is known to lack actual actor authority. In each case, the only possible source of representor authority lies in appointment to the office held. Magelssen's appointment in *The Ocean Frost* as 'vice-president (transportation) and chartering manager' conferred actor authority to conclude certain transactions and accessory representor authority to make statements in connection therewith, but did not confer general apparent representor authority to speak more widely for the principal. In *First Energy*, in contrast, Jamison's appointment as 'senior manager' for an extensive region constituted a representation of authority to sign letters on behalf of the bank including a letter communicating a decision by the bank to do something

---

[59]   ibid, 779. Lord Keith quoted with approval from the judgment of Robert Goff LJ in the Court of Appeal (ibid, 731) that A's argument postulated 'an extraordinary distinction between (1) a case where an agent, having no ostensible authority to enter into the relevant contract, wrongly asserts that he is invested with authority to do so, in which event the principal is not bound, and (2) a case where an agent, having no ostensible authority, wrongly asserts after negotiations that he has gone back to his principal and obtained actual authority, in which event the principal is bound. As a matter of common sense, this is most unlikely to be the law.'

[60]   ibid, 778. See also *Ruben v Great Fingall Consolidated* [1906] AC 439, 447; *Attorney-General for Ceylon v Silva* [1953] AC 461, 480–81.

[61]   *First Energy (UK) Ltd v Hungarian International Bank Ltd* [1993] 2 Lloyd's Rep 194.

that he personally could not authorise by himself. The particular office held by Jamison was, therefore, held to carry general apparent representor authority, in contrast to the position of Magelson in *The Ocean Frost*.[62]

4.28   The Court of Appeal in *First Energy* emphasised commercial realities. A 'senior manager' in charge of the operations of a merchant bank throughout the north of England was in a far more senior position than, for example, the manager of a high-street branch of a retail bank. The natural inference was that such a person enjoyed general authority to speak for the bank, including relaying decisions taken by others higher in the bank's managerial hierarchy. The contrary view 'would defeat the apparent object of appointing a senior manager [for a region] so that local businessmen could deal with him there.'[63] More generally, a third party has to be able to rely on the apparent authority of someone to speak on behalf of a company, and it was simply not realistic to expect a third party in receipt of a communication from a person with the seniority of Jamison to respond by demanding proof of Jamison's authority directly from a relevant company director in London.

4.29   Verification of an agent's authority is, however, far from unknown, with the courts also requiring the third party to exercise diligence as to the authority of the provider of any confirmation to give such reassurance. In *British Bank of the Middle East v Sun Life Assurance Co of Canada (UK) Ltd*,[64] an insurance company's financial undertaking was worded as requiring signature by multiple representatives, but bore the sole signature of a 'unit manager' at the company's City branch in London. By letter to that branch addressed to the 'general manager' of the insurance company, the bank beneficiary of the undertaking sought confirmation of the authority of the named signatory to issue undertakings under his sole signature. Confirmation was duly provided by the 'branch manager', there being no person with the title of general manager, or equivalent, at that branch. The bank was held not entitled to rely on that confirmation. The evidence was clear that a branch manager lacked actual authority to provide the requested confirmation, and the simple fact of answering a letter addressed to senior management of the company could not clothe a middle-ranking manager with authority to speak for the senior management. A Singaporean case, moreover, denies a claim of apparent authority brought by a commercial bank in respect of the conduct of a fraudulent employee of a trading company on the grounds of, in part,

---

[62] In *Skandinaviska Enskilda Banken AB v Asia Pacific Breweries (Singapore) Pte Ltd* [2011] SGCA 22, [2011] 3 SLR 540, the Singapore Court of Appeal distinguished *First Energy* in respect of a company's 'finance manager', as 'not an established title in the corporate sector, unlike corporate titles like "Finance Director", "Chief Financial Officer", "Managing Director", "Chief Executive Officer", "Chairman of the Board of Directors", "President" or "Director". In the present case, [the agent] was not a director . . . but only a finance manager, a position which *prima facie* connotes that the officeholder carries out managerial, rather than executive, functions' (ibid, [7] (Chan Sek Keong CJ), and see ibid, [61]). The Court did not express a view on the title 'senior manager'.

[63] *First Energy (UK) Ltd v Hungarian International Bank Ltd* [1993] 2 Lloyd's Rep 194, 207 (Evans LJ).

[64] *British Bank of the Middle East v Sun Life Assurance Co of Canada (UK) Ltd* [1983] 2 Lloyd's Rep 9.

the commercial power of a bank to seek the clearest evidence from the most senior management of a potential borrower of all requisite authorisations, and also, given the vital economic role of banks, a reasonable expectation of a higher level of financial prudence than might be expected of trading companies.[65]

4.30 *First Energy*, in contrast, questions the realism of expecting a trading company seeking credit to demand from a bank confirmations of specific aspects of the authority of persons the bank has invested with senior managerial positions. It may also be noteworthy that the transaction in *First Energy* constituted a second tranche of interim finance that the bank had already advanced to the claimant to support ongoing negotiations within the defendant bank's ordinary course of business, while the charterparty in *The Ocean Frost* was unprecedented and collateral to a one-off transaction, and contained certain highly unusual features calling for explicit approval from someone with higher managerial authority than that possessed by Magelssen.[66]

4.31 Factually, *First Energy* may perhaps be distinguishable from *The Ocean Frost* on the basis of the seniority of the appointment and scope of the usual accompanying authority of the agent, and the commercial context of dealings between a commercial bank and a small business. There is, nevertheless, a philosophical tension between the two decisions, with the House of Lords focusing on the conduct of the principal while the Court of Appeal concentrated rather on the position as it appeared to the third party. The approach adopted by the House of Lords requires a traditional representation of authority together with reliance and serves to hold a principal to account for creating a misleading impression, while the Court of Appeal favours a more holistic approach based on external appearance and designed to protect and fulfil the reasonable expectations of the third party.[67] In terms of legal principle, if the factual aspects of *First Energy* fail to afford a convincing basis for distinguishing *The Ocean Frost*, the only conclusion must be that the Court of Appeal distinguished apparent representor authority derived from the agent's appointment from apparent actor authority so derived in precisely the manner prohibited by the House of Lords.

---

[65] *Skandinaviska Enskilda Banken AB v Asia Pacific Breweries (Singapore) Pte Ltd* [2009] SGHC 197, [2009] 4 SLR (R) 788, [137]–[139], [2011] SGCA 22, [2011] 3 SLR 540, [94]. See further above, para 4.13.

[66] Notably, a cancellation clause that placed a highly unusual financial risk on the charterers: [1985] 1 Lloyd's Rep 1, 58–59.

[67] Supported by G McMeel, 'Philosophical Foundations of the Law of Agency' (2000) 116 *Law Quarterly Review* 387. *Cf* F Reynolds, 'The Ultimate Apparent Authority' (1994) 110 *Law Quarterly Review* 21.

Undisclosed Principals

4.32　There is a fundamental logical incompatibility between the undisclosed principal and the doctrine of apparent authority. By definition, the third party is unaware that the counterparty is acting as an agent at all. The third party, consequently, cannot be conscious of a representation of authority and cannot, therefore, rely upon any such representation. A third party cannot, therefore, invoke apparent authority against an undisclosed principal by reason of matters said or done by the principal before its existence is revealed.[68] An undisclosed principal may, nevertheless, be estopped from repudiating the unauthorised act of its agent where the circumstances support a different appropriate representation.

4.33　First, where a previously undisclosed principal knows that a third party mistakenly believes a pre-disclosure act to fall within the agent's actual authority and that the third party would incur a detriment were the principal subsequently to deny the authority, the principal must reveal the absence of authority. Failure to do so will be construed as a present representation by the now revealed principal of the agent's authority referring back to the time of the relevant act, a representation that the principal will be estopped from denying.[69]

4.34　Secondly, by virtue of the doctrine of apparent ownership, an undisclosed true owner may represent another to be the owner of property so as to be estopped from denying the latter's ownership and, therefore, right to deal with the property.[70] The representation must, however, be unequivocal and directed at ownership. In particular, a mere transfer of possession will not suffice.[71]

4.35　Thirdly, where an undisclosed principal permits its agent (X) to run a business ostensibly in X's own name, a third party might reasonably assume that X is the owner of the business, so that any transaction entered into with X in the ordinary course of the business is entered into with the person who has the assets of the business available to satisfy liabilities under the transaction. The principal is then estopped from denying that the counterparty to the transaction

---

[68]　*Armstrong v Stokes* (1872) LR 7 QB 598, 604.
[69]　*Spiro v Lintern* [1973] 1 WLR 1002.
[70]　*Eastern Distributors Ltd v Goldring* [1957] 2 QB 600.
[71]　*Farquarson Bros & Co v King & Co* [1902] AC 325. This is consistent with the demise of the personal bankruptcy doctrine of reputed ownership, always subject to exceptions in respect of chattels that commonly saw a divorce of ownership from possession. Indeed, a principle that possession imported a representation of ownership would jeopardize every bailor's title. That it does not led to a series of statutory interventions to generate exceptions to the principle *nemo dat quod non habet* to temper the rights of the true owner of goods in favour of a third party that relies on possession as indicative of a right of disposal in circumstances where no estoppel of ownership arises.

is indeed the owner of the business. As the owner, the principal thereby incurs liability.[72]

4.36 In *Watteau v Fenwick*,[73] the defendant brewery firm bought a public house under an agreement by which the brewery retained the previous owner (Humble) as manager and required most consumables to be purchased from the brewery. The brewery's ownership was not publicised: Humble's name remained above the door to the premises and the alcohol licence remained, and was renewed, in Humble's name. Over a period of time, Humble ordered some goods covered by the agreement from the claimant, but failed to pay for them. Having discovered the true ownership of the public house, the claimant successfully sued the brewery. It was held that a principal is liable for all acts falling 'within the authority usually confided to an agent of that character', notwithstanding any secret restriction on the agent's actual authority, regardless of whether the principal is disclosed or undisclosed.

4.37 Such a bland eliding of disclosed and undisclosed principals is, of course, untenable. The brewery being an undisclosed principal, the decision cannot be accommodated within the doctrine of apparent authority. Indeed, the case has rarely been followed[74] and judicially has been regarded with caution.[75] Nevertheless, the manner in which the business continued to be managed after acquisition by the brewery represented to third parties that Humble was the owner and that the resources of the business owner were, therefore, available to meet contractual liabilities incurred ostensibly by Humble *qua* owner.[76] Such a representation, relating not to authority but to the identity of the business owner, creates an estoppel against the owner in favour of a third party contracting on that basis.[77]

[72] A fortiori where X is the owner of a business and runs it for a time, transacting with a given third party from time to time, before selling the business to Y but, by agreement between X and Y, the sale is kept secret with X continuing to run the business as undisclosed agent for Y (as in *Grinder v Bryans Road Building & Supply Co*, 432 A 2d 453 (Md App 1981)).

[73] *Watteau v Fenwick* [1893] 1 QB 346.

[74] Seemingly the only example is *Kinahan & Co Ltd v Parry* [1911] 1 KB 459; [1910] 2 KB 389 (revd on other grounds [1911] 1 KB 459).

[75] *Rhodian River Shipping Co SA v Halla Maritime Corp (The Rhodian River and Rhodian Sailor)* [1984] 1 Lloyd's Rep 373, 379.

[76] Compare also the statutory doctrine of mercantile agency, whereby an owner of goods who entrusts them to a trader that customarily deals in such goods is bound as against a good faith third party by any disposition of the goods in the ordinary course of the trader's business: Factors Act 1889, s 2(1). The statutory intervention reflects the fact that mere possession of goods does not speak to a right of disposal and is based rather on the placing of goods into a trading context such that third parties would naturally assume a right of disposition.

[77] See M Conant, 'The Objective Theory of Agency: Apparent Authority and the Estoppel of Apparent Ownership' (1968) 47 *Nebraska Law Review* 678, esp 687–88; A Tettenborn, 'Agents, Business Owners and Estoppel' (1998) 57 *Cambridge Law Journal* 274. See also A Goodhart and C Hamson, 'Undisclosed Principals in Contract' (1932) 4 *Cambridge Law Journal* 320, 335–36.

4.38   As a matter of principle, the defendant brewery's liability cannot be sustained on the basis of reciprocity: since an undisclosed principal cannot ratify, there was no possibility of the brewery suing the claimant if, for example, the goods had been defective. The estoppel does, however, prevent the concealed insulation of business assets from business liabilities. It is normal practice for a creditor to demand that a company director pledge his personal wealth by way of guarantee as security for his company's debt; it is not normal for a third party to be compelled to look purely to the limited personal wealth of a company employee, to the exclusion of the company's assets.

4.39   Such a concern is reflected in the Principles of International Commercial Contracts. Although the Unidroit Principles do not generally recognise the undisclosed principal, Article 2.2.4 provides by way of exception that, where an undisclosed agent of a business represents itself to be the owner of the business in contracting with a third party, contractual rights arising against the agent may be exercised against the real owner.

4.40   Two, more generally framed, principles are recognised in the Restatement.[78] First, an undisclosed principal with knowledge of unauthorised acts that cause a detrimental alteration of position by a third party is bound by such acts unless the principal takes reasonable steps to reveal the absence of authority. Secondly, restrictions on the authority of an agent for an undisclosed principal are ineffective against a third party unless they would have been effective had the agency been disclosed. The first principle, is said to be consistent with estoppel (a separate and distinct basis for attribution in the Restatement) and indeed reflects to some extent the first instance of estoppel-based liability of an undisclosed principal discussed above, while the second is based on the reasonable expectation of third parties as engendered by the position in which the principal has chosen to place the agent, and reflects the approach in *Watteau v Fenwick*.

4.41   The Restatement articulates these principles as distinct from either apparent authority or estoppel or indeed any other doctrine. They appear to be examples of a concept of 'inherent agency power', namely the power of an agent to bind its principal purely by virtue of agency status without the support of any doctrine of the general law or any more specific agency law rule of attribution. Resort to such a concept is, however, problematic. If it explains the liability of an undisclosed principal, why does it not apply equally to disclosed principals? Inherent agency power, if it exists, demands recognition as the governing principle in the external relationship. Apparent authority must then be relegated to being merely an example of this greater principle, relegated indeed to redundancy. As a supplement to apparent authority born of desperation to favour third parties, inherent agency power invites objection as devoid of any foundation of coherent principle that would serve as justification and to delineate its extent.

---

[78] Restatement, § 2.06.

5

Ratification

5.1 The doctrine of ratification enables a principal retrospectively to avail itself of an earlier unauthorised act. It permits a principal unilaterally to arrogate to itself attribution of acts by agents beyond the scope of actual authority and persons who lack any agency status at all. Ratification is thus a source both of extended authority and of agency itself.[1]

5.2 The nature of apparent authority in English law restricting the doctrine to the conferral of rights on the third party[2] enhances the significance of the doctrine of ratification. Outside of actual authority, the existence of rights of the principal against the third party depends on ratification. Conversely, in systems where apparent authority constitutes a full authority conferring on the agent the power to create a full legal relationship between principal and third party,[3] the role of ratification is commensurately diminished.

The Nature of Ratification

5.3 Ratification may be characterised as 'a unilateral act of the will [of the principal], namely, the approval after the event of the assumption of an authority which did not exist at the time',[4] although the unilateral nature of the creation of authority can be over-emphasised, since ratification must respond to a prior act of the agent purportedly on behalf of the principal, which prior act may be construed objectively as an expression of willingness to accept authorisation. The principal's intention to ratify must be clearly manifested, but the manifestation need not be communicated to any party that subsequently pleads ratification against the principal.[5] Questions of reliance on the manifestation accordingly do not arise, and the nature of ratification as not based upon estoppel is clearly

---

[1] For ease of exposition, however, the person performing the unauthorised act will be termed an agent.

[2] Above, para 4.4.

[3] For example, the Restatement, the Principles of European Contract Law, and the Draft Common Frame of Reference.

[4] *Harrisons & Crossfield Ltd v London & North-Western Railway Co* [1917] 2 KB 755, 758 (Rowlatt J).

[5] See below, para 5.21.

demonstrated.[6] Equally, it is irrelevant how the manifestation would have been understood, and what response it would have elicited, had it been communicated: 'what matters is the inherent character' of the principal's conduct.[7]

Ratifiable Acts

5.4   A principal obviously cannot claim acts that an agent performs on its own account. Ratification, in consequence, is confined to acts that the agent performs, or purports to perform, on behalf of the principal.[8] It follows that a forgery[9] is not susceptible to ratification, since a forger purports to be the principal rather than to act on the principal's behalf.[10] Likewise, an agent cannot argue that a misdirection of the principal's funds into the agent's own pocket has subsequently been ratified: the agent can be regarded only as misappropriating the funds for itself.[11] There is, however, no impediment to ratification of an act that the agent performs ostensibly on behalf of the principal but in fact in furtherance of a fraud on the principal.[12]

5.5   It follows also that the doctrine of ratification is inapplicable to commission agency. In contracting with the third party, a commission agent acts pursuant to instructions from the principal, but on its own behalf and not on behalf of the principal.[13]

---

   [6] *Harrisons & Crossfield* [1917] 2 KB 755, 758; *Shell Co of Australia Ltd v Nat Shipping Bagging Services Ltd (The Kilmun)* [1988] 2 Lloyd's Rep 1, 11; *National Insurance & Guarantee Corp plc v Imperio Reinsurance Co (UK) Ltd* [1999] Lloyd's Rep IR 249, 260.
   [7] *Shell Co of Australia Ltd v Nat Shipping Bagging Services Ltd (The Kilmun)* [1988] 2 Lloyd's Rep 1, 14 (Lord Donaldson).
   [8] *Jones v Hope* (1880) (1886) 3 TLR 247n, 251. See also DCFR, art II-6:111(1).
   [9] Defined by the Forgery and Counterfeiting Act 1981, s 1 as a false instrument made with the intention of inducing another to accept it as genuine and through its acceptance to occasion prejudice. And see *Demco Investment & Commercial SA v Interamerican Life Assurance (International) Ltd* [2012] EWHC 2053 (Comm), [115]–[116] (upholding the need for an intent that the falseness of the instrument should occasion prejudice).
   [10] *Greenwood v Martins Bank Ltd* [1933] AC 51; [1932] 1 KB 371, 378–9, 385, and so interpreting *Brook v Hook* (1871) LR 6 Ex 89. Likewise *Demco Investment & Commercial SA v Interamerican Life Assurance (International) Ltd* [2012] EWHC 2053 (Comm), [122]. Where, however, (a) to the knowledge of A, B places reliance upon a forgery, (b) A owes B a duty to speak, (c) A fails to disclose the forged nature of the instrument, and (d) B is prejudiced by this non-disclosure, A will be estopped from asserting the forgery: *Greenwood v Martins* [1932] 1 KB 371, affd [1933] AC 51; *Fung Kai Sun v Chan Fui Hing* [1951] AC 489.
   [11] *Imperial Bank of Canada v Begley* [1936] 2 All ER 367, 374. See also *Wilson v Barker & Mitchell* (1833) 4 B & Ad 614 (no ratification of seizure of chattel by agent for own use).
   [12] *Re Tiedemann and Ledermann Frères* [1899] 2 QB 66.
   [13] And see PECL, art 3:207(1), confining ratification to acts performed 'as an agent', and see art 3:102(2) for the distinction between acting 'on instructions and on behalf of, but not in the name of a principal' (commission agency) and acting 'as an agent', albeit unbeknownst to the third party (undisclosed agency). A commission agent does not act 'as an agent, but not in the name of a principal'.

5.6   A principal that has incurred loss or liability may seek the benefit of insurance arranged by another party. Similar issues arise whether the principal asserts that the other party was authorised to obtain the insurance on its behalf and did so, rendering the principal a party to the insurance contract by virtue of prior actual authority, or was not authorised but nevertheless intended to benefit the principal, entitling the principal to engage the contract by ratification. In either case, the question is whether the other party was acting for the principal in obtaining the insurance.[14] The terms of an underlying contract between the principal and the other party may provide cogent evidence. Thus, a clear contractual allocation of risk is inconsistent with an intention to obtain insurance for the benefit of another.[15] Likewise, an express contractual obligation to obtain insurance within certain parameters benefiting the principal indicates that insurance beyond those parameters is not intended to benefit the principal.[16]

5.7   The doctrine of ratification is irrelevant where the agent's lack of authority is known to the third party at the time of the unauthorised act. In such circumstances, the agent cannot realistically purport to act for the principal; at most it can undertake to refer the matter in question to the principal. There is therefore nothing for the principal to ratify. Consequently, acceptance by the agent of an offer 'subject to ratification' has no legal significance. The offer has not been accepted and can be withdrawn until acceptance by the principal.[17]

5.8   Illegality of the unauthorised act does not of itself necessarily preclude ratification.[18] Where, however, the policy underpinning the illegality demands absolute invalidity, ratification would be repugnant to the policy: in this sense, 'life cannot be given by ratification to prohibited transactions'.[19] Accordingly, a transaction in time of war with an enemy alien cannot be ratified after the cessation of hostilities since the policy against trading with the enemy demands an absolute invalidity.[20] Similarly, since the statutory imposition of a licensing requirement for the carrying on of insurance business was designed for the protection of the public, the unlicensed writing of insurance was not just illegal but wholly invalid and not susceptible of ratification.[21] Where ratification of an illegal act is permitted, the principal incurs the consequences of the unlawfulness. Thus,

---

[14]   *National Oilwell (UK) Ltd v Davy Offshore Ltd* [1993] 2 Lloyd's Rep 582, 596–97.

[15]   *Yangtsze Insurance Association v Lukmanjee* [1918] AC 585; *Stone Vickers Ltd v Appledore Ferguson Shipbuilders Ltd* [1992] 2 Lloyd's Rep 578.

[16]   *National Oilwell (UK) Ltd v Davy Offshore Ltd* [1993] 2 Lloyd's Rep 582.

[17]   Any subsequent purported ratification by the principal can take effect only as an acceptance. The controversial proposition that ratification of an unauthorised acceptance can overreach an intervening revocation of the offer (see below, para 5.36) is inapplicable: *Watson v Davies* [1931] 1 Ch 455; *Warehousing & Forwarding Co of East Africa Ltd v Jafferali & Sons Ltd* [1964] AC 1.

[18]   *Bedford Insurance Co Ltd v Instituto de Resseguros do Brasil* [1985] 1 QB 966, 985.

[19]   ibid, 986 (Parker J).

[20]   *Kuernigl v Donnersmarck* [1955] 1 QB 515. See also *Boston Deep Sea Fishing & Ice Co Ltd v Farnham* [1957] 1 WLR 1051.

[21]   *Bedford Insurance Co Ltd v Instituto de Resseguros do Brasil* [1985] 1 QB 966.

ratification of a tortious act renders the principal liable as a tortfeasor.[22] Where, however, the unlawfulness flows from the unauthorised nature of the act, ratification will render the act both authorised and lawful.[23]

Ascertainability of the Principal

5.9   The unauthorised act must be performed on terms that identify or render ascertainable the identity of the purported principal.[24] This enables a judgement to be made on whether a party subsequently purporting to ratify is entitled to do so. Although in the case of authorised acts, an agent may act on behalf of a disclosed but unascertainable principal, or indeed an undisclosed principal, a challenge to the existence of any authority can be resolved by reference to evidence establishing its prior conferral. In the case of unauthorised acts, however, there are no matters outside the act itself to which reference can be made to determine the identity of the person entitled to ratify. In the absence of any designation requirement, the agent would retain the power to attribute the act to unauthorised agency or to its own affairs and, if to agency, to nominate whichever principal it subsequently chose. It could, for example, falsely nominate an entity with no assets amenable to legal process on the part of the third party or in return for reward. The absence of a designation requirement would have the potential, therefore, to facilitate dishonest, corrupt, or capricious conduct on the part of the agent.

5.10   It follows from the designation requirement that an undisclosed principal cannot ratify. This was, indeed, so held by the House of Lords in *Keighley, Maxted & Co v Durant*.[25] The judgments emphasise respect for the terms of the contract as concluded, including the identity of the contracting parties, in accordance with the objective theory of contract formation and interpretation. Ratification might be regarded as an indulgence permitting a principal to benefit from an agent's act notwithstanding the absence of authority, but the indulgence is justified or excused by its assimilation of reality to appearance. It, therefore, supports the objective theory. The undisclosed principal doctrine is a further indulgence, justified on grounds of commercial convenience, permitting the benefit of an act to be claimed in accordance with the agent's concealed intentions but contrary to the

---

[22]   *Bird v Brown* (1854) 4 Ex 786, 799. On ratification and torts, see further below, para 5.16.
[23]   *Whitehead v Taylor* (1839) 10 A & E 210.
[24]   *Watson v Swann* (1862) 11 CB(NS) 756; *Lyell v Kennedy* (1889) 14 App Cas 437; *Eastern Construction Co Ltd v National Trust Co Ltd* [1914] AC 197, 213. It may be that the expression 'terms' is too narrow: a wide range of evidence is admissible to establish the requisite intention to benefit and the designation of the intended beneficiaries: *National Oilwell (UK) Ltd v Davy Offshore Ltd* [1993] 2 Lloyd's Rep 582, 597.
[25]   *Keighley, Maxted & Co v Durant* [1901] AC 240.

objective appearance.[26] For the House of Lords, one indulgence in operation at a time was enough. Such a view is, however, contestable. It is hard to see why, as a matter of contract theory, the objective theory yields to the undisclosed principal doctrine with respect to authorised acts, but prevails with respect to unauthorised acts. However, the more pragmatic concern about bad faith or capricious attribution of the act resonates. Thus, Lord Davey emphasised the 'wide difference between an agency existing at the date of the contract which is susceptible of proof, and a repudiation of which by the agent would be fraudulent, and an intention locked up in the mind of the contractor, which he may either abandon or act on at his own pleasure, and the ascertainment of which involves an enquiry into the state of his mind at the date of the contract.'[27] The former was provable fact, the latter pure speculation.[28]

5.11 The designation may, however, be in extremely broad terms. The standard form of marine insurance policy in use until the 1980s provided that the insurance was taken out in the name of the principal assured and 'all and any other person and persons to whom the [insured property] doth, may or shall appertain, in part or in all'. Such wording was effective to extend the benefit of the insurance to any persons with an interest in the insured property provided the evidence was consistent with an intention on the part of the principal assured to act on their behalf as well as on its own.[29]

5.12 A further issue relates to the time at which it must be possible to determine whether any given individual is eligible to ratify the unauthorised act. The purpose behind the designation rule would indicate that the relevant time is that of the acts relied on as ratification. A contrary view would require the determination to be able to be made at the time of the unauthorised act,[30] which would exclude future members of a designated class. It may be, however, that the unauthorised instrument is susceptible to analysis as an offer open to acceptance by existing or future members of a designated class, generating a separate contract with each class member.[31]

[26] The doctrine is discussed below, para 9.19 st seq.
[27] *Keighley, Maxted & Co v Durant* [1901] AC 240, 256. And see A Goodhart and C Hamson, 'Undisclosed Principals in Contract' (1932) 4 *Cambridge Law Journal* 320, 325–26. *Cf* A Rochvarg, 'Ratification and Undisclosed Principals' (1989) 34 *McGill Law Journal* 287.
[28] The facts may, nevertheless, support an estoppel: *Spiro v Lintern* [1973] 1 WLR 1002, above, para 4.33.
[29] *Watson v Swann* (1862) 11 CB(NS) 756; *Boston Fruit Co v British & Foreign Marine Insurance Co* [1906] AC 336; *National Oilwell (UK) Ltd v Davy Offshore Ltd* [1993] 2 Lloyd's Rep 582, 596–97.
[30] For a dictum of Willes J in support of this view, see *Watson v Swann* (1862) 11 CB(NS) 756, 771. On the facts, however, ratification was in any event precluded since the alleged principal was not in contemplation at the time the contract was concluded. Support for the dictum of Willes J has been expressed in Australia (*Trident General Insurance Co Ltd v McNiece Bros Pty Ltd* (1987) 8 NSWLR 270, 276), but the matter was left open in *National Oilwell (UK) Ltd v Davy Offshore Ltd* [1993] 2 Lloyd's Rep 582, 597.
[31] P Watts and F Reynolds, *Bowstead & Reynolds on Agency*, 19th edn (London, Sweet & Maxwell, 2010) para 2-065. Issues could, however, arise concerning awareness of the offer and what constitutes acceptance.

Competence of the Principal

5.13   It is clear that the principal must be competent to perform the ratified act at the time of the ratification,[32] but it has been asserted that competence is required also at the time of the unauthorised act.[33] Such a second competence proposition is, however, both unnecessary and undesirable. Admittedly, a requirement of competence at the time of the unauthorised act has been invoked in the context of trading with the enemy,[34] where ratification is indeed precluded; however, the preclusion in such cases flows rather from the absolute prohibition demanded by public policy.[35] Again, in respect of insurance contracts, the statutory requirement for an insurable interest, or expectation of acquiring such an interest, at the time of contracting[36] precludes subsequent ratification by a party contemplated as benefiting from the policy according to its wording but lacking the requisite interest or expectation at the time of the unauthorised conclusion of the contract.[37] In contrast, there seems no good reason why a capacity principle designed for protection should be transformed into an absolute barrier denying the protected party a benefit it wishes, in the exercise of true autonomy, to enjoy. Thus, certain acts performed during minority are susceptible to ratification upon the actor's achieving of majority: there is no reason to exclude acts performed through an agent.[38] It is noteworthy that the Restatement confines the competence requirement to the time of ratification.[39]

Existence of the Principal

5.14   A further restriction upon the doctrine of ratification is that the principal must have been in existence at the time of the unauthorised act, a principle that

---

[32]   *Firth v Staines* [1897] 2 QB 70, 75.

[33]   ibid.

[34]   *Boston Deep Sea Fishing & Ice Co Ltd v Farnham* [1957] 1 WLR 1051, 1057–58.

[35]   See above, para 5.8.

[36]   Marine Insurance Act 1906, s 4(2)(a). The formulation of the 1906 Act is considered an accurate statement of general insurance contract law, except perhaps for policies within the Life Assurance Act 1774, in which case the option of an expectation may not be available.

[37]   Insurance is often taken out for the benefit of a designated class, for instance by a head contractor for the benefit of itself and all contractors and subcontractors, existing and future. The commercial value of such cover requires all class members to access it directly as co-assureds rather than rely on derivative rights (for example, by virtue of the Contracts (Rights of Third Parties) Act 1999) that are subject to defences arising out of misconduct of the original assured. For future class members, accessing the policy through agency requires ratification. This may be precluded on the ground either that the class member was not ascertainable as required (above, para 5.12) or lacked an insurable interest at the required time. As noted above (para 5.12) an alternative analysis not reliant on agency may be available and preferable.

[38]   Similarly, mental incapacity at the time of the act should not preclude subsequent ratification. In *Dibbins v Dibbins* [1896] 2 Ch 348, ratification was disputed on the basis of timing; there was no suggestion of *in limine* preclusion by reason of incapacity at the time of the act.

[39]   Restatement, § 4.04(1)(b).

developed in the context of pre-incorporation acts of company promoters. A proposition that promoters cannot bind a company not as yet in existence reflected the entitlement of a newly-formed company to act autonomously without inherited encumbrances.[40] This proposition, however, spawned the further proposition that the company could not ratify pre-incorporation acts of its promoters.[41] This offspring is not justified by autonomy concerns, and has been regretted,[42] but is settled law,[43] accepted seemingly not just in the corporate context but with respect to ratification generally.[44] It reflects the retrospectivity of ratification, whereby a ratified act generally falls to be considered as having been authorised by the principal at the time it was originally performed.[45] Accordingly, in the case of purported conclusion of a contract by an unauthorised acceptance of an offer, ratification engenders a contract concluded at the time not of ratification but of the agent's acceptance. Where, however, the principal did not exist at that time, this is simply not possible.[46]

Knowledge of the Principal

5.15 Ratification requires knowledge by the principal of all essential circumstances regarding the unauthorised act.[47] Knowledge of the unauthorised nature of the act is not, however, required. A principal should know, or be able quickly to determine, whether authority has been conferred; ignorance caused by, for example, organisational dysfunction should not operate to the prejudice of the third party.[48] Nor is knowledge required of the relevant law. Ratification is not a form of

---

[40] *Hutchinson v Surrey Consumers' Gas-Light & Coke Association* (1851) 11 CB 689; *Payne v New South Wales Coal & International Steam Navigation Co* (1854) 10 Exch 283.

[41] *Gunn v London & Lancashire Fire Insurance Co* (1862) 12 CB(NS) 694; *Kelner v Baxter* (1866) LR 2 CP 174.

[42] *Melhado v Porte Alegre, New Hamburgh, & Brazilian Railway Co* (1874) LR 9 CP 503, 505 (in that it precludes any claim for expenses incurred even when the company takes the benefit of the pre-incorporation acts). And see *Re Dale & Plant Ltd* (188) 61 LT (NS) 206, 207 (Kay J: 'I do not see my way to helping the claimant, though I would do so if I could.') Also J Gross, 'Pre-incorporation Contracts' (1971) 87 *Law Quarterly Review* 367.

[43] *Natal Land & Colonization Co Ltd v Pauline Colliery & Development Syndicate Ltd* [1904] AC 120.

[44] *Restatement*, § 4.04(1)(a). But not by the European Principles or Draft CFR: see PECL, art 3:207, Comment B; DCFR, art II-6:111, Comment B.

[45] See below, para 5.25.

[46] The European Principles and Draft CFR, which accept ratification by a principal that was not in existence at the time of the unauthorised act, limit retrospectivity in such a case to the time when the principal came into existence: PECL, art 3:207, Comment B; DCFR art II–6:111, Comment B. Alternatively, it might be possible to adopt a more nuanced approach to retrospectivity (that the *consequences* of the ratified act are worked out *as if* the act had been antecedently authorised). What, however, on either approach would be the third party's position if it discovered the supposed principal's non-existence? Would it be obliged to wait and see whether the principal came into existence and, if so, for how long? Although the time available for ratification is not unlimited (see below, para 5.33 et seq), it might be unreasonable to subject the third party to such uncertainty.

[47] *Eastern Construction Co Ltd v National Trust Co Ltd* [1914] AC 197, 213.

[48] *Ing Re (UK) Ltd v R & V Versicherung AG* [2006] EWHC 1544 (Comm), [2006] 2 All ER (Comm) 870, [155].

election between inconsistent rights, where the effect of the election is to forfeit a right. Such forfeiture requires the election to be fully informed as to the legal rights available and the forfeiture consequential upon the election. Ratification, in contrast, is motivated by a decision that adopting the unauthorised act will benefit the principal without any countervailing relinquishing of alternative rights.[49]

5.16   Where the unauthorised act is unlawful, so that ratification will render the principal liable to answer for that unlawfulness, the knowledge requirement will be carefully scrutinised to ensure that the principal knowingly assumed liability.[50] Where the unauthorised act constitutes commission of a tort, ratification requires full knowledge of the tortious nature of the act. Accordingly, ratification of the misuse of the principal's name in the belief that what was being condoned was a mere irregularity did not constitute ratification of the fraud in fact perpetrated.[51] With respect to torts of strict liability, the authorities are not unanimous,[52] but it is suggested that the nature of ratification as an informed adoption overrides the absence of any fault requirement for the commission of the tort. The critical issue in ratification is not commission of a strict liability tort, but acceptance of responsibility for its commission.

5.17   It is unclear to what extent knowledge includes constructive knowledge. On the general principle that a unilateral mistake as to the meaning of a document is no ground for relief,[53] a principal cannot deny ratification on the basis that ratificatory acts were based on a misunderstanding of the effect of a legal document.[54] More broadly, however, it has been suggested that where the principal has the means of knowledge of a fact and, as between principal and third party, responsibility for the principal's lack of knowledge lies in the circumstances with the principal, the principal's lack of actual knowledge is no bar to ratification.[55] And indeed, any argument for constructive knowledge resonates more strongly as the relevant party is better equipped to ascertain and understand the truth.

5.18   Since the knowledge requirement serves to protect the principal from ill-informed adoptive acts, it can be waived by a clear statement of unqualified adoption that clearly accepts responsibility for whatever the unauthorised act may be.[56]

---

[49]   *SEB Trygg Liv Holding v Manches* [2005] EWCA Civ 1237, [2006] 1 WLR 2276, [46].

[50]   *Suncorp Insurance & Finance v Milano Assicurazioni Spa* [1993] 2 Lloyd's Rep 225, 234(ii).

[51]   *Marsh v Joseph* [1897] 1 Ch 213.

[52]   Compare, for example, *Freeman v Rosher* (1849) 13 QB 780 (unauthorised and unlawful distress constituting trespass not ratified in absence of knowledge of the unlawfulness) and *Hilbery v Hatton* (1864) 2 H & C 822 (unauthorised purchase of goods from seller with no right of sale constituting conversion held to be ratified by principal despite absence of knowledge by principal of the unlawful sale so that principal liable in conversion).

[53]   *Powell v Smith* (1872) LR 14 Eq 85.

[54]   *SEB Trygg Liv Holding v Manches* [2005] EWCA Civ 1237, [2006] 1 WLR 2276, [43].

[55]   *SEB Trygg Liv Holding v Manches* [2005] EWHC 35 (Comm), [2005] 2 Lloyd's Rep 129, [133]–[134], discussed [2005] EWCA Civ 1237, [2006] 1 WLR 2276, [41]–[44].

[56]   *Fitzmaurice v Bayley* (1856) 6 E & B 868; *Marsh v Joseph* [1897] 1 Ch 213, 246–47.

How Ratification is Effected

5.19 Ratificatory acts may be performed by either the principal or any agent with authority to ratify the unauthorised act in question.[57] 'Clear adoptive acts' are required, that afford unequivocal externalised evidence of the intention to ratify.[58] Accordingly, the resumption of possession of a ship after repair did not evidence ratification of an unauthorised variation of the repair contract since taking back and using a chattel after the conferral of an unauthorised service is explicable as merely making the best of the situation.[59] It would, after all, be unreasonable to expect the principal to deny itself use of the chattel for an uncertain and potentially lengthy period.[60] In contrast, the acceptance of goods pursuant to an unauthorised contract of purchase is consistent only with a decision to adopt the transaction.[61]

5.20 It is possible to ratify by silence, by failing to disown an act, but only where ratification is the only reasonable conclusion objectively to be drawn in the circumstances.[62] If the principal, possessed of the requisite knowledge, appreciates that the third party regards it as having adopted an unauthorised act, failure to disown the act within a reasonable time will constitute ratification.[63] But there can be no ratification where the silence is explicable by uncertainty as to the principal's position.[64] Even if it does not constitute ratification, however, silence can give rise to an estoppel where a principal that is aware of the lack of authority owes the third party a duty to disclose material circumstances. In such circumstances, a principal that fails to disclose the agent's lack of authority and permits the third party to act in reliance on the existence of authority will be estopped from asserting the unauthorised nature of the agent's acts.[65] While such circumstances are likely to

---

[57] *Re Portuguese Consolidated Copper Mines Ltd* (1890) 45 Ch D 16, 26–27, 37.

[58] *Eastern Construction Co Ltd v National Trust Co Ltd* [1914] AC 197, 213 (Lord Atkinson).

[59] *Forman & Co Pty Ltd v The Ship 'Liddesdale'* [1900] AC 190.

[60] Compare the general absence of obligation to pay for an unrequested benefit: 'One cleans another's shoes [without being requested]; what can the other do but put them on?' See *Taylor v Laird* (1856) 25 LJ Ex 329, 332 (Pollock CB in the course of argument).

[61] All the more so when reinforced by a refusal to return to the seller: *Waithman v Wakefield* (1807) 1 Camp 120.

[62] *Ing Re (UK) Ltd v R & V Versicherung AG* [2006] EWHC 1544 (Comm), [2006] 2 All ER (Comm) 870, [161].

[63] *Suncorp Insurance & Finance v Milano Assicurazioni Spa* [1993] 2 Lloyd's Rep 225, 234–35, 241.

[64] *Yona International Ltd v La Réunion Française SA d'Assurances et de Réassurances* [1996] 2 Lloyd's Rep 84, 106; *Ing Re (UK) Ltd v R & V Versicherung AG* [2006] EWHC 1544 (Comm), [2006] 2 All ER (Comm) 870, [162].

[65] *Geniki Investments International Ltd v Ellis Stockbrokers Ltd* [2008] EWHC 549 (QB), [2008] 1 BCLC 662, [45]–[46] (customer of stockbroker aware that unauthorised trades being booked to its account not permitted to remain silent and wait to see whether trades prove to be profitable and repudiate if unprofitable, but should disclose to the stockbroking firm the unauthorised conduct of the employee handling the customer's account or be estopped from repudiating the trades on the basis of absence of authority).

establish ratification,[66] estoppel may overcome occasional barriers to ratification, such as problems of lack of competence at the time of the unauthorised act[67] or incomplete knowledge of all material matters.[68]

5.21   Ratification may take effect without communication of the relevant manifestation of the principal's ratificatory intention to any party (agent or third party) that subsequently seeks to invoke it against the principal.[69] Conversely, in the context of estoppel, communication is a prerequisite to the necessary reliance. In practice, however, the requirement of some external manifestation of the intention to ratify means that ratification often will arise from a communication to the subsequently reliant party.[70]

5.22   A principal cannot ratify an unauthorised act in part. Otherwise ratification could operate to impose on a third party a transaction different from the one it understood it had concluded; in particular, selective ratification could fundamentally alter the balance of the bargain between principal and third party. The law, therefore, considers that ratification of any part of the unauthorised act constitutes adoption of the whole.[71]

5.23   It is doubtful whether it is conceptually possible to ratify in advance. The adoption in advance of acts beyond the scope of authority in fact conferred seems inconsistent with the limits imposed upon the authority conferred.[72]

The Retrospectivity of Ratification

5.24   Ratification has a retrospective effect, relating back to the time of the unauthorised act. The precise import of this retrospectivity must, however, be considered carefully.

---

[66] See, indeed, the explicit rejection of estoppel as the operative doctrine in favour of ratification in *Suncorp Insurance & Finance v Milano Assicurazioni Spa* [1993] 2 Lloyd's Rep 225, 234–35.

[67] To the extent that competence at that time is indeed required: see above, para 5.13.

[68] For recognition of estoppel as playing this largely overlapping but occasionally distinct role, see Restatement §4.08.

[69] *Harrisons & Crossfield* [1917] 2 KB 755, 758. See also *National Insurance & Guarantee Corp plc v Imperio Reinsurance Co (UK) Ltd* [1999] Lloyd's Rep IR 249, 260. The same is not true of a decision not to ratify: below, para 5.43.

[70] *Yona International Ltd v La Réunion Française SA d'Assurances et de Réassurances* [1996] 2 Lloyd's Rep 84, 106.

[71] *Re Mawcon Ltd* [1969] 1 WLR 78, 83; *Suncorp Insurance & Finance v Milano Assicurazioni Spa* [1993] 2 Lloyd's Rep 225, 235(vi); *Smith v Henniker-Major & Co* [2002] EWCA Civ 762, [2003] Ch 182, [56].

[72] *Midland Bank Ltd v Reckitt* [1933] AC 1, 18.

Principal and Third Party

5.25 As between principal and third party, ratification precludes either party from asserting the original absence of authority as between themselves. In this sense, the ratified act takes effect as if antecedently authorised[73] and identifies the principal with the original act in time and place: 'by a wholesome and convenient fiction, a person ratifying the act of another, who, without authority, has made a contract openly and avowedly on his behalf, is deemed to be, though in fact he was not, a party to the contract.'[74] Accordingly, unauthorised legal proceedings may be ratified even after the expiry of the limitation period.[75] Similarly, where an agent committed an unauthorised unlawful act within the jurisdiction, ratification rendered the principal guilty of an offence in England, notwithstanding that the ratificatory acts occurred outside the jurisdiction.[76] In contrast, ratification by the Crown of unauthorised tortious acts committed by a naval commander in suppression of the slave trade retrospectively transformed the commission of a tort into an exercise of sovereignty that engaged the defence of act of state.[77]

Principal and Agent

5.26 As between principal and agent, the consequences of ratification are more nuanced. One can proceed in four stages.

5.27 First, risks incidental to authorised acts fall on the principal. Conversely, in the absence of ratification, an unauthorised act outside the agent's actual and apparent authority does not attach in any way to the principal. A decision to ratify should, it is suggested, ordinarily be considered as voluntarily applying the usual incidence of risk to the ratified act. Accordingly, any subsequent losses should be regarded as caused by the principal's decision to ratify. A contrary view – namely, that the principal could ratify at the agent's risk – would require a distinction to be drawn between commercially legitimate and illegitimate assumptions of risk at the agent's expense[78] and would invite disputes regarding the extent to which subsequent losses should be considered as flowing from the agent's unauthorised act or from subsequent acts of the principal.

5.28 Secondly, where the unauthorised act falls within the agent's apparent authority, the principal is bound towards the third party at the third party's election

---

[73] *Koenigsblatt v Sweet* [1923] 2 Ch 314, 325.
[74] *Keighley, Maxsted & Co v Durant* [1901] AC 240, 247 (Lord Macnaghten).
[75] *Presentaciones Musicales SA v Secunda* [1994] Ch 271. See further below, para 5.38.
[76] *Bedford Insurance Co Ltd v Instituto de Resseguros do Brasil* [1985] 1 QB 966.
[77] *Buron v Denman* (1848) 2 Exch 167.
[78] A principal cannot, it is suggested, be entitled to ratify an unauthorised act almost certain to generate a significant loss and then pass that loss on to the agent. But drawing the line between commercially legitimate and illegitimate ratifications invites costly and time-consuming litigation.

but needs to ratify in order to secure reciprocal rights. It is suggested, however, that the same risk analysis should apply since the foundation of apparent authority lies in the principal's holding out of authority, rather than any additional fault of the agent.

5.29   That ratification normally attaches risk to the principal, and, in consequence, precludes the principal from pursuing remedies against the agent, is supported by authority. In *Verschures Creameries Ltd v Hull & Netherlands Steamship Co Ltd*,[79] agents delivered goods to a third party customer, an act that was contrary to the agents' instructions but within their apparent authority. The principal subsequently invoiced the third party, which failed to pay. The principal then sued the customer and recovered judgment for goods sold and delivered. This judgment not being honoured, the principal instituted bankruptcy proceedings against the third party and also sued the agent. Both when invoicing the third party and later when instituting proceedings against it, the principal wrote to the agent expressly reserving its rights against the agent. The Court of Appeal held, however, that the principal could not treat the agent's act as legitimate as against the third party but illegitimate as against the agent: the principal could not assert inconsistent rights.

5.30   Where, moreover, the principal is precluded by ratification from repudiating the agent's act, the agent enjoys the same financial rights in respect of remuneration and indemnity as if the act had been antecedently authorised.[80]

5.31   Thirdly, however, the unauthorised act may exceptionally expose the principal to a particular loss if it fails to honour the agent's act, such as severe and ongoing damage to reputation, for which a damages award against the agent is not an adequate remedy. The existence of such an exception is recognised by a series of first instance decisions, albeit without reference to *Verschures*.[81] In such circumstances, it is suggested, the absence of any commercially realistic alternative may be considered to deprive ratification of its normal causal significance, so that the question of waiver of remedies against the agent then turns on the intention of the principal. Otherwise, the law would permit a commercially involuntary ratification to shield an agent that has failed to respect the limits of its authority, and compel a principal to sacrifice remedy for reputation. Absent such circumstances, however, the principal should not be able to ratify at the agent's risk.

5.32   Fourthly, an agent owes two types of obligation to its principal: performance obligations regulate the scope and fulfilment of the authority conferred,

---

[79]   *Verschures Creameries Ltd v Hull & Netherlands Steamship Co Ltd* [1921] 2 KB 608.

[80]   *Keay v Fenwick* (1876) 1 CPD 745.

[81]   *Suncorp Insurance & Finance v Milano Assicurazioni Spa* [1993] 2 Lloyd's Rep 225, 235(iv). See also *National Insurance & Guarantee Corp plc v Imperio Reinsurance Co (UK) Ltd* [1999] Lloyd's Rep IR 249, 260; *Ing Re (UK) Ltd v R & V Versicherung AG* [2006] EWHC 1544 (Comm), [2006] 2 All ER (Comm) 870, [151]–[152]. Note also *Keighley, Maxsted & Co v Durant* [1901] AC 240, 262 (Lord Lindley): ratification 'is *sometimes* treated as equivalent to a previous authority' (emphasis added).

while fiduciary obligations demand and enforce an obligation of loyalty to the principal.[82] The general proposition that ratification connotes waiver of remedies does not extend to non-compensatory remedies for breach of fiduciary obligations. There is no inconsistency between ratification of an unauthorised act and remedies, whether personal or proprietary, that strip an agent of an illegitimate profit obtained in breach of fiduciary duty. The risk assumed by the principal in conferring authority on an agent does not include the risk of breach of fiduciary duty, and non-compensatory remedies for such breach are not granted in respect of a loss flowing from the ratified act. Ratification of a transaction procured by bribing an agent does not, therefore, shield the agent from the consequences of corruption. Consistently with the prophylactic nature of fiduciary obligations,[83] the principal may sue the agent for a bribe, or any unauthorised profit, notwithstanding ratification.[84] Informed, express, and unequivocal condonation by the principal is required for waiver of non-compensatory remedies for breach of fiduciary obligation.

Unfair Prejudice

5.33   It has always been acknowledged that the liberty to ratify is subject to restrictions; only relatively recently, however, have these restrictions been analysed as instances of a more general principle, namely that ratification is not permitted where it would occasion unfair prejudice to the third party.[85] It is, therefore, through the lens of unfair prejudice that questions such as the length of time for which the principal enjoys the liberty to ratify must be examined.

5.34   Where an act is subject to a time limit, the status of and purpose behind the time limit must be considered in order to determine whether ratification is permitted once the time limit has expired. A time limit stated in a legal instrument such as a contract or statute may constitute a fundamental aspect of the definition of the act. A third party is entitled, once the limit has passed, to consider itself free

---

[82]   See below, ch 6.

[83]   As to which, see below, para 6.39.

[84]   *Logicrose Ltd v Southend United Football Club Ltd* [1988] 1 WLR 1256, 1263. Accordingly, if, in breach of fiduciary duty, an agent sells property to its principal at a profit, the principal is entitled to ratify the contract and hold the agent to account for the profit: *Bentley v Craven* (1853) 18 Beav 75. There is no difference in principle, in this respect, between disloyalty that generates a bribe from a third party equivalent to a premium element in the price the principal is induced to pay to the third party, and disloyalty that generates a profit element in the price the principal is induced to pay directly to the agent. Although see below, para 6.47 (remedies where agent sells property to its principal without disclosure of an interest acquired outside the scope of its fiduciary obligations).

[85]   Especially significant in this regard are *Smith v Henniker-Major & Co* [2002] EWCA Civ 762, [2003] Ch 182; *The Borvigilant* [2003] EWCA Civ 935, [2004] 1 CLC 41. For earlier discussion of similar ideas but under the organising concept of ratification within a reasonable time, see Tan Cheng-Han, 'The Principle in *Bird v Brown* Revisited' (2001) 117 *Law Quarterly Review* 626.

from accomplishment of the act. To permit ratification beyond that limit is to deny the terms of the instrument, to the undue prejudice of the legitimate settled expectations of the third party.[86] Accordingly, where a share purchase option in a partnership agreement was subject to a time limit and time was held to be of the essence, ratification after the limit had passed was not permitted, as incompatible with the significance in the agreement of the time limit.[87]

5.35   Again, where a seller of goods entrusts the goods to a carrier but the buyer becomes insolvent without paying the contract price, the unpaid seller enjoys a right of stoppage in transit,[88] namely a right to instruct a carrier not to deliver the goods to the buyer. By definition, however, the right is to interrupt transit and not to repossess from the buyer.[89] It was, therefore, held in *Bird v Brown*[90] that an unauthorised exercise of the right of stoppage cannot be ratified after termination of the transit. Similarly, in *Walter v James*,[91] the principal revoked his agent's authority to settle a debt owed by the principal to the third party. Considering himself nevertheless morally obliged to the third party to ensure settlement, the agent made a payment to the third party in purported satisfaction of the debt. Subsequently, however, the agent requested that the third party refund the payment, and the third party acquiesced. The principal was held unable subsequently to ratify the agent's payment by way of defence to the third party's action on the revived debt. The unauthorised act having been undone, there was nothing susceptible of ratification. The termination of transit and the undoing of the payment engendered in the third party a legitimate expectation of settled interests; ratification would engender undue prejudice to the third party by disturbing that expectation.

5.36   Considerable difficulty is occasioned by the decision of the Court of Appeal in *Bolton Partners v Lambert*.[92] S was the acting managing director of BP. He received a letter from L offering to lease a factory owned by BP. S responded that he would refer the matter to the directors. Subsequently he wrote again, saying that the directors accepted the offer. In fact, L's offer had been considered not by the board of directors but by a committee with no power to make such decisions. S's letter of acceptance was therefore unauthorised. A draft agreement followed that contained a requirement for a guarantee of the rent. L took objection to this and purported to withdraw his offer. Shortly thereafter, BP's board of directors approved the lease and authorised the issuing of proceedings seeking specific performance. The Court of Appeal held in favour of BP. Although an offer cannot be accepted once it has been revoked, BP's ratification related back to the time of the

---

[86]   *The Borvigilant* [2003] EWCA Civ 935, [2004] 1 CLC 41 [66]–[79] (although the discussion focuses primarily upon third party proprietary rights).

[87]   *Dibbins v Dibbins* [1896] 2 Ch 348.

[88]   Sale of Goods Act 1979, ss 39(1)(b), 44.

[89]   ibid, s 45(1)–(3).

[90]   *Bird v Brown* (1854) 4 Ex 786.

[91]   *Walter v James* (1871) LR 6 Ex 124. See also *Pacific & General Insurance Co Ltd v Hazell* [1997] BCC 400, 416–19.

[92]   *Bolton Partners v Lambert* (1887) 41 Ch D 295.

unauthorised acceptance. A contract was concluded at that moment; L's revocation of the offer was too late.

5.37 The decision is at least questionable,[93] and probably incorrect. First, it is difficult to see why an exercise of a right of stoppage in transit ceases to be ratifiable upon termination of transit while an acceptance does not cease to be ratifiable upon revocation of an offer. If the retrospectivity of ratification cannot reach back past the termination of transit or the reversal of a payment, why can it reach back past the revocation of an offer?[94] In *Bolton v Lambert* itself, the ineffectiveness of ratification in *Bird v Brown* was attributed to the vesting in the buyer of a proprietary right. However, this analysis has since been authoritatively rejected in favour of the seller's being out of time for ratification.[95] *Walter v James*, while apparently accepted as correct,[96] was not discussed.[97] Secondly, the decision privileges the party that operates through an agent. In direct dealings between a party and counterparty, the legally binding engagement of one is matched by the engagement of the other, and revocation of an offer takes unimpeded and immediate effect on communication to the offeree. In indirect dealings through an agent, *Bolton v Lambert* creates the possibility of the third party being bound, while the principal retains the freedom to adopt or reject the contract, although only where the agent lacked both actual and also apparent authority. In such circumstances, however, reciprocity of contractual obligation is transformed into an option at the expense of the third party,[98] although, as discussed below, the modern focus on unfair prejudice may militate against this possibility.[99]

5.38 Where on a true analysis of the instrument a time limit lacks defining significance or no time limit is stated, ratification must occur within a reasonable time, reasonableness being determined by whether it would occasion undue prejudice to the third party to permit ratification after the delay that has occurred.[100] Thus, the law of limitation of action enshrines a fundamental policy against the infinite prolonging of the possibility of litigation on the bases that a never-ending

---

[93] The decision 'presents difficulties': *Fleming v Bank of New Zealand* [1900] AC 577, 587 (Lord Lindley, reserving the case for possible future consideration).

[94] And, indeed, the possibility that it might was cursorily dismissed in *Kidderminster v Hardwick* (1873) LR 9 Ex 13, 22.

[95] *The Borvigilant* [2003] EWCA Civ 935, [2004] 1 CLC 41, [83]–[84].

[96] (1887) 41 Ch D 295, 309.

[97] One factual distinction is that the reversal was by bilateral accord of agent and third party, while in *Bolton v Lambert* it was by unilateral act of the third party. This, however, appears immaterial in terms of legal principle. There is no suggestion in *Walter v James* of the agent's involvement precluding the principal from denying the efficacy of the rescission of the settlement agreement.

[98] For judicial criticism on this basis, see *Re Portuguese Consolidated Copper Mines Ltd* (1890) 45 Ch D 16, 21. Likewise, W Seavey, 'The Rationale of Agency' (1920) 29 *Yale Law Journal* 859, 891.

[99] Below, para 5.41.

[100] *Re Portuguese Consolidated Copper Mines Ltd* (1890) 45 Ch D 16; *The Borvigilant* [2003] EWCA Civ 935, [2004] 1 CLC 41, [73]. That ratification could not prejudice but only benefit the third party will logically extend what is reasonable (*Bedford Insurance Co Ltd v Instituto de Resseguros do Brasil* [1985] 1 QB 966, 987), although an ultimate interest in certainty of rights and liabilities must import some temporal limit.

threat of legal proceedings would be socially and economically corrosive, that individual parties have a right to certainty in their affairs, and that undue delay in the instigating of litigation courts unreliably stale, or incomplete and degraded evidence. These concerns are satisfied whether or not timeously instituted proceedings are authorised. Consequently, the relevant limitation period does not define the proceedings; its expiry does not of itself preclude ratification of the unauthorised instigation of legal proceedings.[101] On the facts, nevertheless, the delay in instituting proceedings may be such as to occasion the third party unfair prejudice were ratification permitted.[102] In such circumstances, ratification will be barred.[103]

5.39 Ratification will generally be precluded where it would divest the third party of an accrued proprietary right. As a matter of principle, however, the divesting of accrued proprietary rights does not constitute an absolute bar to ratification, but constitutes rather a possible example of unfair prejudice. In the leading case of *The Borvigilant*,[104] a tug requisition contract concluded between the owner of an oil tanker and a terminal operator effected a contractual allocation of risk in respect of accidents in the course of towing operations. The contract further provided that the terminal operator could perform its obligations by employing tugs owned by others and that, in such a case, the tanker owner agreed that the tug owner should have the benefit of the terms of the requisition contract. The terminal operator did employ the tugs of another party, one of which collided with the tanker. When the tanker owner sued the tug owner in negligence, the tugowner sought to rely on the risk allocation in the tug requisition contract by way, inter alia, of ratification.[105] The tanker owner argued that such reliance was precluded because the cause of action in negligence accrued before the ratificatory acts. The Court of Appeal held in favour of the tug owner. While a cause of action was a species of personal property right, its accrual did not automatically bar ratification; the question was whether its denial would occasion unfair prejudice to the tanker owner. In practice, the divesting of an accrued property right would constitute unfair prejudice 'in the vast majority of cases', but the case in question illustrated 'the importance of avoiding an inflexible principle.' Allowing ratification on the facts merely held the tanker owner to the risk allocation it had agreed, with respect to parties it had agreed should benefit. This could not be unfair.[106]

---

[101] *Presentaciones Musicales SA v Secunda* [1994] Ch 271.

[102] For example, an important witness may have died (as in *Smith v Henniker-Major & Co* [2002] EWCA Civ 762, [2003] Ch 182) or become otherwise incapacitated from testifying.

[103] *Smith v Henniker-Major & Co* [2002] EWCA Civ 762, [2003] Ch 182, [72]. Prejudice is necessary, but 'the significance of a modest degree of prejudice may be magnified by delay' (ibid, [73] (Robert Walker LJ)).

[104] *The Borvigilant* [2003] EWCA Civ 935, [2004] 1 CLC 41, [66]–[88]. See also *Smith v Henniker-Major & Co* [2002] EWCA Civ 762, [2003] Ch 182, [71].

[105] The tug requisition contract was concluded before the entry into force of the Contracts (Rights of Third Parties) Act 1999.

[106] ibid, [87]–[88] (Clarke LJ). The Court also considered that even if the fact of accrual of property rights did automatically bar ratification, a cause of action was not the type of property right contemplated by the preclusionary rule, but was rather akin to an accrued limitation defence: ibid, [89].

5.40   The exercise of determining whether the circumstances are such as to preclude ratification on the ground of unfair prejudice has been characterised as a 'judgmental application of principle [rather than] an exercise of judicial discretion, although for practical purposes the two are closely akin.'[107] The fact-sensitive flexibility of the concept of unfair prejudice inescapably introduces an element of uncertainty. Two points may be made.

5.41   First, the retrospectivity of ratification raises the prospect of the principal speculating at the expense of the third party. Assuming the unauthorised contract to be subject to market fluctuation, for such period as the principal has the option to ratify, the third party incurs the risk of that fluctuation. A principal-purchaser will ratify if the market rises but decline to ratify if it falls, and conversely in the case of a principal-vendor. Since the possibility of such a strategic (or opportunistic) election arises courtesy only of the conduct of a party purporting to act for the principal, the justification for this incidence of risk is elusive. However, the modern focus on unfair prejudice suggests that the more volatile the market and the greater the (unmerited) opportunity for speculation at the third party's expense the shorter will be the reasonable time for ratification.

5.42   Secondly, under the general law of contract, where an obligation falls to be performed within a reasonable time, the promisee may seek to address the temporal uncertainty by serving a notice calling on the promisor to perform by a specified date. This procedure does not permit the promisee unilaterally to vary the contract by truncating the permitted period for performance below what would be reasonable, but it does permit the promisee to nominate a date with which the promisor must comply within the range of what would be reasonable, and, to that extent, inject certainty into the timing. Provided the notice given is indeed reasonable, non-compliance constitutes a repudiation of the contract.[108] By analogy, it may be possible for a third party that knows of the agent's lack of authority to serve a notice calling on the principal to ratify by a specified date. While the principal is under no obligation to communicate a decision whether or not to ratify, provided the allowed time is not unreasonably short, a failure to ratify may be considered a statement of an intention not to ratify, precluding future ratification.[109]

---

[107] *Smith v Henniker-Major & Co* [2002] EWCA Civ 762, [2003] Ch 182, [82] (Robert Walker LJ).

[108] See E Peel, *Treitel: The Law of Contract*, 13th edn (London, Sweet & Maxwell, 2011), para 18-097.

[109] See para 5.43. Such a development would be consistent with the international instruments, which restrict ratification rights by dedicated (albeit slightly different) notice procedures and also potentially by the overriding requirement of good faith: PECL, arts 2:210, 1:201; PICC, arts 2.2.9, 1.7; DCFR, arts II-6:111(3) (derived from the Unidroit Principles), I-1:103. Note that the context under the European Principles and Draft CFR is the reduced scope for ratification engendered by the nature, in each instrument, of apparent authority as full authority.

Loss of the Right to Ratify

5.43　　According to Lord Atkin, 'ratification cannot take place after the purported principal has by words or conduct intimated to the other party that he does not intend to ratify.'[110] The juridical nature of the operative doctrine is, however, uncertain. On the one hand, no reference is made to reliance by the other party, a basic requirement for the operation of an estoppel. On the other hand, it is unclear why the decision not to ratify requires communication to the other party, rather than merely some external manifestation.[111] The approach of Lord Atkin considers the forfeiture of ratification rights as a form of election,[112] rather than a simple unilateral act of will analogous to ratification itself.[113]

---

[110]　*McEvoy v Belfast Banking Co Ltd* [1935] AC 24, 45.

[111]　A determination not to ratify manifested within the internal accounts of the principal but not communicated, on the facts to the agent but indeed to anyone, may be reversed and ratification permitted: *Simpson v Eggington* (1855) 10 Ex 845.

[112]　For communication and election, see *Scarf v Jardine* (1882) 7 App Cas 345, 360–61.

[113]　See above, para 5.3.

6

Agents' Obligations

6.1   Agency, by definition, is a relationship whereby the principal entrusts the conduct of its affairs to the agent within the parameters of the actual authority conferred. The agent will incur liability to the principal for any losses caused by its failure to comply with the terms of its actual authority, enforceable in accordance with the general law of obligations. However, the control and power over the principal's affairs ceded to the agent place the agent in a position of trust and confidence that equity is astute to ensure is not abused. Fundamental duties of loyalty and fidelity to the principal are enforced through fiduciary obligations that require the highest standards of integrity and probity. This chapter discusses both performance obligations and fiduciary obligations traditionally recognised by English law. In addition, in the particular case of commercial agency, mutual obligations are imposed on both principal and agent under the Commercial Agents Regulations. They are considered in the next chapter.

Performance Obligations

6.2   The scope and standard of an agent's performance obligations depend entirely upon the terms of the actual authority conferred. Assuming that the relationship between principal and agent is contractual, the exercise is one of contractual interpretation.

6.3   A spectrum of scope of authority may be envisaged. At one extreme, the agent may be mandated to perform a clearly and narrowly defined task; at the other extreme, the entire management and conduct of a principal's affairs may be delegated. Depending upon the precise terms of the authority, the agent may be required to follow instructions or to exercise judgement, discretion, and initiative.

6.4   In respect of the standard of obligation assumed, determining whether the agent assumes an unqualified obligation of strict liability, or a qualified obligation to exercise reasonable care, depends upon the true interpretation of the authority. Performance of the essential mandate is a matter of strict liability. An agent mandated to conclude a specified transaction in respect of a specified item of property is clearly in breach of its retainer if it concludes a different transaction in respect of the correct item or the correct transaction in respect of a different item.[1] While a failure to perform the essential mandate is often inherently negligent, liability does not depend on proof of negligence, and proof of absence of negligence does not constitute a defence.[2] Where, however, the principal's complaint is that the mandate has been performed but in an inadequate or inappropriate manner, liability in principle depends on proof of negligence. An agent usually undertakes to exercise reasonable care in acting pursuant to its actual authority.[3]

6.5   Similarly, complaint may not be brought simply for failure to achieve the entrusted goals, but will lie rather for failure to exercise reasonable care in endeavouring to achieve them. Occasionally, however, an agent may be found to have undertaken an unqualified obligation and warranted a particular outcome.[4] In such a case, liability will result from the mere failure to achieve the outcome. Clear evidence will, however, be required for such an unusual – and generally inadvisable – guarantee.

6.6   Precisely what constitutes negligence, and the practicalities of proving it, will be affected by the experience, knowledge, and skill professed by the agent and by reference to which the authority was conferred, and upon the overall context.[5] More is expected of the specialist than the generalist; and the scale of remuneration may be indicative of the level of experience and expertise professed. At some point, indeed, certain errors will be synonymous with negligence. In such circumstances, nevertheless, the distinction between departure from mandate and negligent performance may remain significant; for example, the contract may contain an exemption clause confined, on its true interpretation, to negligent performance. Gratuitous agency, moreover, is not necessarily indicative of a lower level of obligation. Professional services offered on a pro bono basis are accepted as being rendered on the same basis as if remunerated.[6] A social context, reinforced by an absence of payment, may however be incompatible with any assumption of responsibility in association with the rendering of services.[7]

6.7   Notwithstanding the inevitably fact-specific nature of what constitutes negligence, two examples may perhaps be helpful. In *Luxmoore-May v Messenger May*

---

[1] By analogy with an independent expert's departure from instructions (see *Veba Oil Supply & Trading GmbH v Petrotrade Inc (The Robin)* [2001] EWCA Civ 1832, [2002] CLC 405) or an independent contractor's departure from retainer (*Platform Funding Ltd v Bank of Scotland plc* [2008] EWCA Civ 930, [2009] QB 426).

[2] See *Platform Funding Ltd v Bank of Scotland plc* [2008] EWCA Civ 930, [2009] QB 426 (that a surveyor retained by the lender was fraudulently misled by the borrower into valuing the wrong property was no defence to liability for losses accruing to the lender from reliance on the valuation).

[3] *Chapman v Walton* (1833) 10 Bing 57; Supply of Goods and Services Act 1982, s 13.

[4] See the analysis in *Harlow & Jones Ltd v PJ Walker Shipping & Transport Ltd* [1986] 2 Lloyd's Rep 141, 144.

[5] *Duchess of Argyll v Beuselinck* [1972] 2 Lloyd's Rep 172, 183.

[6] *Chancliff Holdings Pty Ltd v Bell* [1999] FCA 1783, [16].

[7] *Chaudhry v Prabakhar* [1988] 3 All ER 718 (duty of care conceded).

Baverstock,[8] the defendant firm of non-specialist, provincial fine-art auctioneers and valuers advised the claimants that two paintings were worth between £30 and £50. Having realised £840 at an auction held by the defendants, the paintings were subsequently attributed to George Stubbs by the leading auction house of Sotheby's and sold for £88,000 to an art dealer who in turn re-sold the paintings to a prominent collector of the works of Stubbs for an undisclosed, but presumably significantly higher, price. The claimants alleged that the defendants had negligently failed to identify the possibility of the paintings having been the work of George Stubbs. The claim failed. The starting point in the analysis was to identify the obligation undertaken by the defendants, namely to formulate a considered opinion as to the sale value of the paintings, taking such further advice as might be appropriate. The requisite standard of care and skill with which this endeavour was to be carried out was that of general provincial auctioneers, not leading specialists. Moreover, the task of valuing pictures of unknown provenance was inherently uncertain, involving opinion and judgement, and open to error. Indeed, despite the subsequent high-price transactions, the true provenance of the paintings had not been established beyond question, with leading experts remaining divided. The defendants had consulted their usual independent valuer and had also taken the painting for a quick free opinion from the leading auction house of Christie's. The court could not conclude that no reasonable auctioneer of the professed expertise of the defendant firm could reasonably have failed to identify the possibility that the paintings were the work of Stubbs.

6.8 In contrast, liability was established in *The Moonacre*.[9] Insurance on a yacht excluded any period while the vessel was laid up out of commission when it was 'used as a houseboat' unless the insurers were notified in advance and an additional premium paid. The vessel was rendered a total loss by fire while laid up with a crew member living on board. Not having been informed of the crew member, the insurers denied liability. The owner sued the broker. The judge acknowledged the broker's status as a general marine broker, professing no specialist expertise with respect to yachts. Equally, however, the broker accepted instructions for the insuring of yachts without professing any special absence of expertise with respect to yachts. The required standard of care, therefore, was not that of a marine broker substantially inexperienced in yachts, but rather that of a broker with 'such general knowledge of the yacht insurance market and the cover available in it as to be able to advise his client on all matters on which a lay client would in the ordinary course of events predictably need advice, in particular in the course of the selection of cover and the completion of the proposal.'[10] The broker attested to his belief that the houseboat clause referred only to residence on board of the owner and the owner's family, and, in particular, did not extend

---

[8] *Luxmoore-May v Messenger May Baverstock* [1990] 1 All ER 1067.
[9] *Sharp v Sphere Drake Insurance plc (The Moonacre)* [1992] 2 Lloyd's Rep 501.
[10] ibid, 523 (Anthony Colman QC, sitting as a Deputy Judge of the High Court).

to the crew. This interpretation, however, was not supported by the ordinary meaning of the policy wording and, as the broker himself admitted, did not represent a general market view among the underwriters. It was, accordingly, negligent for even a non-specialist broker to place the risk on the basis of his own personal belief.

6.9   Where an agent lawfully relies on an independent contractor to assist in the performance of a task entrusted to it, it is not sufficient that the agent exercises reasonable care in the selection of independent contractor. Rather, the undertaking of the agent is that reasonable care will be exercised in performing the entrusted task, so that the agent will incur liability for negligence on the part of the independent contractor.[11] Where, however, the agent's mandate is merely to identify and introduce another party to undertake performance of a service, the agent's obligation is restricted to the exercise of reasonable care in selecting the other party.[12]

6.10   An agent that acts contrary to its instructions clearly acts in breach of duty. However, in the absence of any warranty as to a particular outcome, an agent that exercises reasonable care in unsuccessfully endeavouring to fulfil its instructions incurs no liability for the failure to achieve the object of the conferral of authority, but must inform the principal with reasonable promptness so that the principal has the opportunity to give alternative instructions or adopt alternative measures.[13]

6.11   The terms of any contractual discretion not embraced by a duty to exercise reasonable care, and not otherwise subject to any control providing protection against exercise in accordance with pure whim, should sustain an implied requirement that it be exercised 'honestly and in good faith for the purpose for which it was conferred'.[14] Accordingly, it should, but need only, be exercised in a manner that is not 'capricious, arbitrary or so outrageous in its defiance of reason that it can properly be categorised as perverse'.[15] Thus, an auctioneer that contracted for 'sole and complete discretion' regarding the description of property in its sale catalogue undertook merely not to act capriciously or perversely in describing the principal's property, and did not undertake to exercise reasonable care in so doing.[16] Moreover, faced with a challenge to the exercise of such a discretion, a court must be careful not to usurp the nominated decision-maker by substituting

---

[11]   *Riverstone Meat Co Pty Ltd v Lancashire Shipping Co Ltd (The Muncaster Castle)* [1961] AC 807; *Dow Europe v Novoklav* [1998] 1 Lloyd's Rep 306. See above, para 3.14.

[12]   See above, para 1.30.

[13]   *Youell v Bland Welch & Co Ltd (The Superhulls Cover case) (No 2)* [1990] 2 Lloyd's Rep 431, 446–47; *Aneco Reinsurance Underwriting Ltd v Johnson* [1998] 1 Lloyd's Rep 565, 590.

[14]   *Ludgate Insurance Co Ltd v Citibank NA* [1998] Lloyd's Rep IR 221, [35] (Brooke LJ).

[15]   ibid. See also *Socimer International Bank Ltd v Standard Bank London Ltd (No 2)* [2008] EWCA 116, [2008] 1 Lloyd's Rep 558, [66]; *Compass Group UK & Ireland Ltd v Mid Essex Hospital Services NHS Trust* [2013] EWCA Civ 200, [136].

[16]   *Elidor Investments SA v Christie's, Manson Woods Ltd* [2009] EWHC 3600 (QB).

the parameters of objective reasonableness as determined by the court itself for those of the decision-maker's honesty and subjective rationality.[17]

6.12   More generally, longer-term agency agreements that envisage substantial commitment and sustained cooperation import a spirit of collaboration and joint endeavour to further the common interest that may sustain the implication of a mutual duty of good faith and fair dealing. Such a duty serves to inform and moderate the obligations undertaken and rights enjoyed by the parties to ensure that the agreement operates in a manner consistent with the evolution of an enduring relationship.[18] Such a duty is implied into commercial agency agreements; its import is discussed further in that context.[19]

6.13   Failure to comply with the performance obligations of agency is sanctioned in accordance with the general law of obligations, giving rise to remedies for breach of contract, where the agency is contractual, and in tort.[20]

6.14   Where an agent is under a duty to collect money on behalf of the principal, whether money so collected is subject to a personal duty to account to the principal or whether the principal has a proprietary interest in such money depends upon the true interpretation of the agency agreement.[21] A liberty for the agent to use collected sums for its own benefit in the ordinary course of its business rather than an obligation to credit collected sums to a dedicated account to the benefit of the principal will be indicative of the owing of a personal debt to the principal, rather than the trusteeship of property of the principal.

Fiduciary Obligations

6.15   The conferral of actual authority entails a delegation of the principal's autonomy. For the duration of the authority and within its scope, the agent receives the power to exercise rights of the principal in the principal's place. The agent is placed in a position of power and the principal is rendered correspondingly vulnerable. In such circumstances, and even where the agency is gratuitous,[22] equity considers it appropriate to impose special duties of loyalty (known as 'fiduciary

---

[17]   *Cantor Fitzgerald International v Horkulak* [2004] EWCA Civ 1287, [2005] ICR 402; *WestLB AG v Nomura Bank International plc* [2012] EWCA Civ 495, [32].

[18]   *Yam Seng Pte Ltd v International Trade Corp Ltd* [2013] EWHC 111 (QB), [120]–[152]; [2013] 1 All ER (Comm) 1321.

[19]   See below, ch 7.

[20]   Where, however, a statute imposes a personal – as opposed to vicarious – liability on the principal and the liability is engaged through the conduct of an agent, the maxim *ex turpi causa non oritur actio* will preclude recoupment of any financial penalty from the agent responsible, at least where the liability is based on fault: *Safeway Stores Ltd v Twigger* [2010] EWCA Civ 1472, [2011] 1 CLC 80. Although the principal always has the power unilaterally to revoke the agent's authority: below, paras 11.12–11.13.

[21]   *Angove Pty Ltd v Bailey* [2013] EWHC 215 (Ch), [51].

[22]   *Turnbull v Garden* (1869) 20 LT 218.

duties') to guard against any temptation towards betrayal of the trust reposed by the principal in the agent.[23] A rare exception arises where the authority is granted to secure an existing interest of the agent that exists independently of the agency. In such a case, the purpose of the grant of authority is to benefit the agent, entitling the agent to exercise the authority in its own interest rather than that of the principal.[24] This is discussed in a later chapter.[25]

The Content of Agents' Fiduciary Obligations

6.16   The equitable injunction of loyalty translates primarily into two broad duties, the significance of which lies both in their scope and strictness and also in the remedies by which they are enforced. First, the agent must avoid any conflict that can be avoided between its own interests and those of its principal and must resolve any conflict that does arise in favour of the principal. The duty extends to any engagement in which the agent will or may have a personal interest that will or may conflict with the interests of the principal that the agent is required to promote and safeguard.[26] Secondly,[27] the agent is prohibited from obtaining any benefit from the agency that has not been authorised by the principal.[28]

6.17   Fiduciary duties reflect and embody the principal's entitlement, within the confines of the agency, to the benefit of the agent's services rendered in a spirit of absolute fidelity to the principal's interests: 'if you undertake to act for a man, you must act 100 per cent, body and soul, for him.'[29] An actionable breach depends, accordingly, upon a failure by the agent to meet equity's exacting standards of loyalty. In contrast with a performance obligation, the question is not competence but fidelity: 'A servant who loyally does his incompetent best for his master is not unfaithful and is not guilty of a breach of fiduciary duty.'[30] The agent's performance obligations dictate what the agent must do in order to fulfil its mandate

---

[23]   On the power-liability relationship between principal and agent as the basis for the imposition of fiduciary obligations, see F Dowrick, 'The Relationship of Principal and Agent' (1954) 17 *Modern Law Review* 24. On fiduciary relationships generally, see *Hospital Products Ltd v United States Surgical Corp* (1984) 156 CLR 41, 97; M Conaglen, *Fiduciary Loyalty* (Oxford, Hart Publishing, 2011), pp 61–76.

[24]   *Temple Legal Protection Ltd v QBE Insurance (Europe) Ltd* [2009] EWCA Civ 453, [2009] 1 CLC 553, [50].

[25]   See below, para 11.21 et seq.

[26]   *Aberdeen Rail Co v Blaikie Bros* (1854) 1 Macq 461, 471. A modest gratuity paid in consideration for the excellence of the agent's services, and not to influence any decision, has been held not to give rise to a conflict of interest: *The Parkdale* [1897] P 53 (although the case is also explicable on the basis of implied consent).

[27]   This 'second' duty may in fact merely constitute a particular example of the general injunction against conflict of interest: *Attorney General v Blake* [2001] 1 AC 268, 280.

[28]   The term 'secret profit' is often used but misleading, since the critical issue is informed authorisation based on full disclosure (see below, para 6.21). There is still a breach of fiduciary duty if a profit is disclosed but consent is not given, or consent is obtained based on incomplete disclosure, yet in neither case is the profit truly secret.

[29]   *Imageview Management Ltd v Jack* [2009] EWCA Civ 63, [2009] 1 Lloyd's Rep 436, [6] (Jacob LJ).

[30]   *Bristol & West Building Society v Mothew* [1998] Ch 1, 18 (Millett LJ).

while the agent's fiduciary obligations embody prohibitions designed to guard against any temptation to betray the principal's trust: 'Equity is proscriptive, not prescriptive . . . It tells the fiduciary what he must not do. It does not tell him what he ought to do.'[31]

6.18 An agent is not, however, required to devote 100 per cent of its time to acting for the principal. Equity does not require the agent to offer its principal any possibility of benefit that arises independently of its position as agent and that does not generate any conflict with the principal's interests.[32]

6.19 Assuming the agent's actions contravene equity's standards, the agent's own honest belief that its conduct is permissible is irrelevant.[33] Similarly, equity's exclusive focus on the loyalty of the agent precludes consideration of the impact on the principal's interests of the engagement entered into by the agent.[34] It is, consequently, no defence to an action for breach of fiduciary duty[35] that the agent's conduct did not occasion the principal any prejudice or even that the principal made a profit from the agent's breach of duty;[36] that the agent merely exploited an opportunity that the principal either would have lacked the resources to exploit for itself[37] or would have elected to decline or been otherwise unable to take advantage of for itself;[38] that the agent obtained terms as good as or better than available elsewhere;[39] or that the principal after due consideration elected to maintain the benefit of a transaction procured in breach of duty.[40]

6.20 Acceptance of a bribe constitutes a clear, and serious, breach of fiduciary duty. A bribe consists of an inducement in whatever form given by a third party to an agent that is not disclosed to the principal and that gives rise to a conflict of interest on the part of the agent.[41] It may take the form of a benefit, actual or promised, in cash, in a beneficial opportunity, or in kind,[42] either directly to the agent or made available to another party but nevertheless to the appreciation of

---

[31] *Attorney General v Blake* [1998] Ch 439, 455 (Millett LJ).

[32] The more specific the agent's mandate, the greater the scope for opportunities to arise outside its scope: *Aas v Benham* [1891] 2 Ch 244 (partnership), discussed *O'Donnell v Shanahan* [2009] EWCA Civ 751, [2009] BCC 822 (on the facts, opportunity accrued in the context of the fiduciary position so that relationship to the principal's business irrelevant).

[33] *De Bussche v Alt* (1878) 8 Ch D 286, 316.

[34] *Aberdeen Rail Co v Blaikie Bros* (1854) 1 Macq 461, 471.

[35] Although relevant to the remedies available for breach.

[36] *Parker v McKenna* (1874) LR 10 Ch App 96; *Rhodes v Macalister* (1923) 29 Com Cas 19; *Imageview Management Ltd v Jack* [2009] EWCA Civ 63, [2009] 1 Lloyd's Rep 436, [47]–[49].

[37] *Regal (Hastings) Ltd v Gulliver* (1942) [1967] 2 AC 134n; *Boardman v Phipps* [1967] 2 AC 46.

[38] *Brown v Inland Revenue Commissioners* [1965] AC 244, 257; *Bhullar v Bhullar* [2003] EWCA Civ 424, [2003] 2 BCLC 241, [41].

[39] *Aberdeen Rail Co v Blaikie Bros* (1854) 1 Macq 461, 471.

[40] *Rhodes v Macalister* (1923) 29 Com Cas 19, 28. And we see above, para 5.32.

[41] *Anangel Atlas Compania Naviera SA v Ishikawajima-Harima Heavy Industries Co Ltd* [1990] 1 Lloyd's Rep 167, 171.

[42] *Fiona Trust & Holding Corp v Privalov* [2010] EWHC 3199 (Comm), [73(iii)], [178], [1387].

the agent.[43] Often attracting distinct consideration, for many purposes a bribe is but one type of secret profit, with the consequence that, as between principal and agent, the same principles as regulate breach of fiduciary duty generally are applicable, although the involvement of the third party in the breach of duty raises additional issues. There is, accordingly, no requirement to demonstrate that a bribe had any impact upon the conduct of the agent or the fortunes of the principal.[44] Indeed, it is irrelevant that the agent in fact acted in the principal's best interests;[45] the requisite conflict of interest lies in the temptation of personal gain that deprives the principal of entirely objective, disinterested service.[46] Equally, there is no requirement of an intention on the part of either agent or third party to deceive or harm the principal; in particular, the civil law concept of bribery carries no necessary connotation of intention to corrupt.[47] With respect to the third party (the briber), the essence of bribery lies purely in conferring an inducement on the agent without disclosure to the principal, and a third party that relies on the agent to effect disclosure takes the risk of the agent failing to do so.[48] However, while deceit, corruption, or intention to harm are not required to establish breach of fiduciary duty, their presence may impact upon the remedies awarded or may give rise to additional claims at common law.

6.21 The strictness of fiduciary duties reflects equity's concern that, otherwise, agents might be led astray by temptation.[49] The more an agent's liability for breach of fiduciary duty depends on the outcome of a fact-sensitive enquiry as to the potential for, and probability of, prejudice to the principal, the greater the possibility for a disloyal agent to shelter behind factual uncertainty and the correspondingly more tempting an opportunity for personal advantage may appear. Equity, therefore, adopts a strongly prophylactic approach, precluding any enquiry whatever into the impact of the transaction on the principal's affairs. Instead, an agent that wishes to benefit from its fiduciary position must make full disclosure to the principal of all material circumstances, including precisely what benefit will accrue to the agent, and obtain the principal's informed consent.[50] Disloyalty lies not in active concealment but in failing proactively to make full disclosure.[51]

---

[43] See below, para 6.27.

[44] *Re a Debtor* [1927] 2 Ch 367; *Daraydan Holdings Ltd v Solland International Ltd* [2004] EWHC 622 (Ch), [2005] Ch 119, [53]. Analysis in terms of an irrebuttable legal presumption of inducement to act to the principal's detriment (*Hovenden & Sons v Millhoff* (1900) 83 LT 41; *Industries & General Mortgage Co Ltd v Lewis* [1949] 2 All ER 573) means simply that such inducement forms no part of the definition of bribery: *Mahesan v Malaysia Government Officers' Co-operative Housing Society Ltd* [1979] AC 374, 383.

[45] *Anangel Atlas Compania Naviera SA v Ishikawajima-Harima Heavy Industries Co Ltd* [1990] 1 Lloyd's Rep 167, 171.

[46] *Logicrose Ltd v Southend United Football Club Ltd* [1988] 1 WLR 1256, 1261; *Petrotrade Inc v Smith* [2000] CLC 916, [16]–[17].

[47] *Industries & General Mortgage Co Ltd v Lewis* [1949] 2 All ER 573.

[48] *Logicrose Ltd v Southend United Football Club Ltd* [1988] 1 WLR 1256, 1262.

[49] *Keech v Sandford* (1726) Sel Cas Temp King 61; *Bray v Ford* [1896] AC 44, 51–52.

[50] *Fullwood v Hurley* [1928] 1 KB 498.

[51] *Fiona Trust & Holding Corp v Privalov* [2010] EWHC 3199 (Comm), [1388].

6.22 Where the principal is a company and the board of directors is properly regarded as collectively constituting the company's directing mind and will, disclosure to and consent from one director will serve as disclosure to and consent from the company as a whole,[52] except where the compromised agent is one of the directors, in which case disclosure to and consent from all directors or a properly convened and quorate meeting of the board are required.[53] An agent that acts for more than one principal, such as the parties to a joint venture, must obtain consent from each, unless one principal has authority to grant consent on behalf of all.[54]

6.23 If the benefit to accrue to the agent is somewhat conjectural, such that disclosure would necessarily be materially incomplete,[55] consent should be obtained in principle and an undertaking given, and subsequently honoured, to inform the principal of the precise benefit once known and obtain the principal's consent to that benefit before accepting it.[56] Consent to a reasonable[57] benefit that is customary in a market may be implicit from appointing an agent to act in that market,[58] but merely making a statement that might be considered sufficient to put a principal on enquiry as to benefits accruing to the agent is inadequate as disclosure.[59] Such a statement might suffice to negate liability for fraud, but it will leave an agent liable for breach of fiduciary duty.[60] The burden of proof lies on the principal to prove that profits were indeed earned but on the agent to prove that full disclosure was made and consent granted.[61] Proof is required, moreover, of actual consent; an agent cannot seek to prove that the principal would have consented had disclosure been made.[62]

---

[52] *Jafari-Fini v Skillglass Ltd* [2007] EWCA Civ 261, [98].

[53] *Ross River Ltd v Cambridge City Football Club Ltd* [2007] EWHC 2115 (Ch), [2008] 1 All ER 1004, [213].

[54] *FHR European Ventures LLP v Mankarious* [2011] EWHC 2308 (Ch), [2012] 2 BCLC 39, [83].

[55] While the value of the benefit may be material, if fixed such that the precise monetary value is unknown (for example as a percentage of a profit), disclosure of an honest and realistic estimate of the anticipated scale of benefit should suffice. In certain contexts, it may be sufficient to disclose the existence of a benefit voluntarily but the amount only upon request: see, for example, Office of Fair Trade Guidelines for Credit Brokers and Intermediaries (OFT 1388, November 2011), para 3.7(i)–(k).

[56] *Advanced Realty Funding Corp v Bannink* (1979) 106 DLR (3d) 137, 142.

[57] *De Bussche v Alt* (1878) 8 Ch D 286, 317 (alleged custom for agent engaged to sell at a minimum price to purchase at that price and resell at mark-up for own benefit held to be unacceptable).

[58] *The Parkdale* [1897] P 53. Much depends on the sophistication or vulnerability of the principal: *Hurstanger Ltd v Wilson* [2007] EWCA Civ 299, [2007] 1 WLR 2351, [36]–[37]. In the London insurance market it is customary for a broker (acting as agent for the prospective assured) to be remunerated for services performed to its principal by being afforded the opportunity to bargain with the insurer to be paid a percentage of the premium by way of commission: *Great Western Insurance Co v Cunliffe* (1874) LR 9 Ch App 525. See also *People v Wells Fargo Insurance Services Inc*, 16 NY 3d 169 (2011).

[59] *Dunne v English* (1874) LR 18 Eq 524, 535–36.

[60] *Hurstanger Ltd v Wilson* [2007] EWCA Civ 299, [2007] 1 WLR 2351, [37]–[43].

[61] *Allwood v Clifford* [2002] EMLR 3.

[62] *Murad v Al-Saraj* [2005] EWCA Civ 959, [71]; *Hurstanger Ltd v Wilson* [2007] EWCA Civ 299, [2007] 1 WLR 2351, [35].

6.24 Accordingly, an agent that wishes to act for two principals with conflicting interests must seek the informed consent of both, ensuring that each principal appreciates that it will not be able to assume the normal loyalty and fidelity on the part of the agent to which a principal is normally entitled and which is generally underpinned by the usual range of fiduciary duties.[63] Moreover, even where informed consent has been sought and obtained, the agent must still act in good faith in the interests of each principal. This fiduciary duty of good faith requires the agent not intentionally to further the interests of one principal at the expense of the other. No breach of fiduciary duty will arise unless the agent knows or believes that conduct in the service of one principal is incompatible with its duty of loyalty to the other, although conduct not in breach of fiduciary duty may still constitute a breach of a performance obligation.[64] An agent that finds itself in a position where it cannot serve one principal without breaching its duty of good faith to the other may be able to extricate itself by terminating its service to one in order to act for the other.[65] However, a fiduciary that places itself in a position of owing irreconcilable duties has only itself to blame if a breach of duty and consequent liability prove unavoidable. Thus, a solicitor that undertook to act for both vendor and purchaser in a property development project could not invoke its duty of confidentiality to the purchaser to excuse its non-disclosure to the vendor of the purchaser's criminal record of prohibited activities while an undischarged bankrupt.[66]

6.25 Fiduciary obligations must, however, mould themselves to the agency agreement. 'The fiduciary relationship cannot be superimposed upon the contract in such a way as to alter the operation which the contract was intended to have according to its true construction.'[67] Accordingly, where a principal engages an agent, such as a stockbroker or estate agent, that, in the ordinary course of its business, necessarily represents several principals with conflicting interests and acquires confidential information, the agency agreement must be interpreted as impliedly permitting such conflicts and waiving disclosure of confidential information.[68] It follows also that an agency agreement may expressly grant an agent a liberty not otherwise implicit in the agreement to act in a way that the fiduciary relationship would otherwise prohibit and may contain exemption clauses that

---

[63] *Clark Boyce v Mouat* [1994] 1 AC 428, 435.

[64] *Bristol & West Building Society v Mothew* [1998] Ch 1, 19.

[65] But see below, para 6.29.

[66] *Hilton v Barker Booth & Eastwood* [2005] UKHL 8, [2005] 1 WLR 567, applying *Moody v Cox* [1917] 2 Ch 71. The agent's duty to its principal does not, however, require the disclosure of information confidential to the third party, but rather the payment of compensation to the principal for loss flowing from the breach of duty in acting for the third party: *North & South Trust Co v Berkeley* [1971] 1 WLR 470, 485–86.

[67] *Hospital Products Ltd v United States Surgical Corp* (1984) 156 CLR 41, 97 (Mason J). See also *Henderson v Merrett Syndicates Ltd* [1995] 2 AC 145, 206. For discussion, see M Conaglen, *Fiduciary Loyalty* (Oxford, Hart Publishing, 2011), pp177–85.

[68] *Kelly v Cooper* [1993] AC 205 (PC). On the exceptional nature of such agencies, see *Rossetti Marketing Ltd v Diamond Sofa Co Ltd* [2012] EWCA Civ 1021, [2013] 1 All ER (Comm) 308, [25]–[27].

exclude or limit liability for breach of fiduciary duty. The efficacy of such a contractual challenge to equity's principles will, however, be subject to the closest
scrutiny. In a commercial context, it might be expected that the relevant clauses
would be properly incorporated into the agreement, but, as a matter of interpretation, a court is likely to treat with considerable scepticism a suggestion that a
principal authorised an agent to prefer its own interests over those of the principal
without any restriction or any requirement of disclosure. Any exemption clauses
would necessarily be ineffective on policy grounds to protect the agent against the
consequences of its own fraud,[69] and be construed, at least in the context of
professional agency, as presumptively confined to non-negligent conduct as a
reflection of the inherent unlikelihood that a principal would absolve a professional agent of the consequences of failing to extend the professional standards
and competence the securing of which to the principal's service is the very object
of the agency.[70] In addition, by virtue of section 3 of the Unfair Contract Terms
Act 1977, a clause that purported to modify the fiduciary obligations otherwise
exacted by equity may be open to challenge[71] as unreasonably entitling the agent
'to render a contractual performance substantially different from that which was
reasonably expected' by the principal, and any exemption clause would be open
to challenge as being unreasonable in the context of the agency agreement.

6.26   In the event that an agent, despite its best endeavours, finds itself in a position of actual or potential conflict of interest, it is obliged to prefer the interests of
the principal over its own.[72]

6.27   The restrictions imposed by equity on a fiduciary do not extend to other
persons connected to the fiduciary. An agent's spouse is entitled to deal with the
principal on an arm's-length basis and owes the principal no duty of disclosure by
reason of marital tie to the agent. A court will, however, scrutinise a transaction
carefully to discern whether the apparent counterparty is in truth a front for the
agent.[73]

6.28   The trust and confidence inherent in agency that render it a fiduciary relationship also render unauthorised delegation by the agent a breach of fiduciary
duty.[74] In cases of authorised delegation, the delegate will owe fiduciary duties to

---

[69]   *Pearson (S) & Son Ltd v Dublin Corp* [1907] AC 351.

[70]   As is clearly established in the context of performance obligations: *Canada Steamship Lines Ltd v The King* [1952] AC 192, 208; *HIH Casualty & General Ltd v Chase Manhattan Bank* [2003] UKHL 6, [2003] 1 CLC 358, [11]. It is suggested that a clause is more likely to be construed as addressing performance obligations than fiduciary duties.

[71]   Provided the agent's liability constitutes 'business liability' under s 1(3) of the 1977 Act, and, in accordance with s 3(1), the principal either deals as consumer (as defined by s 12(1)) or on the agent's written standard terms of business.

[72]   *Swain v The Law Society* [1982] 1 WLR 17, 36.

[73]   *Burrell v Burrell's Trustees* [1915] Ch 333. And see below, para 6.41.

[74]   *De Bussche v Alt* (1878) 8 Ch D 286. On authorised and unauthorised delegation, see above, paras 3.12–3.13.

the principal, whether introduced as an agent in direct privity with the principal or knowingly as a sub-agent albeit with no such privity.[75]

6.29   The termination of authority naturally leads to the expiry of fiduciary duties of loyalty,[76] but not where and to the extent that the termination is tainted by conflict of interest.[77] The duration of the disqualification imposed on a fiduciary depends on the reasons underpinning the disqualification, rather than the continuance of the formal relationship. Accordingly, the disqualification from profiting without consent from an opportunity arising out of a fiduciary position cannot be evaded by the simple expedient of terminating the fiduciary relationship.[78] An agent cannot, for example, refrain from informing the principal of a business opportunity in order to usurp it for its own benefit free from fiduciary obligation either on the expiry of a fixed-term agency or after itself instigating the termination of the agency.[79]

6.30   There is, however, no duty, fiduciary or otherwise, that requires an agent to have regard to the principal's interests in lawfully exercising termination rights under the agency; an agent incurs no liability should the timing of its lawful termination of the agency occasion the principal considerable financial loss.[80]

Monitoring and Challenging an Agent's Conduct

6.31   An agent is required to maintain proper records in respect of all dealings and expenses relating to the agency and to produce such records on the principal's demand,[81] and the principal is entitled to apply to the court for the taking of an account in order to determine whether property in respect of which fiduciary duties are owed has been properly managed and expenses properly charged, and thereby the true and accurate position as between the principal and agent. Where a breach of duty has produced a failure to realise proper benefits or to account for benefits improperly obtained by the agent, the account will be surcharged and an account taken as if proper benefits had been realised or the agent had recognised the principal's entitlement to all benefits arising from the agency. Where a breach

---

[75] *Powell v Evan Jones & Co* [1905] 1 KB 11; *Daraydan Holdings Ltd v Solland International Ltd* [2004] EWHC 622 (Ch), [2005] Ch 119, [52].

[76] *Meadow Schama & Co v C Mitchell & Co* (1973) 228 EG 1511; *Attorney-General v Blake* [1998] Ch 439, 453. Contrast the fiduciary duty attaching to confidential information, which derives not from the relationship between principal and agent, but from the information itself, and endures for so long as the information remains confidential: *Blake*, 454.

[77] P Koh, 'Once a Director, Always a Fiduciary?' (2003) 62 *Cambridge Law Journal* 403.

[78] *Carter v Palmer* (1842) 8 C & F 657.

[79] *Industrial Development Consultants Ltd v Cooley* [1972] 1 WLR 443; *CMS Dolphin Ltd v Simonet* [2002] BCC 600.

[80] *CMS Dolphin Ltd v Simonet* [2002] BCC 600, [95].

[81] *Yasuda Fire & Marine Insurance Co of Europe Ltd v Orion Marine Insurance Underwriting Agency Ltd* [1995] QB 174 (see above, para 1.17). On the nature of the obligation as flowing from an agent as an accounting party, see *Paragon Finance plc v DB Thakerar & Co* [1999] 1 All ER 400, 416.

of duty has produced an improper benefit, as where the agent has made an unauthorised but successful investment, the principal may elect not to falsify the account, in which case the investment will be treated as duly made on behalf of the principal and associated expenditure will be allowed in taking the account. Assuming the taking of account procedure reveals a need to rectify the position as between principal and agent, the necessary substantive remedies will follow.[82]

Remedies Arising out of Breach of Fiduciary Obligation

6.32   A breach of fiduciary obligation may give rise to a range of remedies. It is necessary to consider the consequences for the agency relationship, the consequences for any transaction induced in breach of fiduciary duty, consequential financial remedies against the agent, and remedies that may be pursued against the third party.

Remedies in Respect of the Agency Relationship

6.33   Since fiduciary duties manifest the trust and confidence fundamental to an agency relationship, breach of fiduciary duty is generally repugnant to the relationship and entitles the principal to terminate the agency forthwith.[83] The right of termination is, however, sensitive to the circumstances surrounding the breach of duty and will not be available in every case.[84] A possible example would arise where the agent intervenes in good faith and for the benefit of the principal to enable an opportunity to be exploited that the principal lacks the resources to exploit alone but falls foul of equity's prophylactic severity regarding unauthorised profits.

6.34   With respect to remuneration, since an agent is not entitled to say that services rendered in breach of fiduciary duty entitle it to any reward, no commission or other remuneration is payable in respect of services tainted by the breach of duty, regardless of whether the principal in fact benefits from the services,[85]

---

[82]   *Ultraframe (UK) Ltd v Fielding* [2005] EWHC 1638 (Ch), [1513]–[1514].

[83]   *Swale v Ipswich Tannary Ltd* (1906) 11 Com Cas 88; *Rhodes v Macalister* (1923) 29 Com Cas 19, 29.

[84]   *Crocs Europe BV v Anderson* [2012] EWCA Civ 1400, [2013] 1 Lloyd's Rep 1, [48].

[85]   *Andrews v Ramsay & Co* [1903] 2 KB 635; *Imageview Management Ltd v Jack* [2009] EWCA Civ 63, [2009] 1 Lloyd's Rep 436. See also *Tesco Stores Ltd v Pook* [2003] EWHC 823 (implied forfeiture of participation in share profits scheme). In *Keppel v Wheeler* [1927] 1 KB 577, a selling agent procured an agreement subject to contract to sell but, in the mistaken belief that its agency duties had terminated, informed the purchaser rather than the principal of a later higher offer and acted for the purchaser in reselling the property at the higher figure. The agent was held liable in damages for the difference between the two selling prices, but entitled to its commission from the principal on the sale. References in judgments to the agent's good faith may be read as suggesting that commission is forfeit only in cases of moral turpitude (*Kelly v Cooper* [1993] AC 205, 216–17 (PC)), but the case may be explained on the basis that the principal elected to claim damages for breach of contract rather than pursue a remedy for breach of fiduciary duty (see *Imageview Management Ltd v Jack* [2009] EWCA Civ 63, [2009] 1 Lloyd's Rep 436, [44] (Jacob LJ): 'just an honest breach of contract').

although, as noted below,[86] in deserving cases an allowance may be made in the context of an account of profits. Remuneration, however, remains payable where the breach does not impugn the relevant service. Accordingly, a bona fide failure, when seeking reimbursement in respect of ancillary expenses incurred in the course of executing its authority, to account for discounts received from third parties did not prejudice the agent's entitlement to commission in respect of the primary transaction, the agent's performance of which was independent of and had been unaffected by the breach of duty.[87]

Remedies in Respect of a Transaction Induced in Breach of Fiduciary Duty

6.35   Where an agent in breach of fiduciary duty procures a contract between the principal and the agent itself, the transaction is voidable, in accordance with the general proposition that consent induced by fraud or other wrongdoing remains effective as consent, notwithstanding that the wrongdoing may have remedial consequences, including the right in respect of any resulting transaction or disposition subsequently to withdraw consent with retrospective effect through the remedy of rescission.[88] Where the agent's conduct amounts to fraud, the principal may rescind the contract at common law as of right. Where the agent's conduct constitutes a non-fraudulent breach of fiduciary duty, the principal may rescind the contract in equity, subject to the discretion of the court to decline to confirm.[89] In either event, the right to rescind is subject to the normal bars of affirmation, impossibility of counter-restitution, intervention of third party rights, and lapse of time.[90] In *Kimber v Barber*,[91] A, through a nominee, purchased shares that it knew P wished to acquire and then, without disclosing its interest, offered to procure a sale of the shares to P at a price that represented a 50 per cent mark-up on the acquisition price. The resulting sale to P was held to be voidable, but rescission was barred by P's resale of many of the shares to a bona fide purchaser. P was awarded a financial remedy.

6.36   Where an agent in breach of fiduciary duty procures the conclusion of a contract directly between principal and third party, the breach of fiduciary duty will render the contract voidable only if known to the third party. Rescission as of right at common law will be available where the third party's conduct amounts to fraud – typically, bribery of the agent.[92] Rescission subject to the discretion of the

---

[86] See para 6.44.

[87] *Hippisley v Knee Bros* [1905] 1 KB 1. *Aliter* if the discount had been received from the other party to the principal transaction, even in the absence of any moral turpitude on the part of the agent: ibid.

[88] *Shogun Finance Ltd v Hudson* [2003] UKHL 62, [2004] 1 AC 919, [6]–[8].

[89] *TSB Bank plc v Camfield* [1995] 1 WLR 430, 438–39; *Hurstanger Ltd v Wilson* [2007] EWCA Civ 299, [2007] 1 WLR 2351, [47], [50].

[90] *Guinness plc v Saunders* [1990] 2 AC 663, 697–98. Albeit that the operation of the bars may vary between common law and equity: *Alati v Kruger* (1955) 94 CLR 216, 223–24.

[91] *Kimber v Barber* (1872) LR 8 Ch App 56.

[92] *Panama & South Pacific Telegraph Co v India Rubber, Gutta Percha & Telegraph Works Co* (1875) 10 Ch App 515, 525; *Hovenden & Sons v Millhoff* (1900) 83 LT 41, 43; *Re a Debtor* [1927] 2 Ch 367; *Taylor v Walker* [1958] 1 Lloyd's Rep 490, 509–13; *Logicrose Ltd v Southend United Football Club Ltd* [1988] 1 WLR 1256.

court will be available in equity where the third party's conduct falls short of fraud but nevertheless exposes the third party to accessory liability in equity for dishonest assistance in breach of fiduciary duty.[93]

6.37 Where the contract generated by a breach of fiduciary duty is concluded not directly between principal and third party but instead by the agent itself purportedly acting on behalf of the principal, it is difficult to see why, as a matter of principle, there should be any difference in result or even analysis. In law, however, analysis in terms of consent induced by fraud or other wrongdoing is displaced in favour of application of the ordinary rules of authority.[94] The contract will clearly fall outside the agent's actual authority, but the principal will be bound to the third party provided the contract falls within the agent's apparent authority. In this regard, the critical question is likely to be whether, in the light of the third party's knowledge of the circumstances, it is plausible for the third party to claim reliance upon the representation of authority upon which apparent authority is based.[95] In practice, this may reflect the test for accessory liability.[96] The consequence, however, may be different. Accessory liability affords the principal the option of rescission, albeit that the right to rescind may be barred. Known absence of authority denies any contract between the principal and third party, enabling a principal to disown the contract without the need to rescind but denying the principal the option to hold the third party to the transaction as the agent's overt pursuit of its own interests would preclude ratification.[97] It is regrettable, if not unique, for the technicalities of how a wrong is perpetrated to affect the rights of the victim as against a wrongdoer.[98]

Consequential Financial Remedies against the Agent

6.38 The financial liabilities of an agent in breach of fiduciary duty give rise to questions of both the extent of the liability and whether the principal may avail itself of not only personal but also proprietary remedies.

---

[93] *Logicrose Ltd v Southend United Football Club Ltd* [1988] 1 WLR 1256, 1261. As to accessory liability for dishonest assistance, see below, paras 6.62–6.63.

[94] *Criterion Properties plc v Stratford UK Properties LLC* [2004] UKHL 28, [2004] 1 WLR 1846.

[95] *Hopkins v TL Dallas Group Ltd* [2004] EWHC 1379 (Ch).

[96] Both tests are subjective: see above, para 4.12 (apparent authority); below, para 6.62 (accessory liability for dishonest assistance). The European Principles likewise adopt a subjective approach to avoidance against a third party on the basis of an agent's conflict of interest, although this is inconsistent with its objective approach to the reliance requirement of apparent authority: PECL, arts 3:205(1) ('knew or could not have been unaware'), 3:201(3) ('reasonably and in good faith'). The Unidroit Principles import constructive knowledge into both apparent authority and avoidance against third parties in cases of conflict of interest: PICC, arts 2.2.5(2), 2.2.7(1).

[97] Above, para 5.7.

[98] For another example of English law ignoring the substance of fraud in favour of the form in which it is cloaked, with remedial consequences, see *Shogun Finance Ltd v Hudson* [2003] UKHL 62, [2004] 1 AC 919.

Account of Profits

6.39   An agent cannot be permitted to retain any benefits gained from a breach of fiduciary duty. The remedy of an account of profits is a personal equitable remedy designed to compel a defaulting fiduciary to disgorge all profits made in breach of fiduciary duty, extending even to profits to which consent would have been given if requested. It is not a compensatory remedy: the only question is whether the profit was made in breach of duty, not whether it corresponds to a loss incurred by the principal. As with the strictness of fiduciary obligation, so the scope of the account of profits remedy possesses a degree of prophylaxis that reflects equity's concern to deter any betrayal of trust: better a windfall to the principal than a penny of disloyally made profit to the agent.[99] Accordingly, where an agent diverts business opportunities to its own benefit, it is accountable for all profits flowing from exploitation of those opportunities.[100] A causal link between the breach of fiduciary duty and the profit must, however, be established.[101] The agent must account for:

> the profits properly attributable to the breach of fiduciary duty, taking into account the expenses connected with those profits, and a reasonable allowance for overheads (but not necessarily salary for the wrongdoer), together with a sum to take account of other benefits derived from those contracts. For example, other contracts might not have been won, or profits made on them, without (e.g.) the opportunity or cash-flow benefit which flowed from contracts unlawfully obtained. There must, however, be some reasonable connection between the breach of duty and the profits for which the fiduciary is accountable.[102]

6.40   Again, where an agent diverts an opportunity to represent a third party from its principal to a business on its own account, it will be liable to account for the resulting profits but only for such period of time as the third party would otherwise have retained the principal as its representative.[103] Where the agent illegitimately mixes property belonging to the principal with its own, the agent carries the burden of identifying property and profits not tainted by breach of fiduciary duty.[104]

6.41   An agent is not liable for profits accruing to the benefit of another, including a company in which the agent has a substantial, even a controlling, interest.[105]

---

[99]   *Reading v Attorney-General* [1951] AC 507; *Industrial Development Consultants Ltd v Cooley* [1972] 1 WLR 443. On the importance of a strict approach, see M Conaglen, 'The Extent of Fiduciary Accounting and the Importance of Authorisation Mechanisms' (2011) 70 *Cambridge Law Journal* 548; I Samet, 'Guarding the Fidiciary's Conscience – A Justification for a Stringent Profit-Stripping Rule' (2008) 28 *Oxford Journal of Legal Studies* 763.

[100]   *Industrial Development Consultants Ltd v Cooley* [1972] 1 WLR 443.

[101]   *Murad v Al-Saraj* [2005] EWCA Civ 959.

[102]   *CMS Dolphin Ltd v Simonet* [2002] BCC 600, [97] (Lawrence Collins J).

[103]   *Warman International Ltd v Dwyer* (1995) 192 CLR 544, 565.

[104]   ibid, 562.

[105]   *Regal (Hastings) Ltd v Gulliver* [1967] 2 AC 134, 151–52; *Ultraframe (UK) Ltd v Fielding* [2005] EWHC 1638 (Ch), [1561]–[1576]; *National Grid Electricity Transmission plc v McKenzie* [2009] EWHC 1857 (Ch), [117]. *Aliter* if profits channelled through a formal partnership or joint venture: *Imperial Mercantile Association v Coleman* (1873) LR 6 HL 189; *National Grid v McKenzie*, [118].

Profits cannot, however, be sheltered behind a company that is a mere cloak for, and creature of, the agent, employed as a device to disguise the breach of duty.[106]

6.42 The precise reach of the account of profits has, however, yet to be clearly tested in cases where the defaulting agent invests an unauthorised profit and the investment proves to be successful, generating secondary profits. The mere fact of investing the illegitimate gain is no bar to the remedy: a defaulting agent has no entitlement to a change of position defence. The question is whether, despite the requisite causal connection with the breach of duty that yielded the original illegitimate seed corn, disgorgement of profits will be precluded at some stage of remove from the breach even though they would not have been generated without the breach of duty. In this sense, it is asked whether the account of profits is subject to a remoteness of gain limitation.[107] Such a limitation denying recovery beyond the original gain would, it is suggested, be inconsistent with the prophylaxis that underpins equity's entire approach to the regulation of fiduciaries. Moreover, as already seen,[108] in the diverted business opportunity cases the defaulting agent is required to account not simply for the value of the opportunity but for all profits made in successfully exploiting the opportunity. In terms of reach of personal remedy against a defaulting fiduciary, there is, it is suggested, no justification for any categorical distinction between profiting by exploiting and profiting by investing.[109]

Money Had and Received

6.43 In respect of a bribe, as an alternative to the equitable remedy of an account of profits, the principal may claim the value of the bribe at common law by way of an action for money had and received.[110] The principal is entitled to the bribe as against the agent regardless of whether the principal elects to adopt or rescind any transaction resulting from the bribe.[111]

Equitable Allowance

6.44 The combination of the severity of the fiduciary obligation of loyalty and the remedy of an account of profits can threaten injustice. Thus, for example,[112]

---

[106] *Gencor ACP Ltd v Dalby* [2000] 2 BCLC 734; *Trustor AB v Smallbone (No 2)* [2001] 1 WLR 1177. Likewise in respect of profits received by another natural person but over which the agent retains de facto control and from which the agents therefore receives benefit: *Fiona Trust & Holding Corp v Privalov* [2010] EWHC 3199 (Comm), [1538]–[1541].

[107] P Birks, *An Introduction to the Law of Restitution* (Oxford, Oxford University Press, 1985) p 351.

[108] Above, para 6.39.

[109] Cautious support for extended personal remedies was expressed in *Sinclair Investments (UK) Ltd v Versailles Trade Finance Ltd* [2011] EWCA Civ 347, [2011] 3 WLR 1153, [53], [79], [90]. An absence of such extended reach was assumed by the Privy Council in *Attorney-General for Hong Kong v Reid* [1994] 1 AC 324, and see *Lister & Co v Stubbs* (1890) 45 Ch D 1, 15. And see below, para 6.58.

[110] *Boston Deep Sea Fishing & Ice Co v Ansell* (1888) 39 Ch D 339, 367; *Mahesan v Malaysia Government Officers' Co-operative Housing Society Ltd* [1979] AC 374.

[111] *Logicrose Ltd v Southend United Football Club Ltd* [1988] 1 WLR 1256, 1262–63.

[112] As in *Boardman v Phipps* [1967] 2 AC 46.

where the agent in good faith makes available its own resources to exploit for the benefit of itself and the principal an opportunity the principal lacks the resources to exploit solely for itself, the agent, not having obtained the principal's prior consent, commits a breach of fiduciary duty and is prima facie liable to account for the entirety of the benefit accruing to itself, notwithstanding the benefit it has enabled the principal to obtain. Sensitive, however, to the possibility of fervour for agent loyalty being transformed into an instrument for unjust enrichment of the principal, equity recognises the possibility of a discretionary[113] allowance reflecting the time, expertise and financial resources contributed by the agent[114] and extending in appropriate circumstances beyond reimbursing the agent's contribution to awarding a profit element.[115] The discretion is not in principle dependent upon the moral blamelessness of the agent,[116] but is generally to be exercise sparingly and will certainly be more readily and more generously exercised where the agent acted in good faith.[117] In the particular case of company directors, however, it is doubtful whether it would ever be appropriate to grant an allowance as it would constitute remuneration not contemplated by the company's constitution as set forth in the company's articles of association.[118] In all cases, the agent carries the burden of proving that the circumstances warrant an allowance.[119]

Equitable Compensation

6.45 In contrast to the disgorgement nature of an account of profits, the remedy of equitable compensation requires the agent to restore to the principal all loss that would not have been incurred but for the breach of fiduciary duty.[120] In the event that the breach of duty occasions the principal no loss (a question determined as at the date of judgment, not the date of breach of duty), equitable compensation cannot be claimed.[121] The remedy is, therefore, of utility where the breach occasions the principal loss without or in excess of any profits for which the agent must account. In appropriate circumstances, notably acceptance of a

---

[113] *Murad v Al-Saraj* [2005] EWCA Civ 959, [88].

[114] *Re Jarvis* [1958] 1 WLR 815, 820; *Boardman v Phipps* [1964] 1 WLR 993, 1018, [1967] 2 AC 46; *Warman International Ltd v Dwyer* (1995) 192 CLR 544, 562.

[115] *O'Sullivan v Management Agency and Music Ltd* [1985] QB 428. However, awarding the agent the fee the principal would have agreed to pay had full disclosure been made (as considered appropriate on the facts in *Accidia Foundation v Simon C Dickinson Ltd* [2010] EWHC 3058 (Ch), [94]–[95]) seems inconsistent with equity's strict policy of deterrence.

[116] *O'Sullivan v Management Agency and Music Ltd* [1985] QB 428.

[117] *Imageview Management Ltd v Jack* [2009] EWCA Civ 63, [2009] 1 Lloyd's Rep 436, [56].

[118] *Guinness plc v Saunders* [1990] 2 AC 663. Although it is unclear why a company's articles of association should in this context be elevated above any other agreement between principal and agent governing an agent's remuneration.

[119] *Imageview Management Ltd v Jack* [2009] EWCA Civ 63, [2009] 1 Lloyd's Rep 436, [56].

[120] The remedy appears to be available in the event of any breach of fiduciary duty without proof of any subjective wrongdoing: *Swindle v Harrison* [1997] 4 All ER 705, 728.

[121] *Target Holdings Ltd v Redferns* [1996] 1 AC 421; *Gwembe Valley Development Co Ltd v Koshy (No 3)* [2003] EWCA Civ 1048, [2004] 1 BCLC 131, [47]. And see M Conaglen, *Fiduciary Loyalty* (Oxford, Hart Publishing, 2011), pp 90–94.

bribe, the principal also has the option of seeking compensation for all harm caused through an action for damages in tort for fraud.[122] Loss recoverable by a compensatory remedy includes all costs incurred in identifying and unravelling the breach of duty.[123]

No Double Recovery

6.46 Assuming a loss-causing breach, both disgorgement and compensatory remedies are in principle available, but double recovery is prohibited. To the extent that pursuing both would result in double recovery, the principal must elect between the remedies. Where litigation is pursued with both remedies being claimed, the principal must elect at judgment, but will be permitted a short but reasonable time to consider the alternatives once judgment has been handed down.[124] In *Mahesan v Malaysia Government Officers' Co-operative Housing Society Ltd*,[125] the agent fraudulently colluded with a third party for land to be sold to the principal at an increased price. Having discovered land for sale, the agent arranged for it to be purchased by the third party for $456,000. Three months later and after $45,000 had been spent to evict squatters, the land was resold to the principal for $944,000. The transaction, therefore, yielded a profit of $443,000 out of which the agent received $122,000. The principal was held entitled to a disgorgement remedy in the measure of $122,000 or a compensatory remedy in the measure of $443,000, but not both since recovery of the former served to reduce the loss in respect of which the latter was awarded.

Sale by Agent to Principal

6.47 In the absence of full disclosure, sale by an agent to its principal of property in respect of which it already owed fiduciary duties to the principal at the time of its acquisition clearly involves a breach of fiduciary duty that renders the agent accountable for any profit it has made on the transaction.[126] The property is treated as having been originally acquired on behalf of the principal; the agent is, therefore, entitled to reimbursement of the acquisition cost but to nothing more.[127] Similarly, where an agent is instructed to purchase property of a type at the most advantageous market terms, sale to the principal of the agent's own property will render the agent liable to account for any profit in excess of a

---

[122] Reference is sometimes made to liability in the tort of deceit, but 'the claim based on bribery is not a species of deceit but a special form of fraud where there is no representation made to the principal of the agent let alone reliance': *Petrotrade Inc v Smith* [2000] CLC 916, [19] (David Smith J), rejecting any suggestion of an implied representation of no breach of duty.

[123] *National Grid Electricity Transmission plc v McKenzie* [2009] EWHC 1817 (Ch), [160].

[124] *United Australia Ltd v Barclays Bank Ltd* [1941] AC 1; *Mahesan v Malaysia Government Officers' Co-operative Housing Society Ltd* [1979] AC 374; *Tang Man Sit v Capacious Investments Ltd* [1996] 1 AC 514; *National Grid Electricity Transmission plc v McKenzie* [2009] EWHC 1817 (Ch), [54].

[125] *Mahesan v Malaysia Government Officers' Co-operative Housing Society Ltd* [1979] AC 374.

[126] *Bentley v Craven* (1853) 18 Beav 75.

[127] *Re Ambrose Lake Tin & Copper Mining Co* (1880) 14 Ch D 390, 398.

reasonable market price.[128] In either case, the principal can rescind the contract, but, through the remedy of an account of profits, has the option of retaining the property on, in effect, modified terms.[129] The position is different, however, where the agent is instructed to acquire a specific item of property in which it so happens the agent has a pre-existing interest acquired before the inception, or otherwise outside the scope, of any fiduciary duties owed to the principal. Non-disclosure of the agent's interest is a breach of fiduciary duty rendering the contract voidable.[130] The facts may, however, preclude rescission and the mere fact that sale to the principal generates, in comparison with the original acquisition cost, a profit accruing to the agent does not render the agent accountable to the principal for that profit where the agent's interest in the property arose outside the agent's fiduciary duties.[131] Where, however, it can be shown that the contract price exceeded a fair market price,[132] it has been persuasively argued that the principal should be entitled to equitable compensation equivalent to the loss represented by the excess,[133] although where on the facts the breach of duty lies solely in non-disclosure of the agent's interest the requisite causal link between breach of duty and loss may be absent.[134]

Proprietary Remedies

6.48   In addition to the personal remedies already discussed, a breach of fiduciary duty may entitle the principal to a proprietary remedy. There is, however, considerable uncertainty in the law. The chief significance relates to insolvency of the agent: a proprietary claim will confer priority on the principal over otherwise equal-ranking personal claims of other creditors. It may be helpful to distinguish four situations.

6.49   First, the agent misappropriates an asset in which the principal had a pre-existing proprietary interest, and the principal can identify the asset itself either remaining in the hands of the agent or as followed into the hands of a third party, or a substitute asset identified in accordance with orthodox principles of tracing.

---

[128]   *Re Cape Breton* (1885) 29 Ch D 795, 811; *Cavendish Bentinck v Fenn* (1887) 12 App Cas 652, 659.

[129]   *Cavendish Bentinck v Fenn* (1887) 12 App Cas 652, 659.

[130]   *Re Cape Breton* (1885) 29 Ch D 795; *Armstrong v Jackson* [1917] 2 KB 822, 824–25.

[131]   *Re Cape Breton* (1885) 29 Ch D 795; *Ladywell Mining Co v Brookes* (1887) 35 Ch D 400; *Burland v Earle* [1902] AC 83, 98–99.

[132]   Although on a sale of a specific item in respect of which there is no market, such proof may be elusive (see *Cavendish Bentinck v Fenn* (1887) 12 App Cas 652), and the courts consider that judicial determination of an appropriate price would constitute illegitimate imposition on the parties of a contract they did not make: *Cook v Deeks* [1916] 1 AC 554, 564.

[133]   M Conaglan, 'Equitable Compensation for Breach of Fiduciary Dealing Rules' (2003) 119 *Law Quarterly Review* 246; and similarly M Conaglen, *Fiduciary Loyalty* (Oxford, Hart Publishing, 2011), pp 87–90.

[134]   On the need for causation, see above, para 6.45. Causation may be easier to establish in respect of the extent of the agent's profit than the mere fact of the agent's interest. If the agent knew the price was excessive, the principal could claim the excess at common law in deceit or in equity through either an account of profits or equitable compensation.

There is no doubt that a principal enjoys a proprietary remedy in this situation: the asset or traced substitute belongs to the principal in accordance with orthodox property law and is, therefore, unavailable for appropriation in discharge of the insolvent agent's liabilities.[135] Similarly, an agent that makes an unauthorised investment of money held on behalf of the principal holds any profits on trust for the principal.[136]

6.50 Secondly, the agent, without proper authorisation, diverts to its own benefit an opportunity that fiduciary law dictates should be exploited for the benefit of, or at least offered to, the principal. Authority holds that the agent is a trustee of the fruits of the opportunity. For example, company directors who negotiated a contract on behalf of the company but then signed the contract on behalf of themselves rather than the company were held to be constructive trustees of the contract and of all profits derived from it.[137]

6.51 Thirdly, an agent negotiating a contract with a third party profits without authorisation from agreeing a higher price to be paid by its principal or a lower price to be paid by the third party. In such a case, the unauthorised profit accruing to the agent is in effect funded by the excess paid or the discount forfeited by the principal. In this situation, English authority denies the principal a proprietary remedy. Notably, in *Metropolitan Bank v Heiron*,[138] the third party paid the agent a sum of money to induce the principal to settle a claim against the third party. The third party was clearly prepared to settle the claim for the amount of the inducement payment plus the agreed settlement figure. The agent, however, failed to disclose or account to the principal for the inducement payment; in effect, therefore, to the extent of that payment the principal received a lower sum in settlement of the claim. The principal, however, failed in a claim to recover the inducement payment. By the time the claim was brought, a personal action against the agent was time-barred; so the principal's entitlement to the payment depended on establishing a proprietary claim, which the Court of Appeal denied. In *Lister & Co v Stubbs*,[139] the third party bribed the agent to place with it orders for large quantities of goods on behalf of the principal. Much of the bribe money was then invested in freehold property and other investments. In connection with a claim for the original bribes and all profits generated from the bribes, the claimant sought interlocutory relief requiring the agent to identify and restrain from dealing with all assets derived from the bribes. This, it was considered, depended on the principal being able to assert a proprietary claim in respect of such assets, which the Court of Appeal again denied. In both *Heiron* and *Stubbs*, the Court of

---

[135] *Foskett v McKeown* [2001] 1 AC 102.

[136] *Brown v Inland Revenue Commissioners* [1965] AC 244.

[137] *Cook v Deeks* [1916] 1 AC 554. See also *Industrial Development Consultants Ltd v Cooley* [1972] 1 WLR 443.

[138] *Metropolitan Bank v Heiron* (1880) 5 Ex D 319. Likewise *Gwembe Valley Development Co Ltd v Koshy* [2003] EWCA Civ 1048, [2004] 1 BCLC 131.

[139] *Lister & Co v Stubbs* (1890) 45 Ch D 1.

Appeal denied that the agent's fraud generated a relationship between the agent and principal other than that of debtor and creditor. The agent had not subverted property of the principal, and the principal's remedies were purely personal. The opportunity that generates a proprietary claim is an opportunity to obtain property that is denied by the breach of duty, not an opportunity to obtain on more advantageous terms the same transaction that is in fact obtained. Put another way, the basis of a proprietary claim is the deprivation of an asset, and not simply the commission of a wrong.[140]

6.52   Fourthly, the benefit accruing to the agent does not reflect any reduction in benefit that otherwise should have accrued to the principal. In *Sinclair Investments (UK) Ltd v Versailles Trade Finance Group plc*,[141] the fiduciary's fraudulent breach of duty created a false impression of profitability of a company, which in turn enhanced the share price of that company's parent company, of which the fiduciary was the principal shareholder. The fiduciary was then able to profit by selling some of his shares in the parent company. These shares were not property belonging to the principal or a traceable substitute for any such property, nor had they been acquired in the exercise of an opportunity subject to fiduciary obligations. Consequently, following English authority including *Heiron* and *Stubbs*,[142] the Court of Appeal denied the principal any proprietary claim to the proceeds of sale of the shares.

6.53   In so doing, the Court of Appeal declined to follow the contrary Privy Council decision in *Attorney-General for Hong Kong v Reid*,[143] in which the Government of Hong Kong claimed a proprietary remedy in respect of property purchased by a corrupt fiduciary with bribe money. The bribes having been paid to pervert the course of justice by influencing decisions as to whether to bring criminal prosecutions, they could not be said to be even indirectly funded by the

---

[140]   *Paragon Finance plc v D B Thakerar & Co* [1999] 1 All ER 400, 408–09; *Foskett v McKeown* [2001] AC 1 AC 102, 130; *Sinclair Investments (UK) Ltd v Versailles Trade Finance Group plc* [2011] EWCA 347, [2012] Ch 453, [80]; *Cadogan Petroleum plc v Tolley* [2011] EWHC 2286 (Ch). It has been suggested that *Lister v Stubbs* is distinguishable and that a proprietary remedy will lie where, in a case involving a sale to the principal, the agent is bribed to agree an inflated price, and the bribe paid out of that price can be tracked back to the extra consideration provided by the principal (*Daraydan Holdings Ltd v Solland International Ltd* [2004] EWHC 622 (Ch), [2005] Ch 119, [87]), but any such distinction has subsequently been denied in the absence of rescission of the sale contract: *Cadogan*, [36].

[141]   *Sinclair Investments (UK) Ltd v Versailles Trade Finance Group plc* [2011] EWCA 347, [2012] Ch 453.

[142]   And also the decision of the House of Lords in *Tyrrell v Bank of London* (1862) 10 HLC 26, in which a fiduciary profited without authorisation from the acquisition of a plot of land with the intention of reselling part to the principal to serve as its business premises and retaining the remainder. Profits generated from the resold part were held on trust for the principal. The more contentious aspect of the litigation, however, concerned the remaining land. The *ratio decidendi* of the case attracts, of course, the precedent value to be accorded all decisions of the House of Lords, but precisely what the *ratio* is has attracted differing views. The better view, it is suggested, is that the House of Lords held the fiduciary accountable for the value of the remaining land but denied any proprietary remedy in respect of it. This reading of the decision has been denied by the Privy Council (*Attorney-General for Hong Kong v Reid* [1994] 1 AC 324, 333 (discussed below)) but accepted by the Court of Appeal in *Sinclair v Versailles* [2011] EWCA 347, [2012] Ch 453, [60]–[61].

[143]   *Attorney-General for Hong Kong v Reid* [1994] 1 AC 324.

principal. Nevertheless, the Privy Council held that a proprietary interest in the illegitimate gain vested in the principal immediately upon its receipt by the fiduciary. Equity simply did not permit the defaulting fiduciary to assert that it had profited in breach of fiduciary duty: any gain within the scope of its fiduciary duties had to be treated as acquired by the fiduciary on behalf of, and therefore held as constructive trustee for, the principal.[144] In so holding, the Privy Council either dismissed as not truly in point or considered wrongly decided any (apparently) contrary authority. In particular, *Lister v Stubbs* was wrong.

6.54 In *Sinclair v Versailles*, the Court of Appeal considered that it was not free to follow *Reid* as a matter of precedent but also that as a matter of principle the view adopted in *Reid* was highly questionable.

6.55 Recognition of a proprietary remedy confers on the principal priority in the fiduciary's insolvency. Insolvency law adopts a policy of equality of distribution subject to proprietary claims; insolvency law defers to property law subject only to exceptional cases where the property right is created in such a way as unfairly to deplete the insolvent estate. Proprietary remedies are afforded priority as a consequence of that deference. Absent the misappropriation of property in which the principal had a pre-existing proprietary right, or the illegitimate acquisition of property by the subversion of an opportunity for the correct exploitation of which the fiduciary was accountable to the principal, the question arising is the extent to which recognition should be given to property rights in the proceeds of fiduciary wrongdoing: in particular, whether breach of fiduciary duty is a sufficient justification of itself to promote the principal from unsecured debtor to beneficiary under a constructive trust.[145]

6.56 According to the Privy Council in *Reid*, the principal enjoys a proprietary right in an illegitimate gain immediately upon its receipt by a defaulting fiduciary simply by virtue of the maxim that equity looks on as done that which ought to be done. Ignoring the fact that what should have been done was to decline the illegitimate gain in the first place or obtain informed consent from the principal, the Privy Council declared that, since the defaulting fiduciary should have accounted for the gain to the principal, in equity such accounting was considered to have been accomplished so that the gain was held by the fiduciary as constructive trustee for the benefit of the principal.

---

[144] For support that the fundamental issue is equity's core technique in enforcing fiduciary loyalty, see, notably, P Millett, 'Bribes and Secret Commissions' [1993] *Restitution Law Review* 7; P McGrath, 'Constructive Trusts: An Analysis of *Sinclair v Versailles*' [2012] *Lloyd's Maritime and Commercial Law Quarterly* 516, 521, 532–36.

[145] On one view, insolvency consequences should be ignored in deciding whether or not proprietary claims exist: see, for example, P McGrath, 'Constructive Trusts: An Analysis of *Sinclair v Versailles*' [2012] *Lloyd's Maritime and Commercial Law Quarterly* 516, 521. For a convincing refutation, see C Rotherham, 'Policy and Proprietary Remedies: Are We All Formalists Now?' (2012) 65 *Current Legal Problems* 529. Such consequences were clearly recognised in *Sinclair v Versailles* itself: [2011] EWCA 347, [2012] Ch 453, [54], [83].

6.57   This approach has the effect of denying any fundamental distinction between fiduciary wrongdoing and a usurpation of property rights. On the approach adopted in *Reid*, any transgression of equity's fiduciary rules triggers a proprietary claim in respect of any resulting benefit; whenever there is a liability to account, the principal will have a proprietary claim.[146] However, the application of the equitable maxim can only be justified on the basis of an implied undertaking in the agency agreement to transfer to the principal all illegitimate gains, so that equity would fasten upon the gain immediately upon receipt and treat its transfer as accomplished.[147] Such an implication would be a purely instrumental invention,[148] designed to generate a proprietary claim. It requires normative justification.

6.58   Certainly, the entire tenor of the law on fiduciary obligations requires that a defaulting fiduciary should not be permitted to retain any benefit from the breach of duty. Accordingly, the fiduciary should be compelled to disgorge not only any original illegitimate gain received, but also any second-generation benefits obtained through exploiting or investing the original gain.[149] The Privy Council assumed that personal remedies are confined to the original value received. If true, the policy of disgorgement would indeed provide a powerful reason for recognition of a proprietary claim. However, that personal claims are indeed currently so limited, or, if so limited, could not be extended, is open to significant doubt.[150] And assuming that the policy of disgorgement can be satisfied by personal remedies, a normative justification for recognising a proprietary claim is absent,[151] and the resultant

---

[146]   *Halifax Building Society v Thomas* [1996] Ch 217, 229.

[147]   Such automatic attachment to after-acquired property was recognised in *Holroyd v Marshall* (1862) 10 HL Cas 191 and forms the basis of all security rights over future property. The language of the Privy Council's judgment, however, is redolent rather of a simple obligation of repayment of debt, to which, the obligation not being specifically enforceable, the maxim could not attach.

[148]   An illegitimate gain 'could not possibly be said to be an asset which the fiduciary was under a duty to take for the beneficiary': *Sinclair Investments (UK) Ltd v Versailles Trade Finance Ltd* [2011] EWCA Civ 347, [2012] Ch 453, [80] (Lord Neuberger MR). It would, however, still be an institutional trust and not, therefore, offend against the current rejection of discretionary, remedial trusts. For such rejection, see *Halifax Building Society v Thomas* [1996] Ch 217, 229; *Re Polly Peck International plc (No 2)* [1998] 3 All ER 812.

[149]   It is uncontroversial that the denial of this policy in *Lister & Co v Stubbs* (1890) 45 Ch D 1, 15 is unsustainable.

[150]   See above, para 6.42. And see G Virgo, *The Principles of the Law of Restitution*, 2nd edn (Oxford, Oxford University Press, 2006) pp 524–25 (and generally on proprietary relief, p 519 et seq). Others disagree: see notably Lord Millett, 'Bribes and Secret Commissions Again' (2012) 71 *Cambridge Law Journal* 583, 603 (in an article maintaining his opposition to *Lister v Stubbs* and criticising its resurrection in *Sinclair v Versailles*).

[151]   *Sinclair Investments (UK) Ltd v Versailles Trade Finance Ltd* [2011] EWCA Civ 347, [2012] Ch 453, [53]. If it were felt that personal remedies could not fully satisfy the disgorgement policy (because, for example, of difficulties in quantifying the illegitimate gain), adoption of a remedial approach to proprietary remedies (contrary to current principle) would permit such remedies, as a general proposition, to be awarded outside of insolvency where there are no priority concerns and refused where the defaulting fiduciary is insolvent: see P Ridge, 'Justifying the Remedies for Dishonest Assistance' (2008) 124 *Law Quarterly Review* 445, 460–67. And see also the measured discussion in A Hicks, 'The Remedial Principle of *Keech v Sandford* Reconsidered' (2010) 69 *Cambridge Law Journal* 287, esp 316–19.

conferral of priority on the principal, an otherwise unsecured creditor in respect of the illegitimate gain, over the agent's other unsecured creditors is arbitrary and contrary to a principled, transparent and fair ordering of the agent's insolvency.[152] There is simply no reason why the victim of a breach of fiduciary duty should enjoy priority over the claims of victims of other forms of wrongdoing, or indeed the holders of equitable rights securing a provision of new value.[153]

6.59 It is suggested, therefore, that the Privy Council in *Reid* fell into error: personal remedies should be extended beyond the original illegitimate gain so as to respond more fully to the policy of disgorgement; recognition of a proprietary remedy in English law would then be both contrary to authority and unjustifiable.[154]

Third Party Accessory Liability for Breach of Fiduciary Duty

6.60 Not only the agent but also, in appropriate circumstances, the third party may incur liability in connection with a breach of fiduciary duty by the agent. Such liability may arise at common law or in equity. In each case, the agent's state of mind with respect to its conduct that constitutes a breach of duty is irrelevant (indeed, the agent may not even be aware that its conduct constitutes a breach of duty). The focus is entirely upon the third party.[155] There must, however, be a breach of duty by the agent; third party liability is parasitic upon a breach by the agent and may, accordingly, be termed accessory liability. The enforceability of the liability of an agent for breach of duty and of the accessory liability of a third party are, nevertheless, independent. Where an agent wrongfully diverts a business opportunity to a third party, the subsequent insolvency of the third party is irrelevant to the agent's liability for breach of duty.[156]

Accessory Liability at Common Law in Tort

6.61 Assuming the relationship between the principal and agent to be contractual, a third party may incur liability in the tort of inducing a breach of contract.

---

[152] R Goode, 'Property and Unjust Enrichment', in A Burrows (ed), *Essays on the Law of Restitution* (Oxford, Oxford University Press, 1991) ch 9, pp 215, 240–42. And see *Various Customers of BA Peters plc v Moriarty* [2008] EWCA Civ 1604, [2010] 1 BCLC 142, [21].

[153] *Sinclair Investments (UK) Ltd v Versailles Trade Finance Ltd* [2011] EWCA Civ 347, [2012] Ch 453, [54], [83].

[154] See R Goode, 'Proprietary Liability for Secret Profits – A Reply' (2011) 127 *Law Quarterly Review* 493. Subject perhaps to a fundamental change of policy with respect to remedial proprietary remedies: see above, fn 151. One consequence of the law as upheld in *Sinclair v Versailles* is the need to distinguish factually between opportunity cases and other cases involving breach of fiduciary duty. In *FHR European Ventures LLP v Mankarious* [2013] EWCA Civ 17, [2013] 1 Lloyd's Rep 416, a differently constituted Court of Appeal, while acknowledging the constraints of precedent, appears to have felt less sympathetic towards *Lister v Stubbs*, regretted the need to distinguish opportunity cases from others (ibid, [116]), and classified as within the opportunity category a case that, with respect, involved a simple bribe. Permission to appeal to the Supreme Court has been sought.

[155] *Royal Brunei Airlines Sdn Bhd v Tan* [1995] 2 AC 378 (rejecting the view that accessory liability is confined to dishonest breaches of fiduciary duty).

[156] *CMS Dolphin Ltd v Simonet* [2002] BCC 600.

Accordingly, a third party that with knowledge of the contract acts in such a way as is calculated to result in a breach of contract by the agent will incur liability in damages for resulting loss to the principal.[157] Bribery of an agent will also result in tortious liability for fraud.[158]

Accessory Liability in Equity for Assistance

6.62 Accessory liability in equity is referred to traditionally as 'knowing assistance', and more recently as 'dishonest assistance'. A third party will incur accessory liability where, in the light of all the circumstances known to the third party, its interaction with the agent would be considered by ordinary honest people to transgress the normal standards of honest conduct. The test for knowledge is subjective: the circumstances must be within the third party's actual knowledge, although this extends to matters of which the third party is aware as a realistic possibility but deliberately refuses to seek confirmation. Constructive knowledge – that a reasonable person in the position of the third party would have known of the circumstances – does not suffice. Given the requisite knowledge, however, the touchstone of liability is objective: the standard is that of hypothetical honest people.[159] A third party will, therefore, incur liability if hypothetical honest people with the knowledge of the third party would decline to act, seek further information or advice, or insist on further information or advice being obtained. It is irrelevant whether the third party itself either regarded its conduct as dishonest or, seemingly, realised that its conduct was dishonest by the standards of ordinary honest people.[160] Indeed, requiring such subjective realisation would produce an

---

[157] *Twinsectra Ltd v Yardley* [2002] 2 AC 164, [128].

[158] Although note the possibility of disclosure to the principal sufficient to negate fraud while inadequate to avoid liability based on an unauthorised profit accruing to the agent: *Hurstanger Ltd v Wilson* [2007] EWCA Civ 299, [2007] 1 WLR 2351, [37]–[43]. On the nature of this fraud liability, see above, para 6.45.

[159] The opinion of any body of real people is not decisive. Ultimately, the objective standard is determined by the court (*Starglade Properties Ltd v Nash* [2010] EWCA Civ 1314, [2011] Lloyd's Rep FC 102, [32]), although the court will doubtless be cognisant of, and perhaps influenced by, prevailing mores.

[160] Apart from the second half of this sentence, it is uncontroversial that the principles stated so far in this paragraph were articulated by the Privy Council in *Royal Brunei Airlines Sdn Bhd v Tan* [1995] 2 AC 378 and confirmed by the House of Lords in *Twinsectra Ltd v Yardley* [2002] 2 AC 164. Whether the third party need realise its conduct was dishonest by the standards of ordinary people has proved more difficult. In *Twinsectra*, a majority of the House of Lords appeared to consider that such subjective realisation of objective dishonesty was required (and indeed that the Privy Council had so ruled in *Royal Brunei*). Subsequently, however, in *Barlow Clowes International Ltd v Eurotrust International Ltd* [2005] UKPC 37, [2006] 1 WLR 1476 the Privy Council considered that *Royal Brunei* had held that subjective realisation of objective dishonesty was not required and that *Twinsectra*, properly interpreted, approved *Royal Brunei*. The former, it is suggested, is correct, the latter expedient: the primacy which *Twinsectra* as a decision of the House of Lords must be accorded in English law cannot be denied by a conflicting decision of the Privy Council, but there is leeway for an English court to accept a Privy Council view on the interpretation of a House of Lords decision. In *Abou-Rahmah v Abacha* [2006] EWCA Civ 1492, [2007] 1 Lloyd's Rep 115, [59(a)], [69], Arden LJ considered that that leeway should be accepted. Although the other members of the court reserved their position (see ibid, [23], [91]), the approach of Arden LJ has been followed at first instance: *Aerostar Maintenance International Ltd v Wilson* [2010] EWHC 2032 (Ch), [184]–[185]; *Novoship (UK) Ltd v Mikhaylyuk* [2012] EWHC 3586 (Comm), [91].

illogical disparity between common law liability for inducing a breach of contract based on unadorned intentional wrongdoing and, uncharacteristically, more relaxed equitable liability for knowing assistance in a breach of fiduciary duty requiring subjective appreciation of dishonesty.[161]

6.63 The stringency with which equity demands the loyalty of an agent to its principal calls for the strongest deterrents against knowing participation in a breach of fiduciary duty. Accordingly, equitable accessory liability may be sanctioned by either an account of profits accruing to the third party[162] or equitable compensation for loss sustained by the principal.[163] In cases of bribery, the agent and third party are jointly and severally liable to the principal for the bribe by way of either an account of profits or an action for money had and received.[164] As with a defaulting agent, the principal is required to elect as against the third party between a disgorgement remedy and a compensatory remedy in so far as cumulative remedies would produce double recovery.[165] The principal may combine remedies against the agent and third party subject again to restrictions against double recovery. Accordingly, the principal is entitled to accounts of profits as against both the agent and the third party,[166] but cannot recover twice in respect of, for example, a profit accruing initially to the third party and remitted to the agent.

Third Party Liability for Receipt

6.64 While dishonest assistance requires complicity in the breach of fiduciary duty, third party liability may also arise by virtue of receipt of money or property the transfer of which was effected in or procured by a breach of fiduciary duty.

6.65 Where the receipt occurs pursuant to a contract concluded on behalf of the principal by the agent, the critical question, as observed above, is whether the transaction fell within the agent's apparent authority.[167] If it did, the third party's

---

[161] *Twinsectra Ltd v Yardley* [2002] 2 AC 164, [127]–[132]. See also *Royal Brunei Airlines Sdn Bhd v Tan* [1995] 2 AC 378, 387.

[162] *Fyffes Group Ltd v Tomlinson* [2000] 2 Lloyd's Rep 643, 668–72; *Fiona Trust & Holding Corp v Privalov* [2010] EWHC 3199, [62]–[66]. As with an agent's liability to account, it is irrelevant whether the profits would have accrued even in the absence of accessory liability: *Fiona Trust & Holding Corp v Privalov* [2010] EWHC 3199 (Comm), [67].

[163] *Fyffes Group Ltd v Tomlinson* [2000] 2 Lloyd's Rep 643, 660.

[164] *Mahesan v Malaysia Government Officers' Co-operative Housing Society Ltd* [1979] AC 374; *Logicrose Ltd v Southend United Football Club Ltd* [1988] 1 WLR 1256, 1264. Where a third party pays over a bribe, whether to the agent or some other party for payment over to the agent, but the attempt at bribery proves unsuccessful, the principle of *ex turpi causa non oritur actio* precludes recovery of the bribe by the third party: *Nayyar v Denton Wilde Sapte* [2009] EWHC 3218 (QB), [2010] Lloyd's Rep PN 139.

[165] *Mahesan v Malaysia Government Officers' Co-operative Housing Society Ltd* [1979] AC 374.

[166] But the agent and third party are each liable to account only for their own profits; there is no joint and several liability to account for their combined profits: *Ultraframe (UK) Ltd v Fielding* [2005] EWHC 1638 (Ch), [1600]; *Novoship (UK) Ltd v Mikhaylyuk* [2012] EWHC 3586 (Comm), [95]–[100].

[167] *Criterion Properties plc v Stratford UK Properties LLC* [2004] UKHL 28, [2004] 1 WLR 1846.

rights as recipient cannot be impugned. Otherwise, however, chattels transferred will remain the property of the principal, so that their retention against the will of the principal or disposal by the third party will generate liability in the tort of conversion. Money traceable at common law into the hands of the third party in its original or a substituted form is recoverable at common law by way of a restitutionary action for money had and received. In principle, liability is strict, but the third party will have a defence where in good faith it gave valuable consideration in return for the money or where and to the extent that it has changed its position in good faith as a result of receiving the money.[168]

6.66   Tracing at common law is, however, defeated in the common situation where the principal's money is mixed with other funds. Equitable tracing, conversely, acknowledges no such restriction. Nevertheless, equity restricts recovery to cases of 'knowing receipt', requiring proof of sufficient knowledge on the part of the recipient of the circumstances surrounding the transfer as to render it unconscionable for the recipient to retain the money or property transferred or the benefit of having subsequently transferred the money or property again.[169] This, however, merely replicates the enquiry into the recipient's state of mind undertaken to establish apparent authority: absence of honest or rational belief in the agent's authority will render receipt unconscionable.[170] Knowing receipt will again be in issue where the agent's intervention induces the principal to contract directly with the third party recipient.

6.67   Knowing receipt entitles the principal to exercise both a personal remedy against the recipient to repay a sum equal to that received and also a proprietary remedy over the received fund and traceable assets representing that fund.

---

[168]   *Lipkin Gorman v Karpnale Ltd* [1991] 2 AC 548.

[169]   *Bank of Credit and Commerce International (Overseas) Ltd v Akindele* [2001] Ch 437; *Charter plc v City Index Ltd* [2007] EWCA Civ 1382, [2008] Ch 313, [7]–[8]. The vague concept of 'unconscionability' displaces a previously articulated distinction between subjective awareness of improper transfer and an objective proposition that the recipient ought to have been aware of the improper nature of the transfer, the former being sufficient and the latter insufficient for receipt-based liability. The suggestion may be that some commercial recipients should incur liability based on (egregious) negligence. An alternative analysis favours abandoning altogether any enquiry into the recipient's knowledge in favour of strict restitutionary liability moderated by restitutionary defences, notably change of position: Lord Nicholls, 'Knowing Receipt: The Need for a New Landmark', in Cornish et al (eds), *Restitution: Past, Present and Future* (Oxford, Hart Publishing, 1998) ch 15; *Twinsectra Ltd v Yardley* [2002] 2 AC 164, [105]. This alternative analysis was doubted by Nourse LJ in *Akindele* ([2001] Ch 437, 455–56), pointing out that the change of position defence retains considerations of culpable knowledge but with an undesirable change in the burden of proof.

[170]   *Thanakharn Kasikorn Thai Chamkat (Mahachon) v Akai Holdings Ltd* [2010] HKFCA 64, [2011] 1 HKC 357, [135]–[137], [147].

7

Mutual Obligations in Commercial Agency

7.1   In cases of commercial agency, the obligations discussed in the previous chapter are supplemented by reciprocal obligations imposed by the Commercial Agents Regulations. By virtue of regulation 3(1), 'in performing his activities a commercial agent must look after the interests of his principal and act dutifully and in good faith', while regulation 4(1) provides that 'in his relations with his commercial agent a principal must act dutifully and in good faith.' These obligations are explicitly stated to be non-derogable.[1]

The Import of the Obligations

7.2   The central tenet of the mandatory regime is a reciprocal obligation to act dutifully and in good faith. This reflects the essence of commercial agency as a joint engagement in developing a business. Both parties must pledge to furthering the joint endeavour not just according to the terms, express and implied, of the agency agreement[2] but in a general spirit of mutual cooperation, and faithfulness and commitment to the common purpose. The reciprocal obligation is not, however, fiduciary: the Regulations require not that a party act exclusively in the interests of the other, but that the agency agreement be pursued to the mutual benefit of both.[3] Conversely, the good faith requirement is not simply one of subjective integrity: conduct must be reasonable in the context of the agency and consistent with the justified expectations of the other party. Conduct that, viewed objectively, is clearly unjustifiably prejudicial to the agency breaches the good faith

---

[1] Commercial Agents Regulations, reg 5(1).

[2] *Rossetti Marketing Ltd v Diamond Sofa Co Ltd* [2011] EWHC 2482 (QB), [2012] 1 All ER (Comm) 18, [55]: the obligations imposed by the Commercial Agents Regulations mould themselves to the agreement concluded by the parties, requiring loyalty to the bargain as struck by the principal and agent.

[3] DCFR, art IV.E-2:201, Comment D. Indeed, for the principal to require the agent to act wholly in the principal's interest would contravene the obligation of good faith owed by the principal to the agent. Cf *Rossetti Marketing Ltd v Diamond Sofa Co Ltd* [2011] EWHC 2482 (QB), [2012] 1 All ER (Comm) 18, [41], considering, wrongly it is suggested, that the reference in reg 3(1) to acting dutifully connotes loyalty and reflects the fiduciary obligations of common law. This is not to deny that particular conduct of an agent may constitute both a breach of the obligation to act dutifully and in good faith under the regulations and also a breach of fiduciary duty.

obligation under regulation 4, notwithstanding that the relevant party honestly believes its conduct appropriate in the circumstances.[4] An analogy may be drawn with the implied, reciprocal, non-fiduciary obligation in a contract of employment to act with mutual trust and confidence,[5] the approved formulation of this obligation being that each party 'shall not, without reasonable and proper cause, conduct itself in a manner calculated and likely to destroy or seriously damage the relationship of confidence and trust between employer and employee'.[6] Accordingly, where an agent was achieving a declining level of sales but refused to engage in discussions about performance, a decision by the principal unilaterally to make a rational and proportionate reduction in the range of the agent's activities did not constitute a breach of the reciprocal obligation.[7]

7.3   The reciprocal obligation operates within the context of the agency agreement; it does not provide a basis for the imposition of additional duties beyond the scope of the agreement. Moreover, while the contract cannot detract from the obligation of good faith, the more detailed the contractual prescription of the parties' respective rights and obligations, the more reduced the scope for additional specific manifestations of good faith within the parameters of the agreement.[8]

7.4   The obligation of good faith impacts upon the exercise of contractual discretions not embraced by a duty to exercise reasonable care. At common law, the decision-maker is required merely to avoid capriciousness and perversity.[9] Under the Regulations, however, good faith requires that any discretion should be exercised consistently with furthering the objectives of the agency, unless it is apparent that those objectives are no longer commercially sensible, or unless other interests are such as to justify a decision not to further the agency. Where, for example, the principal has more than one commercial agency agreement but unexpected demand produces a shortfall in capacity to supply all potential customers introduced by the agents, good faith would prohibit the principal from, for example, favouring one agency at the expense of the other purely in order to further its own financial interests. The principal's good faith obligation under one agency would not, however, require the ignoring of obligations under other contracts and would not preclude any reasonable apportionment of the available goods between the agencies.

---

[4] On good faith obligations in contracts generally, supporting the views expressed in this paragraph, see *Overlook v Foxtel* [2002] NSWSC 17; *Gold Group Properties Ltd v BDW Trading Ltd* [2010] EWHC 1632 (TCC). And see above, para 6.12.

[5] *Vick v Vogle-Gapes Ltd* [2006] EWHC 1665 (TCC), [85]–[86]; *Crocs Europe BV v Anderson* [2012] EWCA Civ 1400, [2013] 1 Lloyd's Rep 1, [56].

[6] *Malik v Bank of Credit & Commerce International SA* [1998] AC 20, 45.

[7] *Vick v Vogle-Gapes Ltd* [2006] EWHC 1665 (TCC).

[8] *Npower Direct Ltd v South of Scotland Power Ltd* [2005] EWHC 2123 (Comm), [153]–[156]. *Cf* above, para 6.25.

[9] Above, para 6.11.

7.5   The Regulations provide expressly that a commercial agent mandated to negotiate, or negotiate and conclude, transactions must make proper efforts to honour that mandate.[10] The agent must, therefore, engage proactively in endeavouring to develop the business, taking active steps to identify potential new customers and persuade them of the attractiveness of the principal's goods. In addition, a principal is expressly required to inform the agent within a reasonable time of acceptance or refusal of any transaction negotiated by the agent or any failure to fulfil a transaction concluded by the agent.[11] No restriction is articulated regarding the principal's discretion to decide how to respond to a proposed transaction or whether to fulfil a concluded transaction. The express requirement to inform of the decision taken might indicate that the silence with respect to the process by which the decision is arrived at is indicative of the absence of any limitation on that process. It is suggested, however, that the reciprocity of the good faith obligation dictates that an agent's obligation to make proper efforts to procure a potential transaction should be matched by an obligation to decline that transaction only on proper grounds.[12] It then follows that the agent should be entitled to an indication of the principal's reasons for declining or failing to perform a transaction sufficient to enable the agent to monitor the propriety of the principal's decision-making.[13] The principal should also forewarn the agent should it foresee an inability to meet the demand that the agent is likely to generate.[14]

7.6   Good faith also requires that each party should disclose to the other all information relevant to the conduct and prospects of the agency. In particular, the principal should notify the agent within a reasonable period if it anticipates that the volume of transactions will be significantly lower than the agent could reasonably have expected.[15] Similarly, the agent may be required to notify the principal should it become apparent that generating transactions will prove significantly more difficult than anticipated.

---

[10]   reg 3(2)(a).

[11]   reg 4(3).

[12]   *Page v Combined Shipping & Trading Co Ltd* [1996] CLC 1952 (good arguable case that under the Regulations the principal could not exercise a discretion as to the volume of transactions accepted under the agency so as to accept no transactions at all or only a derisory number). And see the ICC Model Commercial Agency Contract, art 4.2 (obligation not to reject orders unreasonably).

[13]   DCFR, art IV.E-3:308, Comment A, adopts a different approach, suggesting that the principal need not provide any reasons for individual decisions but must inform the agent more generally if it will refuse a certain type of customer or contract. Comment B, however, accepts and asserts the legitimate interest of the agent in being able to determine whether the principal has refused to contract or perform arbitrarily or in bad faith, the satisfaction of which requires the approach suggested in the text.

[14]   DCFR, art IV.E-3:309.

[15]   Commercial Agents Regulations, reg 4(2)(b).

Remedies for Breach

7.7   In accordance with the silence of the Directive on the matter, regulation 5(2) provides that the consequences of breach of the obligations prescribed by regulations 3 and 4 are determined by the applicable law of the commercial agency contract. Under English law, the Regulations will be considered to create mandatory implied contractual terms, with breach sanctioned in accordance with the principles of general contract law.[16] In view of the variable nature, extent and gravity of potential breaches, the implied obligations should be considered innominate, with the result that whether a breach is repudiatory, entitling the innocent party to elect to treat the contract as discharged, will depend on an assessment of the gravity of the breach in all the circumstances.[17] Any loss occasioned by a breach will be recoverable as damages for breach of contract.

---

[16] That the good faith obligation under the Regulations is not fiduciary, see above, para 7.2. The same conduct may constitute a breach of both a fiduciary obligation and the contractual good faith obligation implied by the Regulations, in which case any combination of remedies that does not produce double recovery will be available.

[17] *Crocs Europe BV v Anderson* [2012] EWCA Civ 1400, [2013] 1 Lloyd's Rep 1.

8

An Agent's Financial Rights Against the Principal

8.1 At common law, an agent enjoys remuneration rights dependent upon the terms of its agreement with the principal, together with a possible indemnity against expenses and liabilities incurred in the course of the agency, with the benefit of a possessory lien to secure its entitlements. Commercial agents benefit from a partly mandatory regime to the extent that they are remunerated by commission.

Remuneration: Entitlement and Discretion

8.2 An agent's remuneration may be expressed as to the whole or in part in discretionary terms. In such a case, it must be determined as a matter of interpretation whether the agent has an entitlement to some reward and the discretion is confined to amount, or whether the discretion relates more fundamentally to whether the agent is to receive any reward at all. Any such discretion imposes no obligation to arrive at an objectively reasonable decision, but merely a duty to act in a manner that is neither perverse nor irrational.[1] Accordingly, an agreement that 'the amount of remuneration I am to receive I leave entirely for you to determine' clearly contemplated that the agent's services were not to be gratuitous but confined the agent's entitlement to a genuine consideration by the principal of an appropriate amount.[2] Conversely, a principal was held entitled to decline to pay anything by way of a discretionary commission where the commission was payable in excess of a fixed fee and intended to reflect profits generated by the agent's services, which had in fact failed to generate any profits.[3]

---

[1] See above, para 6.11.
[2] *Bryant v Flight* (1839) 5 M & W 114. Likewise *Horkulak v Cantor Fitzgerald International* [2004] EWCA Civ 1287, [2005] ICR 402.
[3] *Kofi Sunkersette Obu v Strauss & Co Ltd* [1951] AC 243 (PC). For a discretion to treat the agent's services as entirely gratuitous, see *Taylor v Brewer* (1813) 1 M & S 290 ('such remuneration as should be deemed right').

8.3   Where the agency agreement is contractual and the contract is silent as to remuneration, there is an implied term that the agent will receive reasonable remuneration.[4] The agent is, therefore, entitled to remuneration calculated on an objectively reasonable basis and not merely to a proper consideration of the matter by the principal. Accordingly, in the event of dispute, it falls to the court to determine for itself on the basis of all relevant circumstances what the remuneration should be, as opposed to ascertaining what the principal in a proper exercise of its discretion would have decided.[5] Particular relevance will be afforded to a figure that was clearly in the contemplation of the parties themselves as appropriate even if there was no final agreement on the remuneration payable either at all or in respect of the services subsequently rendered by the agent.[6]

8.4   Commercial agency by definition is not gratuitous.[7] A commercial agent is entitled to whatever remuneration has been agreed. In default of agreement, it is entitled to the remuneration 'customarily allowed', or, in the absence of any custom, to whatever is reasonable.[8]

Earning Remuneration

8.5   To earn the agreed remuneration, whatever has been agreed as the trigger for remuneration must first occur. An auctioneer retained to sell by auction is not entitled to the agreed commission if, an attempt to sell by auction proving abortive, it procures a private sale.[9] Likewise, an agent retained to procure the sale of an identified property is not entitled to the agreed remuneration where a prospective purchaser introduced by the agent does not proceed to purchase the property, but instead an associated company acquires a controlling interest in the holding company of the property owner. Notwithstanding the commercially identical result, the agency agreement clearly contemplates a transfer of title in the property by the property owner, whereas the agent's intervention has produced a transfer of a different interest by a different entity.[10] And again, commission payable in respect of a project introduced by the agent is not earned where the agent introduces a further party that in turn introduces the principal to a project,[11] nor where

---

[4] Supply of Goods and Services Act 1982, s 15.
[5] *Socimer International Bank Ltd v Standard Bank London Ltd (No 2)* [2008] EWCA Civ 116, [2008] 1 Lloyd's Rep 558, [66].
[6] *Allan v Leo Lines Ltd* [1957] 1 Lloyd's Rep 127, 134; *Berezovsky v Edmiston & Co Ltd* [2011] EWCA Civ 431, [2011] 1 CLC 922.
[7] Commercial Agents Regulations, reg 2(2).
[8] ibid, reg 6(1).
[9] *Marsh v Jelf* (1862) 3 F & F 234.
[10] *Estafnous v London & Leeds Business Centres Ltd* [2011] EWCA Civ 1157.
[11] *Wollenberg v Casinos Austria International Holding GmbH* [2011] EWHC 103 (Ch).

an agent retained to find a purchaser introduces a party who undertakes in turn to find a purchaser but subsequently purchases for itself.[12]

8.6 Commonly, an agent is retained to procure transactions. In such a case, subject to contrary intention, remuneration will be payable not simply if the principal enters into the contemplated transaction but if the principal's so doing was the result of intervention by the agent that qualifies as the transaction's 'effective cause'. This proposition reflects the natural interpretation of the agency agreement: the agent should receive remuneration not simply if a particular transaction happens to ensue but if the agent has earned it by engaging the principal and third party with the transaction.[13] A lesser requirement, moreover, would court the risk of being satisfied in respect of any one transaction by more than one agent, rendering the principal liable to pay multiple remunerations. Such a risk is so clearly contrary to the natural intentions of a principal and to the logical understanding of a reasonable agent that it not only sustains effective causation as a principle of presumptive interpretation,[14] but militates strongly against any conclusion of its satisfaction on any given set of facts by more than one agent.[15] The effective cause, accordingly, is not merely an occurrence without which the transaction will not occur (a 'but for' cause), but is the engagement with the third party that really brings about the transaction.[16]

8.7 Similar reasoning underpins the analysis where the agent is engaged to introduce a counterparty to a transaction, such as a purchaser. The concept of 'introduction' imports causation and the reference to a transactional counterparty involves contractual status, so that remuneration is earned by introducing a counterparty that, as a real consequence of the agent's intervention, contracts with the principal;[17] put another way, the requirement is not that the third party merely be made acquainted with the principal, but that the third party be led into, or brought to, the specified transaction.[18]

---

[12] *Barnett v Isaacson* (1888) 4 TLR 645.

[13] *MSM Consulting Ltd v United Republic of Tanzania* [2009] EWHC 121 (QB), (2009) 123 Con LR 154, [142]. And see the discussion (albeit in the context of chargeability of services to value added tax) of the distinction between bringing parties together and mechanical behaviour as a mere conduit in *Royal Bank of Scotland v Commissioners for Her Majesty's Revenue & Customs* [2012] EWHC 9 (Ch), [2012] STC 797, [41]–[49].

[14] *Cooper (Brian) & Co v Fairview Estates (Investments) Ltd* [1987] 1 EGLR 18; *County Homesearch Co (Thames & Chilterns) Ltd v Cowham* [2008] EWCA Civ 26, [2008] 1 WLR 909 [14].

[15] Or by the same agent twice in respect of the same intervention. In *Millar v Radford* (1903) 19 TLR 575, an agent instructed to find a tenant or purchaser found a tenant and received commission. When the tenant subsequently purchased the property without any further intervention by the agent, the agent's claim for further commission was rejected. The original intervention could not be considered a cause of the purchase.

[16] *Green v Bartlett* (1863) 14 CB(NS) 681, 685; *McNeil v Law Union & Rock Insurance Co Ltd* (1925) 23 Ll L Rep 314, 316. Accidental overhearing by the third party of a conversation between the agent and another party does not constitute an engagement with the third party: *Coles v Enoch* [1939] 3 All ER 327.

[17] *Foxtons Ltd v Bicknell* [2008] EWCA Civ 419, [2008] 2 EGLR 23.

[18] *John D Wood & Co v Dantata* [1987] 2 EGLR 23, 25; *Nahum v Royal Holloway & Bedford New College* [1999] EMLR 252, 261. Creating an advertisement that causes the third party to approach the

8.8   Whether the agent is retained to 'find' or 'introduce' a counterparty, there is no requirement that the agent should conduct all the negotiations between the initial engagement of the third party with the transaction and its eventual conclusion. Provided the transaction concluded is that in which the agent awakened the third party's interest, the agent's intervention will usually retain its causal potency notwithstanding that the principal and third party elect to negotiate the details of the transaction directly with one another or through a different agent:[19] 'if an agent [retained to find a purchaser] brings a person into relation with his principal as an intending purchaser, the agent has done the most effective, and, possibly, the most laborious and expensive, part of his work'.[20] Were it otherwise, the principal could take the benefit of the agent's industry but easily avoid paying the agreed remuneration.[21]

8.9   In a case where the principal ultimately contracts with a third party originally introduced by one agent but only after a further intervention by another agent (both agents being retained to find or introduce a counterparty), any inference in favour of the causal efficacy of the original introduction may be displaced on the facts where that introduction failed to generate any lasting, productive interest.[22] Accordingly, where an introduction by one agent foundered on a demand from the principal vendor for a non-refundable deposit that was completely unacceptable to the introduced purchaser, a second introduction of the same purchaser, after the collapse of a rival bid, on terms not involving the deposit was considered to be the effective cause of the resulting sale. The demand for a deposit had constituted an insurmountable obstacle to proceeding upon the first introduction, and, by the time the demand had been dropped, the negotiations were proceeding upon the second introduction.[23] Similarly, the subsequent intervention was considered to be the effective cause where the third party's former wife for whom property was proposed for purchase emphatically rejected it after a visit arranged by one agent, but changed her mind and accepted it after a second visit arranged some weeks later by another agent.[24]

---

principal directly will suffice: *Burney v London Mews Co Ltd* [2003] EWCA Civ 766, [28]. In the case of purchase by a partnership, interaction between the agent and one member of the partnership will suffice, and nor does it matter that the purchaser under the sale contract is expressed to be one of the (other) partners: *Christie Owen v Davies plc v RAOBGLE Trust Corp* [2011] EWCA Civ 1151, [2011] NPC 104.

[19]   *Allan v Leo Lines Ltd* [1957] 1 Lloyd's Rep 127; *Nahum v Royal Holloway and Bedford New College* [1999] EMLR 252, 26l; *Berezovsky v Edmiston & Co Ltd (The Darius)* [2010] EWHC 1883 (Comm), [2010] 2 CLC 126, [40]–[41], [47]–[48], [53].

[20]   *Burchell v Gowrie & Blockhouse Collieries Ltd* [1910] AC 614, 625 (Lord Atkinson).

[21]   As was attempted in *McNeil v Law Union & Rock Insurance Co Ltd* (1925) 23 Ll L Rep 314; *Charania v Harbour Estates Ltd* [2009] EWCA Civ 1123.

[22]   It goes too far to require that all interest arising from the original introduction should have entirely evaporated: *Chasen Ryder & Co v Hedges* [1993] 1 EGLR 47, 48.

[23]   *HRL Property Management Services Ltd v Chequers of Kensington Ltd* (QB, 27 October 2000).

[24]   *Foxtons Ltd v Bicknell* [2008] EWCA Civ 419, [2008] 2 EGLR 23. See also *Glentree Estates Ltd v Holbeton Ltd* [2011] EWCA Civ 755.

8.10 The effective cause requirement representing the presumed interpretation of an agency agreement, it can be displaced by evidence of contrary intention. This is most clearly the case where remuneration is not linked to any intervention of the agent at all.[25] Alternatively, exclusion of any effective cause requirement may be the logical inference to draw from the terms of the agreement. Thus, where a sole agency[26] to 'introduce an applicant who subsequently purchases' provided for a reduced fee where the principal sold privately, a requirement that an introduction by the agent constituted an effective cause of the purchase would have produced the bizarre consequence that a fee would have been payable in the event of an introduction that constituted an effective cause or a private sale without any introduction at all, but not in the intermediate case of an introduction that failed to qualify as an effective cause. A fee was, therefore, payable in the event of conclusion by the principal of a sale contract with any counterparty introduced by the agent, irrespective of whether the introduction constituted an effective cause of the contract.[27] Again, the nature of the agent's services may render probable a significant lapse of time between the agent's intervention and any resulting transaction so that the agent's intervention is unlikely to qualify as an effective cause. In such a case, an interpretation of the agency agreement that applies the effective cause doctrine imports an improbable assumption by the agent of risk of non-payment for services rendered.[28] Moreover, although the presumption in favour of the effective cause requirement is strong, it will be weakened where the terms of the agency either prohibit or militate against the retaining of another agent, so that, realistically, any concern about multiple remunerations is absent.[29]

8.11 Although it is theoretically possible for the intervention of more than one agent each to qualify as a transaction's effective cause,[30] as noted above, the concern to avoid liability for the resulting multiple remunerations that underpins the very concept renders extremely improbable a factual conclusion of multiple effective causes. Liability to more than one agent may, however, more readily be incurred where the agents are retained on different terms such that at least one need not satisfy the effective cause test. Thus, where the claimant auctioneers were entitled to commission on the sale of property within a specified period of time whether or not effected by the auctioneers and a sale ensued during that period

[25] *Thorpe & Partners v Snook* (1983) 266 EG 440; *Bernard Marcus & Co v Ashraf* [1988] 1 EGLR 7 (see below, para 8.11).

[26] See further below, para 8.19.

[27] *Glentree Estates Ltd v Favermead Ltd* [2010] EWCA Civ 1473, [2011] EGLR 23.

[28] *Watersheds v Simms* [2009] EWHC 713 (QB).

[29] *County Homesearch Co (Thames & Chilterns) Ltd v Cowham* [2008] EWCA Civ 26, [2008] 1 WLR 909, [17]. See also *Cooper (Brian) & Co v Fairview Estates (Investments) Ltd* [1987] 1 EGLR 18.

[30] It suffices in principle for an agent's intervention to constitute 'an', rather than 'the', effective cause of the transaction: *Nahum v Royal Holloway & Bedford New College* [1999] EMLR 252, 267; *Aboualsaud v Aboukhater* [2007] EWHC 2122 (QB), [125]). For division of shipbroking commission in accordance with custom, see *Burnett v Bouch* (1840) 9 Car & P 620; *Hill v Kitching* (1846) 2 Car & K 278.

through another firm to which the principal paid commission, the principal was held liable to pay commission to the claimants as well.[31]

8.12   Where remuneration is earned upon the conclusion of a contract, the contract must be legally enforceable. Accordingly, no remuneration will be payable in respect of a contract voidable for misrepresentation, even if the misrepresentor is the principal.[32]

8.13   Accomplishing that which earns remuneration does not necessarily exhaust the agent's obligations under the agency agreement. Thus, a broker in the London insurance market earns its remuneration once the risk has been placed and insurance cover secured, even though the broker may undertake further duties during the lifetime of the insurance.[33] The agent's remuneration is earned and payable, notwithstanding that further duties remain to be performed. In the event of culpable non-performance of those further duties by the agent, however, remuneration remaining to be paid will be susceptible to a set-off against the agent's liability in damages.[34]

8.14   The agency agreement may, nevertheless, distinguish between the earning of remuneration and when it is payable, postponing payment to the fulfilment of some further condition. Where in such a case remuneration has been earned, the fact that the agency terminates before the remuneration becomes payable does not prejudice the agent's entitlement to payment once the condition for payment is fulfilled.[35]

8.15   In the case of sales of land, the contract is concluded upon 'exchange of contracts', with payment and transfer of title ensuing by way of 'completion'. Although remuneration is earned upon exchange of contracts, the presumed intention that an agent will be paid out of the purchase money results in remuneration being considered at common law to be payable only upon completion.[36] However, the terms of estate agency agreements commonly provide for remuneration to be payable upon exchange of contracts, allocating to the principal the risk that the third party resiles from the contract after exchange,[37] or the contract proves abortive for some other reason.

---

[31]   *Bernard Marcus & Co v Ashraf* [1988] 1 EGLR 7. See also *Lordsgate Properties v Balcombe* [1985] 1 EGLR 20.

[32]   *John D Wood & Co (Residential & Agricultural) Ltd v Craze* [2007] EWHC 2658 (QB), [2008] 1 EGLR 17, [44]–[45] (but see below, para 8.26). A fortiori where entitlement to remuneration is conditional upon a 'binding contract': *Peter Long & Partners v Burns* [1956] 1 WLR 1083.

[33]   *Velos Group Ltd v Harbour Insurance Services Ltd* [1997] 2 Lloyd's Rep 461. See also *Explora Group plc v Hesco Bastion Ltd* [2005] EWCA Civ 646, [65] (commission earned on making introductions; performance of marketing obligations not a prerequisite).

[34]   As in the context of unlawful repudiation of the agency: below, para 11.9.

[35]   *Explora Group plc v Hesco Bastion Ltd* [2005] EWCA Civ 646 [65], [85]; *Proactive Sports Management Ltd v Rooney* [2011] EWCA Civ 1444, [2012] 2 All ER (Comm) 815, [44]–[48]. In the event of termination by reason of unlawful repudiation by the agent, the agent's entitlement to remuneration will be subject to a set-off of liability in damages for breach of contract: *Explora v Hesco*, [85].

[36]   *Foxtons Ltd v Thesleff* [2005] EWCA Civ 514, [2005] 2 EGLR 29, [16].

[37]   *Midgley Estates Ltd v Hand* [1952] 2 QB 432; *Foxtons Ltd v O'Reardon* [2011] EWHC 2946 (QB).

8.16   Should an agent's services in purported fulfilment of the agency agreement fail to earn remuneration in accordance with its terms, no claim will lie instead for a quantum meruit in respect of those services. Such a claim may be brought, however, in respect of additional services performed by the agent at the request of the principal falling outside the agency agreement and in respect of which no fee was agreed.[38]

Entitlement to Earn Commission

8.17   Outside of agency undertaken in a social or family context, an agent expects to earn remuneration in respect of the services it performs. Where, however, the agent's remuneration is contingent upon achieving a certain result, such expectation is only partially underpinned by legal right.

Exclusivity Clauses

8.18   At common law, the fact of engaging an agent to achieve a specified goal precludes the principal neither from engaging one or more rival agents to compete to earn the remuneration on offer nor from proceeding itself to achieve the specified goal without the intervention of any agent.[39] An agent, therefore, incurs the risk of undertaking considerable work only to be denied remuneration because the principal elects to proceed through another agent or through its own efforts.

8.19   In response, the agency agreement may confer complete or partial exclusivity upon the agent.[40] Through what may be termed 'sole agency', the principal confers partial exclusivity by undertaking either not to proceed through another agent or to pay the first agent the agreed remuneration should it do so, but retains the right to proceed autonomously through a privately arranged transaction without liability. Where the agency is 'sole and exclusive', the principal confers complete exclusivity by undertaking to proceed neither through another agent nor by private transaction, or to pay the agent the agreed remuneration should it do so.[41] The existence and degree of exclusivity granted may be reflected in the level of remuneration payable, a higher fee in the absence of exclusivity reflecting the enhanced risk assumed by the agent of unremunerated services.

[38] *Luxor (Eastbourne) Ltd v Cooper* [1941] AC 108, 125, 140–41; *Cooke v Hopper* [2012] EWCA Civ 175.

[39] Likewise DCFR, art IV.D-3:301.

[40] See *Great Estates Group Ltd v Digby* [2011] EWCA Civ 1120, [2012] 2 All ER (Comm) 361, [6], [23]–[24], [27].

[41] An agreement that disables the principal from itself acting is subject to the doctrine of restraint of trade but is unlikely to be invalidated by it: *Proactive Sports Management Ltd v Rooney* [2011] EWCA Civ 1444, [2012] 2 All ER (Comm) 815.

8.20   Where a principal contracts in breach of an exclusivity clause, the agent will be entitled to damages in accordance with general principles of contract law, provided it can show that it had a real and substantial, and not just a speculative, prospect of earning remuneration under the agreement.[42]

Implied Terms not to Inhibit the Earning of Remuneration

8.21   Where an agency agreement does not contain an express restriction on the principal's continued autonomy over its affairs, any implied restriction must fairly reflect the true interpretation of the agreement.

8.22   Where, for example, an agent is retained to find a potential counterparty – without assuming any obligation to endeavour to do so – but is not authorised to conclude a contract, and remuneration is payable upon the conclusion of a contract, the principal retains the liberty to decline to enter into any proposed transaction or to contract other than through the agent. In *Luxor (Eastbourne) Ltd v Cooper*,[43] estate agents retained to sell two cinemas with commission payable on completion of the sale duly introduced a prospective purchaser prepared to pay the desired price, but the principal preferred to sell by private transaction to another purchaser. The House of Lords declined to recognise an implied term that the principal would not without good reason decline to contract with a purchaser introduced pursuant to the agency agreement. Two factors in particular were emphasised. First, what, as between principal and agent, might constitute good reason for declining to contract with the introduced third party was inherently so uncertain as to render the clause impossible for a court to supervise and therefore unworkable. Secondly, the ease with which the risk to the agent could be reduced by an exclusivity clause[44] or eliminated by divorcing the entitlement to remuneration from the principal's response to a possible transaction indicated that the absence of such drafting should be considered as reflecting a deliberate assumption of risk on the part of the agent that could not be disturbed. Such factors militate also against an implied term that the principal would consider any proposed transaction properly and not reject arbitrarily, capriciously or perversely.[45]

8.23   Emphasis, however, was also placed on the unilateral nature of estate agency contracts: the agent undertakes no legal obligations to expend resources in endeav-

---

[42]   *Nicholas Prestige Homes v Neal* [2010] EWCA Civ 1552; *Great Estates Group Ltd v Digby* [2011] EWCA Civ 1120, [2012] 2 All ER (Comm) 361, [29].

[43]   [1941] AC 108.

[44]   Such a clause does not address the possibility of the principal electing not to proceed at all, but that risk is small at least with respect to assets in which the principal has a purely commercial interest and might in any event be considered a risk the agent generally has to assume and does assume in the absence of cogent evidence of contrary intention.

[45]   The judgments indeed recognise that the agent is exposed to the arbitrary whim of the principal, but consider that a professional agent should understand the risk it is assuming and contract for express protection if the risk is unacceptable.

ouring to accomplish the purpose of the agency. The agreement is merely that if the agent is successful in achieving the specified result, a reward will be payable.[46] In contrast, an agency agreement may oblige the agent to employ its best endeavours to achieve the purpose of the agency, for example to generate customers for the principal's business. It is strongly arguable that the express imposition of such an obligation on the agent may sustain a reciprocal implied promise that the principal will not arbitrarily decline the fruits of such an obligation, and will not otherwise act capriciously so as to deny the agent the benefit it reasonably expected to have a fair opportunity to derive from the assumption and fulfilment of its obligations. The question, therefore, would be not whether the principal's refusal was objectively reasonable, but merely whether the proposed transaction was given proper consideration. Such a minimal implication fairly reflects the cooperative nature of bilateral agency contracts.[47] In cases of commercial agency indeed, a failure by the principal at least to give proper consideration to transactions negotiated by the agent would be inconsistent with the mutual obligation of good faith under regulation 4 of the Commercial Agents Regulations.[48] It would be incongruous were the same provision to be considered incompatible with agency agreements falling outside the Regulations: an obligation inherent in agency agreements to develop markets in goods cannot be repudiated as unworkable and contrary to the natural understanding of parallel agreements to develop markets in services.

8.24   Where an agent is to receive a percentage of the receipts or profits accruing to the principal over the lifetime of a contract concluded or procured by the agent, the principal is free to act lawfully in respect of the contract in a way that impacts adversely upon the remuneration payable to the agent. Accordingly, where a shipbroker was to receive a percentage of the hire earned and paid under an 18-month time charterparty, the shipowners were entitled to sell the ship to the charterers after four months, terminating the charterparty and the earning of hire that would generate remuneration for the shipbroker. No term could be implied denying the shipowners the right to dispose lawfully of their own property as they so desired.[49]

8.25   Similarly, a fixed-term agency to generate orders for the principal's business of itself imports no obligation to maintain any particular level of business activity, or even to carry on trading, for the duration of the term. The opportunity to earn commission is an incentive, not an entitlement. A principal remains free to operate or run down its business activities in accordance with its own interests, subject only, it is suggested, to the minimal constraint of refraining from capricious neglect of the agency.[50]

---

[46]   [1941] AC 108, 117, 120–21, 124–25.
[47]   Indeed, a stronger implied term not to refuse reasonable orders has been conceded: *Alpha Lettings Ltd v Neptune Research & Development Inc* [2003] EWCA Civ 704, [33].
[48]   See above, para 7.2 et seq.
[49]   *French (L) & Co Ltd v Leeston Shipping Co Ltd* [1922] 1 AC 451.
[50]   *Ex p Maclure* (1870) LR 5 Ch 737; *Rhodes v Forwood* (1876) 1 App Cas 256. Of course, the true interpretation of the agency agreement may support the assumption of an obligation to maintain trading for a specified period: *Reigate v Union Manufacturing Co (Ramsgate) Ltd* [1918] 1 KB 592.

8.26   The agency agreement will, nevertheless, commonly sustain an implication that the principal will not act unlawfully so as to frustrate the purpose of the agency.[51] Accordingly, the principal incurred liability where commission for introducing a purchaser was payable on contract performance according to the weight of goods shipped, but unlawful failure by the principal to ship any goods deprived the agents of their commission;[52] and, similarly, where the agent's remuneration depended on the conclusion of a legally enforceable contract but fraudulent misrepresentation on the part of the principal vitiated any transaction procured by the agent.[53] In the latter case, moreover, since the relevant issue is whether the principal acts unlawfully rather than whether it knowingly so acts, any misrepresentation that denied remuneration should incur liability.

8.27   Sometimes, however, the terms of the agency agreement will deny any such implication. In an atypical case,[54] A transferred to P exclusive rights to purchase a specified property. This contract provided for A to receive a fee from P not 'on completion of the sale' but 'if we complete', and contemplated the provision by P of a substantial deposit to the vendor that would be forfeit on failure to complete. P elected not to complete, forfeiting the deposit. A's claim for damages for breach of an implied term not to act unlawfully so as to frustrate A's remuneration rights was unsuccessful. The fee clause clearly offered no assurance of completion. Moreover, it was improbable that the parties would contemplate both forfeiture of the deposit and payment of A's fee.

8.28   Whatever the position of the principal, there is no basis for implying a promise on the part of the third party to the agent not to act unlawfully so as to frustrate the agency. Consequently, where the agent's commission is dependent on performance of the procured contract but breach of contract by the third party results in non-performance, the agent has no action against the third party for breach of an implied collateral contract.[55]

Commercial Agency

8.29   Part III of the Commercial Agents Regulations contains a set of provisions (in regulations 7–12) applicable to the extent that any commercial agent is remunerated by commission.[56]

---

[51]   *Luxor (Eastbourne) Ltd v Cooper* [1941] AC 108, 142, 149–50.
[52]   *Alpha Trading Ltd v Dunnshaw-Patten Ltd* [1981] QB 290. See also *Moundreas & Co SA v Navimpex Centrala Navala* [1985] 2 Lloyd's Rep 515.
[53]   *John D Wood & Co (Residential & Agricultural) Ltd v Craze* [2007] EWHC 2658 (QB), [2008] 1 EGLR 17, [67]–[68].
[54]   *Adler v Ananhall Advisory & Consultancy Services Ltd* [2009] EWCA Civ 586.
[55]   *Marcan Shipping (London) Ltd v Polish Steamship Co (The Manifest Likowy)* [1989] 2 Lloyd's Rep 138.
[56]   Commercial Agents Regulations, reg 6(3).

Remuneration by Commission

8.30 Commission is defined for the purposes of the Regulations as meaning 'any part of the remuneration of a commercial agent which varies with the number or value of business transactions'.[57] This excludes not only remuneration by salary, which may in any event denote status as an employee (which is by definition incompatible with commercial agency[58]), but also consideration for an agent's services in the form of the opportunity to profit by way of mark-up in the price negotiated with the third party.[59] First, remuneration connotes payment by the principal, as opposed to an opportunity to contract for profit determined by negotiation between the agent and third party.[60] Secondly, mark-up lacks the immediate connection to the number and value of business transactions envisaged by the definition in the Regulations. Thirdly, a number of the provisions in the Regulations that address commission contemplate or clearly require that the principal should be able to calculate the amount of commission due to the agent, which is not possible where the return to the agent depends on a mark-up unknown to the principal.[61]

Entitlement to Commission (1): Transactions Concluded during the Agency

8.31 A commercial agent's entitlement to commission in respect of transactions concluded during the period of the agency contract[62] extends to three categories of transaction. The first category, as stated in regulation 7(1)(a), is based on proved causation, embracing transactions 'concluded as a result of [the agent's] action'. The concept of 'action' clearly embraces the negotiating or negotiating and concluding of contracts that commercial agents must by definition be authorised to undertake[63] and may extend to further acts that lead to transactions being concluded between third parties and the principal that do not constitute negotiation, notwithstanding the broad meaning attributed to that term.[64] The causation language of the Regulations, it has been suggested, requires that the agent has

---

[57] ibid, reg 2(1).

[58] ibid.

[59] *Mercantile International Group plc v Chuan Soon Huat Industrial Group plc* [2001] CLC 1222, [122]–[123]. On mark-up generally as remuneration, see above, para 1.28.

[60] See also *AMB Imballagi Plastici SRT v Pacflex Ltd* [1999] 2 All ER (Comm) 249, 252.

[61] Commercial Agents Regulations, regs 7, 8, 12.

[62] This refers to the period during which the agency contract in fact endured, not the period during which it should have endured up to lawful termination. Consequently, reg 7 will cease to apply (and reg 8, discussed below, will commence) on acceptance by the agent of a repudiatory breach by the principal: *Roy v MR Pearlman Ltd* [1999] 2 CMLR 1155, [31]–[32].

[63] Commercial Agents Regulations, reg 2(1).

[64] Above, paras 2.34–2.35. Possibilities include canvassing activities of locating and introducing potential counterparties (although it is suggested above that they do constitute negotiation), general marketing activities, or creating a website for promoting and selling the principal's goods.

'contributed to the conclusion of the contract between the customer and the principal in an identifiable, considerable and useful manner', although not that the agent's intervention with the customer was directed at procuring 'a particular contract'.[65] This would suggest a lower causal threshold than that imported by the effective cause doctrine of common law. Actions amounting to negotiating or negotiating and concluding contracts will meet the causal requirement of regulation 7(1)(a); other interventions may elicit doubt.

8.32   The second category is based on extending the causal reach of procuring a contractual relationship between the principal and third parties. It embraces, by virtue of regulation 7(1)(b), transactions 'concluded with a third party whom [the agent] has previously acquired as a customer for transactions of the same kind.' The agent accordingly receives credit for an original intervention that produced a customer in respect of further transactions with the principal whether or not the agent had any further input. They are presumed to be attributable to the agent's original intervention, the concept of 'acquisition as a customer' logically importing the same causal link between the agent's intervention and the original contract with the principal as pertains in regulation 7(1)(a).

8.33   The third category applies, by virtue of regulation 7(2), where the commercial agent enjoys 'an exclusive right to a specific geographical area or to a specific group of customers'. The agent is entitled to commission in respect of any transaction concluded during the period of the agency agreement with a customer belonging to the area or group, as the case may be. There is no requirement of any proved causal link between the activity of the agent and the transaction,[66] but the exclusive nature of the agency provides a basis for inferring that the transaction is attributable to the efforts of the agent in promoting the principal's goods. In this respect, regulation 7(2) may be regarded as based upon deemed causation.

8.34   Regulation 7(2) applies only to agents that enjoy exclusive representation rights, but the Regulations provide no definition of 'exclusive'. It would, however, be consistent with a deemed causation basis for regulation 7(2) to embrace partial exclusivity (or 'sole agency'), where the principal retains the right to transact directly with third parties.[67]

8.35   A commercial customer 'belongs' to an area, for the purposes of regulation 7(2), provided that it carries on its business activities there, irrespective of where the customer has its legal seat or central office. Where a customer pursues business

---

[65]   DCFR, art IV.E-3:301, Comment C.

[66]   Case C-104/95 *Kontogeorgas v Kartonpak AE* [1996] ECR I-6643.

[67]   Thus, the ICC Model Commercial Agency Contract contemplates territorial exclusivity but permits the principal to deal directly with customers in the relevant territory, provided the agent is informed. The agent is entitled to commission on such transactions subject to contracting out in the context of internet sales (see below, para 8.47): arts 1.1, 13. In *Edwards v International Connection (UK) Ltd* (Central London Cty Ct, 25 November 2005) an argument that a commercial agent's exclusivity did not extend to sales directly by the principal (termed 'in-house sales') was rejected on the facts.

activities both within and outside the relevant area, the centre of gravity of the transaction will need to be determined by reference to the place where negotiations took place with the agent or should, in the ordinary course of events, have taken place, the location from which the order was placed, and the place of delivery of the goods.[68] Provided the customer belongs to the specified area or group, it is irrelevant that the customer may be purchasing the goods for resale outside the specified area or group.[69]

8.36 On its wording, regulation 7(2) requires merely a concluded transaction involving a third party belonging to the designated geographical area or group. There is no express reference to any involvement of the principal. Nevertheless, in the context of Part III of the Regulations (that addresses remuneration),[70] it is clear that an entitlement to commission accrues only in respect of transactions where the principal has a direct or indirect involvement. Accordingly, no entitlement arises where third parties place orders with suppliers of the principal's goods that are genuinely independent of the principal or its subsidiaries.[71]

Entitlement to Commission (2): Transactions Concluded after the Agency

8.37 Notwithstanding the termination of the agency agreement, the Commercial Agents Regulations provide for a continuing entitlement to commission in two situations. The first involves post-termination transactions that satisfy conditions of causation and timing; the second involves post-termination acceptance of pre-termination orders.

Causation and Timing

8.38 By virtue of regulation 8(a), commission is payable where a transaction, albeit concluded after termination of the agency, is 'mainly attributable to' the efforts of the agent during the period of the agency and the transaction is entered into 'within a reasonable period' of the agency's termination.

8.39 The causation language of regulation 8(a) imports a two-stage test. First, the agent's intervention must in isolation satisfy the threshold causal potency of regulation 7(a). Given that both provisions are based on proved causation, it would be most incongruous were an agent to receive credit for a transaction concluded after cessation of the agency on the basis of a more tenuous link than that required for a transaction concluded while the agency was still alive. Secondly, the causative potency of the agent's intervention must outweigh the cumulative

---

[68] Case C-104/95 *Kontogeorgas v Kartonpak AE* [1996] ECR I-6643 [27]–[30].
[69] *Edwards v International Connection (UK) Ltd* (Central London Cty Ct, 25 November 2005), [31].
[70] In particular, regs 10 and 11; as to which, see below, paras 8.44–8.46.
[71] Case C-19/07 *Chevassus-Marche (Heirs of Paul) v Groupe Danone* [2008] 1 Lloyd's Rep 475.

potency of all other factors, whether pre- or post-termination, that contributed to the conclusion of the transaction. At this stage, assuming there is another causally relevant intervention, the doctrine of effective cause may assist by way at least of analogy in determining whether the original intervention retains predominant causal potency.[72]

8.40   What constitutes a reasonable time after the termination of the agency within which transactions must be concluded for commission to be payable under regulation 8(a) may be determined by the parties in the agency agreement.[73] In default of such accord, the question is necessarily one of fact, to be determined with regard to the nature of the agency, the knowledge and expertise of any successor agent, the product, and the customer base. One may contrast an agency for sophisticated industrial machinery that will tend to generate fewer but high-value transactions that will require nurturing through a prolonged gestation period with an agency for low value, high turnover goods in a market where new products are regularly introduced and customers' interest will readily lapse if not constantly refreshed. In the former, a reasonable time may extend to a couple of years, while in the latter it may expire after a few months.[74]

8.41   The two requirements of causation and timeliness are independent and must each be satisfied.[75] Commission will not be payable in respect of transactions mainly attributable to the agent's intervention where they are concluded after the expiry of a reasonable time, nor in respect of transactions concluded within a reasonable time of the agency's termination but in the absence of the requisite causal link.

8.42   Given that the transaction contemplated by regulation 8 is concluded after the expiry of the original agency, the transaction may be the product of the efforts of both the original agent and a successor agent. In principle, where the intervention of the original agent constitutes the predominant cause of the transaction, commission is payable in full to the original agent under regulation 8(a) and not at all to the successor under regulation 7.[76] By way of exception, commission may be shared where the respective contributions of the two agents render division equitable.[77] There is, however, no provision for reduction of commission where the agent's intervention is supplemented by a subsequent intervention on the part of the principal.

---

[72] See the discussion of the doctrine of effective cause in the context of successive interventions by different agents: above, para 8.9.

[73] *Vick v Vogle-Gapes Ltd* [2006] EWHC 1665 (TCC), [131].

[74] *cp Ingmar GB Ltd v Eaton Leonard Inc* [2001] CLC 1825 (agency for 'sophisticated tube and pipe bending machines and associated equipment mainly designed for the aircraft and automotive industries': 21 months within a reasonable period) and *Tigana Ltd v Decoro Ltd* [2003] EWHC 23 (QB), [2003] ECC 23 (leather furniture: nine months' limit)

[75] *Tigana Ltd v Decoro Ltd* [2003] EWHC 23 (QB), [2003] ECC 23, [64] ('conjunctive and cumulative': Davis J).

[76] Commercial Agents Regulations, reg 9(1).

[77] ibid.

Pre-termination Orders

8.43 By virtue of regulation 8(b), commission is payable in respect of trans-actions concluded after termination of the agency in a second situation. This arises where one of the three possibilities under regulation 7 is satisfied and the order of the third party reaches the principal or the commercial agent before termination of the agency. A principal cannot, therefore, postpone accepting a third party's order until after an agency terminates in order to avoid paying commission, conduct that would in any event contravene the obligation to act in good faith under regulation 4.[78]

When Commission Due and Payable

8.44 Assuming that a transaction falls within regulation 7 or 8, commission accrues due, subject to contrary intention, on the earliest of three occurrences, namely when the principal executed[79] or should have executed the transaction and when the third party executed the transaction.[80] In any event, commission accrues due, on a non-derogable basis, no later than the time when the trans-action is executed by the third party or would have been had the principal duly performed its part of the contract.[81] If, however, a transaction fails by reason of non-performance on the part of the third party not itself justified by non-performance by the principal, no commission will be due: the agent takes the risk of transaction failure because the third party proves unreliable.

8.45 In default of an agreement more favourable to the agent, commission that has accrued due is then payable on a quarterly basis, with payment required no later than the last day of the month following the quarter in which the commission accrues due.[82] By that date, the principal must supply the agent with a statement of commission due, which the agent is entitled to check by reference to all information available to the principal.[83] Both the right to the statement and the right to check are non-derogable.[84]

Loss of the Right to Commission

8.46 By virtue of regulation 11(1), the agent will forfeit earned commission only if and to the extent that it is 'established that the contract between principal and third party will not be executed . . . due to a reason for which the principal is not

---

[78] As to which, see above, ch 7.
[79] Meaning performed.
[80] Commercial Agents Regulations, reg 10(1).
[81] ibid, reg 10(2), (4).
[82] ibid, reg 10(3), (4).
[83] ibid, reg 12(1), (2).
[84] ibid, reg 12(3).

to blame.'[85] The term 'established' appears to denote that the non-execution is a matter of fact rather than conjecture.[86] The reference to 'blame' does not connote that the principal is legally at fault for the non-performance, but merely that the non-performance is attributable to the principal as a factual proposition.[87] It follows that the principal will need to insure against the risk of having to pay commission despite not receiving the benefit of the transaction either because of legally culpable non-performance by the third party or because the contract is frustrated. Any commission already received by the agent before extinction of the right to receive it must be repaid.[88]

Whether Non-Derogable

8.47   As indicated in the course of discussion, a number of the provisions in the Commercial Agents Regulations relating to commission are explicitly stated to be non-derogable, at least to the detriment of the agent.[89] No such status, however, is accorded to the principal provisions that govern the agent's entitlement to commission. Regulations 7–9 and 10(1) are merely default provisions, applicable in the absence of contrary intention. Accordingly, the parties remain free to determine for themselves the basis on and the extent to which and the time at which the agent will become entitled to commission. For example, the ICC Model Commercial Agency Contract, which is based upon a grant of territorial exclusivity subject to a continued right for the principal to deal directly with customers in the relevant territory,[90] modifies regulation 7(2) by permitting contracting out of any right to commission with respect to sales by the principal through its internet website.[91] In respect of transactions concluded after the termination of the agency and resulting from orders received before termination, the Model Contract modifies regulation 8(b), imposing a temporal limitation that restricts the agent's entitlement to commission to sales concluded not more than six months after termination.[92] The agency agreement might also seek to avoid possible disputes under regulation 8(a) regarding the causal potency of the agent's intervention or what constitutes a reasonable time by dispensing with any need for causation but restricting the entitlement to transactions concluded within a specified period of short duration. The Model Contract does not do so, but does introduce a requirement of written notification to the principal before

---

[85]   Any derogation therefrom to the agent's detriment is void: reg 11(3).

[86]   *cf* the proposition of contract law that an anticipatory breach 'must be proved in fact and not in supposition': *Universal Cargo Carriers Corp v Citati* [1957] 2 QB 401, 450 (Devlin J).

[87]   P Watts and F Reynolds (eds), *Bowstead & Reynolds on Agency,* 19th edn (London, Sweet & Maxwell, 2010) para 11-032 (citing the French text of the Directive).

[88]   Commercial Agents Regulations, reg 11(2).

[89]   ibid, regs 10(2), (3) (see reg 10(4)), reg 11(1) (see reg 11(3)), regs 12(1), (2) (see reg 12(3)).

[90]   arts 1.1, 13.

[91]   art 13.4.B.

[92]   art 19.1.

termination of the agency of the pending negotiations that may result in commission-generating sales.[93]

8.48 It should be emphasised, however, that while the conferral of commission rights is ultimately a matter for contract, any provision that has the effect of reducing the rights conferred other than in accordance with regulation 11(1) is void.[94]

Indemnity

8.49 In addition to any remuneration, the agent may also be entitled to an indemnity in respect of expenses, liabilities and losses incurred by the agent while acting within the scope of its actual authority. Accordingly, where the custom of a port rendered personally liable an agent that booked space on a vessel for its principal's goods where the goods arrived late and the vessel departed without them, the custom was considered reasonable so that the incurring of liability fell within the agent's implied actual authority entitling the agent to indemnification from the principal.[95]

8.50 Where the agency is contractual, the indemnity may be conferred by an express or implied term of the agency agreement. Alternatively, the agent, on the true interpretation of the agreement, may assume the risk of wasted expenditure to be offset against the benefit that it is contemplated will accrue to the agent through the agency.[96]

Agent's Lien

8.51 As security for its entitlements against the principal by way of remuneration and indemnity, as a matter of common law the agent enjoys a possessory lien over its principal's chattels unless otherwise agreed.[97]

8.52 A common law possessory lien confers a right to retain possession; the lienee does not enjoy a right to sell the retained property and apply the proceeds

---

[93] art 19.2.
[94] Commercial Agents Regulations, reg 11(3). On reg 11(1), see above, para 8.46.
[95] *Anglo Overseas Transport Ltd v Titan Industrial Corp (UK) Ltd* [1959] 2 Lloyd's Rep 152.
[96] The ICC Model Commercial Agency Contract expressly provides that expenses are presumptively covered by commission: art 15.4. Likewise DCFR, art IV.D-2:103(1).
[97] *Rolls Razor Ltd v Cox* [1967] 1 QB 552.

in discharge of the secured debt.[98] It is a right to inconvenience and embarrass by withholding possession of goods, documents, or money in the lienee's possession.[99] The lien has priority over third party rights subsequently acquired in the property for valuable consideration in good faith and without notice of the lien,[100] and affords protection in insolvency,[101] but is circumscribed by the rights of the lienor. Accordingly, the lien is subject to any third party rights to which the property is already subject at the time the lienee acquires possession.[102]

8.53   A possessory lien is either particular or general. A particular lien is confined to property connected to the financial rights the agent seeks to enforce. A general lien entitles retention of property irrespective of whether there is any connection between the financial claim and the property. In principle, an agent's lien is particular, but a general lien may be conferred by agreement[103] or by custom. Bankers and solicitors by custom enjoy general liens.

8.54   For an agent to acquire a lien over an item of property, it must both obtain possession and incur the financial right against the principal in its capacity as agent. Accordingly, a factor[104] had no lien over an insurance policy that came into his possession while performing non-factorial services.[105] And no lien can arise in respect of rights against the principal that antedate the engagement to act as agent.[106]

8.55   Because an agent's lien is based on possession, it is lost if the agent voluntarily relinquishes possession.[107] It will also be lost if waived by the agent, for example by the taking of alternative security inconsistent with the retention of a lien.[108]

8.56   A sub-agent's claim for remuneration and indemnity lies against the agent. Nevertheless, a sub-agent enjoys a lien over the property of the principal, pro-

---

[98]   *Thames Iron Works Co v Patent Derrick Co* (1860) 1 J & H 93. Although a right of sale may be conferred by contract: British International Freight Association Standard Trading Conditions (2005 edition), cll 8, 10.

[99]   *Ismail v Richards Butler* [1996] 2 All ER 506, 514.

[100]   *West of England Bank v Batchelor* (1882) 51 LJ Ch 199.

[101]   *Uniserve Ltd v Croxen* [2012] EWHC 1190 (Ch) (efficacy of contractual general lien in administration).

[102]   *Peat v Clayton* [1906] 1 Ch 659; *Withers LLP v Rybak* [2011] EWCA Civ 1419, [2012] 1 WLR 1748 (money subject to a court order).

[103]   *George Barker (Transport) Ltd v Eynon* [1974] 1 WLR 462. See also the British International Freight Association Standard Trading Conditions (2005 edn), cl 8.

[104]   An agent whose normal business is the disposal of goods entrusted to his possession by the principal.

[105]   *Dixon v Stansfield* (1850) 10 CB 398.

[106]   *Houghten v Matthews* (1803) 3 B & P 485.

[107]   *Legg v Evans* (1840) 6 M & W 36, 42.

[108]   *Capital Finance Co Ltd v Stokes* [1969] 1 Ch 261. The inconsistency must, however, be unequivocal: 'the no man's land of doubt belongs to the lienee' (*Metall Market OOO v Vitorio Shipping Co Ltd (The Lehmann Timber)* [2012] EWHC 844 (Comm), [2012] 2 All ER (Comm) 577, [23] (Popplewell J)).

vided the engagement of a sub-agent is within the agent's actual authority.[109] Where the principal is undisclosed at the time of engagement of the sub-agent, a lien over the principal's property can be exercised in respect of claims arising against the agent before the existence of the principal is revealed, regardless of whether the principal's property comes into the hands of the agent before or after revelation of the principal's existence. No lien exists, however, in respect of claims against the agent arising after such revelation.[110]

[109] *Solly v Rathbone* (1814) 2 M & S 298.
[110] *Mann v Forrester* (1814) 4 Camp 60.

9

Agency and Contract

9.1 Where an agent concludes a contract while acting on the instructions of a principal, the third party may be aware of the principal's existence and identity, or the principal's identity or its very existence may not be revealed. The agent, moreover, may or may not have authority to generate privity of contract between principal and third party.

Disclosed and Undisclosed Agency

9.2 The distinction between disclosed and undisclosed agency depends on the third party's awareness of the existence of a principal or possibility of a principal at the time of conclusion of the contract. Awareness denotes actual knowledge: constructive notice is insufficient. A third party that wishes to take advantage of the truncated nature of an undisclosed principal's contractual rights need not demonstrate that it lacked the means of discovering the principal's existence.[1] Where, however, the counterparty is known to act sometimes as principal and sometimes as agent, a third party that contracts without clarification of the capacity in which the counterparty is acting on this particular occasion must accept the consequences of whichever role the counterparty is in fact assuming. Accordingly, where the counterparty is in fact acting as agent, the principal will enjoy the full enforcement rights of a disclosed principal. A third party that wishes to ensure it is dealing with the counterparty as principal and not as an agent must obtain an assurance from the counterparty that it is acting on its own behalf.[2] All the more where the third party knows of the existence but not the identity of the principal: such an unidentified principal is disclosed.[3]

---

[1] *Borries v Imperial Ottoman Bank* (1873) LR 9 CP 38; *Greer v Downs Supply Co* [1927] 2 KB 28.
[2] *Baring v Corrie* (1818) 2 B & Ald 137; *Cooke & Sons v Eshelby* (1887) 12 App Cas 271.
[3] *Semenza v Brinsley* (1865) 18 CB(NS) 467.

Undisclosed Agency, the Doctrine of the Undisclosed Principal, and Commission Agency

9.3 Undisclosed agency is a factual situation where, as just discussed, the third party is unaware of the existence of a principal. The doctrine of the undisclosed principal is a legal doctrine belonging to the external aspect of undisclosed agency that addresses the rights and liabilities that arise as between either the undisclosed principal or the agent on the one hand, and the third party on the other. That is not to deny that undisclosed agency has both internal and external aspects, but the undisclosed nature of an agency does not affect the internal aspect. It does, however, impact upon the external aspect, and it is that external aspect that the undisclosed principal doctrine addresses. The doctrine applies where the principal authorises the agent to bring the principal into contractual relations with the third party either without revealing the principal's existence and the agent so acts, or on a disclosed principal basis but the agent ostensibly acts on its own behalf. Crucial to the generation of contractual rights between the undisclosed principal and the third party, and to the operation of the undisclosed principal doctrine, is the principal's conferral of actual authority on the agent to bring the principal, notwithstanding non-disclosure of its existence, into contractual privity with the third party.[4]

9.4 Commission agency, in contrast, arises where the principal instructs the agent to contract with the third party on the agent's own behalf and does not authorise the creation of contractual relations between itself and the third party.[5] There is, therefore, no external aspect to commission agency. Consequently, while on the facts commission agency may be disclosed or undisclosed, it is of no import. The agency relationship between the principal and the commission agent and the contractual relationship between the third party and the commission agent acting in its own name and on its own behalf are unaffected by disclosure or non-disclosure of the existence of a principal, and there is no relationship between the principal and third party. The doctrine of the undisclosed principal, as a doctrine predicated upon the generation by an agent of legal relations between an undisclosed principal and third party, is, therefore, inapplicable to commission agency.[6]

---

[4] *Hutton v Bulloch* (1874) 9 QB 572; *Garnac Grain Co Inc v HMF Faure & Fairclough Ltd* [1966] 1 QB 650, 684.

[5] See above, para 1.8.

[6] Contrast the European Principles, which assimilate commission and undisclosed agency (although defined to exclude constructive notice of the principal's existence) under the concept of 'indirect representation' (PECL, art 3:102(2)), under which contractual rights and obligations arise initially between intermediary and third party. Only upon insolvency or fundamental non-performance by the intermediary are the principal and third party entitled to demand disclosure from the intermediary of the other's identity and address, and then to exercise rights against that other: PECL, arts 3:301–3:304.

Disclosed Agency

9.5   Where an agent successfully procures the conclusion of an authorised contract on behalf of a disclosed principal, different analyses are possible as to the
standing in relation to the contract of the principal and the agent.

Contract Between Principal and Third Party; Agent No Standing

9.6   An agent that acts pursuant to its actual authority in concluding a contract
overtly on behalf of its principal normally generates a contract between its
principal and the third party in respect of which the agent has no standing. This
is consistent with general principles of contract law under which the assumption
of contractual rights and liabilities depends upon a manifestation of consent,
objectively construed, to the privileges and obligations of a legally enforceable
agreement. An agent acting overtly on behalf of another offers no manifestation
of personal consent to a contractual relationship. Consequently, rights of
performance, variation, termination, and enforcement lie with the principal, and
may be exercised without consultation of, or even informing, the agent, although
the principal may of course authorise the agent to exercise any such rights on its
behalf.[7] Likewise, obligations under the contract and liability for non-performance
lie with the principal to the exclusion of the agent.

9.7   Where an agent acts without actual authority in purporting to conclude a
contract on behalf of the principal, whether the principal is bound by the agent's
acts depends at the third party's election on the doctrine of apparent authority,[8]
or at the principal's election on the doctrine of ratification.[9] Irrespective of the
principal's position, however, the agent still offers no personal engagement to –
and cannot therefore incur any direct contractual liability in respect of – the proposed transaction, but may incur collateral liability to the third party for breach of
warranty of authority.[10]

9.8   Where a party purports to act on behalf of a disclosed but unidentified principal, and even signs the contract 'as agent', that party may subsequently reveal
that in truth it was acting for itself and assume the status of principal in relation to

---

[7] An agent authorised to enforce the principal's rights under the contract would of course have to
bring proceedings in the name of the principal. At common law, moreover, an agent cannot be authorised to enforce its principal's contractual rights in its own name even by an express term of the contract (*Gray v Pearson* (1870) LR 5 CP 568; *Evans v Harper* (1875) 1 QBD 45), although this is now
subject to the Contracts (Rights of Third Parties) Act 1999.

[8] Discussed above, ch 4.

[9] Discussed above, ch 5.

[10] *Jenkins v Hutchinson* (1839) 13 QB 744. On liability for breach of warranty of authority, see
below, paras 9.46–9.53.

the contract. Accordingly, where a charterparty is concluded between 'X (agents of the charterer)' and Z (shipowners), and further provides that 'this charter being entered into on behalf of others, all liability of agents shall cease on shipment of cargo', it is permitted to X to reveal that it has chartered the vessel on its own behalf and to enforce the contract as principal.[11] Any contractual ascription of status as agent, whether in the body of the contract or the signature, is understood as denying liability in so far as the designated party is acting in the capacity of agent[12] but as leaving open the possibility of that party's qualifying as principal.

9.9 Of course, a previously purported agent claiming entitlement to engage with the contract on its own behalf must be able to conform to any contractually stipulated precondition for principal status. Consequently, where the supposed principal is identified in the contract, evidence is admissible to demonstrate that the principal's identity was financially, commercially, or otherwise material such that the third party would not have contracted had the true identity of the principal been revealed, excluding the agent from status as contracting party.[13] Moreover, subject to any possibility of apparent authority or ratification, no contract will arise with the supposed principal. In consequence, there will be no contract at all, although the agent will again be subject to liability for breach of warranty of authority.

Contract Attracting Personal Engagement of the Agent

9.10 By way of exception to the general position described in the previous section, an agent concluding a contract overtly on behalf of its principal may offer a manifestation of personal engagement with the contract so as to enjoy enforcement rights and incur liability. If so, such engagement may be as the sole contracting party to the exclusion of the principal, either because the agent was engaged as a commission agent with no authority to create contractual privity between principal and third party, or because, notwithstanding authority to create privity, the contract in fact concluded by the agent on its true interpretation precludes attachment to any party other than a stipulated counterparty, namely the agent. Alternatively, the engagement of the agent may be additional to that of the principal: authorised by the principal to create contractual privity between itself and the third party, the agent duly does so while also adding its own personal engagement.

9.11 Whether an agent engages personally with a contract depends entirely on the true interpretation of the contract as a whole in accordance with the holistic approach to interpretation of modern contract law.[14] Subject always to

---

[11] *Schmaltz v Avery* (1851) 16 QB 655; *Harper & Co v Vigers Bros* [1909] 2 KB 549.
[12] *Oglesby v Yglesias* (1858) E B & E 930.
[13] *Rayner v Grote* (1846) 15 M & W 359; *Gewa Chartering BV v Remco Shipping Lines Ltd (The Remco)* [1984] 2 Lloyd's Rep 205.
[14] *Tudor Marine Ltd v Tradax Export SA (The Virgo)* [1976] 2 Lloyd's Rep 135.

that reservation, several general propositions may be derived from the case law. First, in commercial contracts especially, the terms in which a party signs a contract carry particular significance. Signature of a contract in one's own name without qualification naturally denotes acceptance of personal engagement with the contract, subject to clear contrary evidence elsewhere in the document.[15] Secondly, references to agency in the body of the contract of themselves are ambiguous, capable either of merely describing the internal relationship between two parties, or of denoting the legal capacity in which the named party is acting in relation to the transaction. Consequently, a statement that a contract is concluded 'between X, agent for Y' will not negate the assumption of contractual responsibility denoted by X's unqualified signature.[16] Indeed, thirdly, an unqualified signature as a contracting party is not inconsistent with an indication elsewhere in the contract that a different party has that status since the signature may be read as an acceptance of liability as if a contracting party.[17] In contrast, fourthly, a statement in the operative part of a contract of acting 'on account of' another may be construed as an unambiguous assertion of legal capacity of engagement with the contract, overriding an unqualified signature.[18] Fifthly, moreover, in the interests of commercial certainty, signature of a commercial contract 'as agent' will be upheld as manifesting a deliberate intention to exclude personal liability on the contract.[19]

9.12 Assuming the agent to have engaged personally with the contract, the position of the principal depends on whether the agent was authorised to create privity between principal and third party and upon whether the contract, on its true interpretation, admits of engagement by the principal in addition to the agent.[20] Given the preparedness of English law to recognise contractual status in respect of an undisclosed principal, the natural inference, subject to contrary intention, is that the personal engagement of an agent acting for a disclosed principal and authorised to generate privity between principal and third party will be in addition to, and not to the exclusion of, that of the principal.[21]

---

[15] *Internaut Shipping GmbH v Fercometal SARL (The Elikon)* [2003] EWCA Civ 812, [2003] 2 Lloyd's Rep 430, [53]; *Hamid v Francis Bradshaw Partnership* [2013] EWCA Civ 470.

[16] *Parker v Winlow* (1857) 9 Ex 942. See also *Brandt (HO) & Co v Morris (HN) & Co Ltd* [1917] 2 KB 784.

[17] *Internaut Shipping GmbH v Fercometal SARL (The Elikon)* [2003] EWCA Civ 812, [2003] 2 Lloyd's Rep 430, [50]–[51]. *A fortiori*, knowledge on the part of the third party that the signatory acts pursuant to authority of another (as opposed to signs in the capacity as agent for another) does not deny the contractual assumption of responsibility: *Hyundai Merchant Marine Co Ltd v Dartbrook Coal (Sales) Pty Ltd* [2006] FCA 1324, (2006) 236 ALR 115, [106].

[18] *Gadd v Houghton* (1876) 1 Ex D 357. Contrast the identification of the assured under a political risks policy as 'X Bank a/c Y' followed by the address of the bank, where the reference to 'a/c Y' served merely to identify the transaction in respect of which the policy provided cover: *Punjab National Bank v de Boinville* [1992] 1 Lloyd's Rep 7.

[19] *Universal Steam Navigation Co Ltd v James McKelvie & Co* [1923] AC 492.

[20] *The Swan* [1968] 1 Lloyd's Rep 5, 12.

[21] *Higgins v Senior* (1841) 8 M & W 834, 844; *Young v Schuler* (1887) 11 QBD 651. The matter may be put beyond doubt by signature explicitly on behalf of both the agent personally and the principal: *International Railway Co v Niagara Parks Commission* [1941] AC 328. Judgments upholding the liability

9.13 Agents acting for foreign principals have attracted particular consideration. Contracting with a counterparty in another jurisdiction typically presents enhanced difficulties in assessing the counterparty's reliability and solvency, and in the enforcing of legal rights should disputes arise. At one time, therefore, trade usage was said to give rise, subject to contrary indication, to a factual inference that an agent acting in England for a foreign principal undertook personal liability on the contract, and indeed that the correct analysis was one of commission agency, denying any contractual privity between principal and third party.[22] Such parochial trade usage, however, has not endured into the modern, innately international, commercial world. Nevertheless, the underlying concerns remain valid, and the impact of the geographical remoteness of a foreign principal on assessment as a contractual counterparty and potential adversary in a dispute resolution process may be relevant as part of the factual matrix taken into account in the interpretation of a contract with respect to assumption of liability by the agent and the principal.[23]

9.14 Wherever the principal has no direct status on the contract, it is always possible that the principal may be empowered to enforce the contract by virtue of the Contracts (Rights of Third Parties) Act 1999 as an identified third party to the contract intended to receive the benefit of one or more of its terms.[24] Under the 1999 Act, however, the principal remains a stranger to the contract and immune from liability under it.

Unidentified Principals

9.15 An agent may conclude a contract on behalf of a disclosed principal without revealing the principal's identity either because the principal has instructed the agent to keep its identity concealed or because the agent elects not to disclose the principal's identity. In either case, the contract clearly takes effect between principal and third party. However, the normal approach to disclosed principals and contractual liability requires some modification; otherwise, the third party's enforcement rights can be frustrated by the simple expedient of a continuing refusal to reveal the identity of the party against whom they lie. There are two possible solutions.

---

of an agent on a contract where the status of the principal is not in issue should be considered carefully before being regarded as denying contractual standing to the principal.

[22] *Smyth v Anderson* (1849) 7 CB 21, 33; *Armstrong v Stokes* (1872) LR 7 QB 598, 605; *Elbinger Action-Gesellschaft v Claye* (1873) LR 8 QB 313, 317; *Robinson v Mollett* (1875) LR 7 HL 802, 809–10.

[23] *Teheran-Europe Co Ltd v ST Belton (Tractors) Ltd* [1968] 2 QB 545.

[24] On the concept of identification, see Contracts (Rights of Third Parties) Act 1999, s 1(3).

9.16   The first is to consider that an agent that acts for an unidentified principal assumes personal liability on the contract from the outset, at least subject to contrary intention. This is the approach of the Restatement,[25] on the basis that the third party's decision to contract is unlikely to be based solely on a consideration of the principal's solvency or reliability of performance. Not knowing the principal's identity, the third party can rely at most on unverifiable reassurances and statements of general description from the agent and on any general reputation of the agent as acting for solvent and reliable principals.[26] The second possible solution acknowledges the normal incidence of liability, confined to the principal, as initially applicable but imposes on the agent an obligation to reveal the identity of the principal within a reasonable time on demand of the third party. This approach is adopted by the European Principles and Draft CFR, which contemplate that in the event of non-compliance, the agent becomes personally liable on the contract.[27] A variant would confine the third party's right to disclosure to situations where the operation or enforcement of the contract required knowledge of the principal's identity, and restrict the remedies for breach to damages for consequential loss.

9.17   The traditional position of English law differs from that adopted by the Restatement: that an agent acts for an unidentified principal does not give rise to any inference of assumption of personal engagement with the contract, although it is a factor that can be taken into account.[28] All depends on the true interpretation of the contract, which is approached without any prior assumption. More recently, however, a preparedness to move towards the approach of the Restatement has been evinced, considering an agent for an unidentified principal at least to undertake liability on the contract[29] in the absence of clear contrary intention.[30] Moreover, market customs have been proved rendering the agent liable on the contract either from the beginning, effectively the surety of its principal,[31] or, reflecting the approach of the European Principles, in the event of failure to disclose the principal's identity within a certain time.[32]

---

[25]   Restatement, § 6.02(2).

[26]   Restatement, § 6.02, Comment (b).

[27]   PECL, art 3:203; DCFR, art II-6:108.

[28]   *Vlassopulos (N & J) Ltd v Ney Shipping Ltd (The Santa Carina)* [1977] 1 Lloyd's Rep 478, in which the commercial context clearly indicated that brokers on the Baltic Exchange acted purely as agents in ordering bunkers, with no assumption of personal responsibility. *Cf Short v Spackman* (1831) 2 B & Ad 962 (clear assumption of contractual status by agent for unidentified principal).

[29]   The question of standing to enforce the contract against the third party has not been in issue.

[30]   *Seatrade Groningen BV v Geest Industries Ltd (The Frost Express)* [1996] 2 Lloyd's Rep 375, 381. In *Teheran-Europe Co Ltd v ST Belton (Tractors) Ltd* [1968] 2 QB 53, [1968] 2 QB 545, it was common ground on the facts that the agent incurred liability, although disputed whether as commission agent or, as held, on a contract between principal and third party.

[31]   *Imperial Bank v London & St Katharine Docks Co* (1877) 5 Ch D 195; *Cory Bros Shipping Ltd v Baldan Ltd* [1997] 2 Lloyd's Rep 58, 62–63.

[32]   *Hutchinson v Tatham* (1873) LR 8 CP 482.

9.18 It is highly improbable that the courts would be prepared to countenance the disappearance of the third party's enforcement rights into a legal black hole of agency without clear evidence that the third party genuinely assumed that risk.[33] The courts might indeed adopt the position of the Restatement, at least as an interpretative presumption. Alternatively, the neutral traditional approach to interpretation might be supplemented by an implied undertaking (being an extrapolation from an absence of original contractual liability of the agent, non-disclosure of the principal's identity, and the extreme unlikelihood of the third party's assumption of obligations while countenancing a lack of reciprocity) either in the contract or collateral thereto[34] to disclose the principal's identity within a reasonable time when demanded by the principal in order to enforce rights under the contract.

The Doctrine of the Undisclosed Principal

9.19 Even where the third party contracts in ignorance that the counterparty with which it has negotiated is acting not on its own behalf but as an agent, once revealed a previously undisclosed principal generally has standing to enforce the contract and is subject to its liabilities. Exceptionally, however, the possibility of an undisclosed principal is excluded by the terms of the contract. More generally, while non-disclosure of the true contracting counterparty is generally accepted as legitimate, the third party enjoys protection against unfair prejudice that might thereby arise.

Origins, Justification, and Theoretical Analysis

9.20 The origins of the undisclosed principal doctrine appear to lie in the practice for a geographically remote principal to consign goods for sale to a selling agent. Concerns regarding remote, especially foreign, contracting counterparties required contractual rights enforceable against a known local party such that an agent entrusted with possession of goods for sale, known as a factor, was considered to have implied actual authority to sell the goods in its own name and ostensibly on its own behalf.[35] However, the absence of enforceable rights on the part of the principal against the third party could leave the principal exposed should the factor become insolvent or otherwise cease to engage with the contract. Thus, the principal required standing to intervene and collect outstanding

---

[33] Compare the reluctance of the courts to allow the loss sustained by a third party under a contract for its benefit to disappear into the legal black hole created where the loss is sustained by a party devoid of entitlement to sue. See, eg, *Offer-Hoar v Larkstore Ltd* [2006] EWCA Civ 1079, [2006] 1 WLR 2926, [85].

[34] See, by analogy, the agent's implied warranty of authority: below, para 9.46 et seq.

[35] *The Matchless* (1822) 1 Hagg 97, 100–01; *Stevens v Biller* (1883) 25 Ch D 31.

debts under the contract should the factor no longer exact payment. It was, more-over, considered unacceptable that one who instigates a transaction for personal benefit should be shielded from liabilities on the transaction by the undisclosed interposition of an agent. By the end of the eighteenth century, therefore, both rights and liabilities of an undisclosed principal were clearly recognised.[36]

9.21   Today, the doctrine of the undisclosed principal continues to be regarded as reflecting valuable commercial convenience,[37] although changes in commercial trading practice marginalise the original source of its utility. Instead, the doctrine reflects the reality of the transaction as perceived from the side of the principal and agent while acknowledging the widespread commercial practice of contract-ing through intermediaries,[38] protects the principal whose agent omits to disclose the fact of agency,[39] and provides the third party with the benefit of an additional potential defendant to satisfy claims arising out of the contract.

9.22   The doctrine also affords a principal two specific benefits. First, where the third party would refuse to contract with the principal even though the identity of the contracting counterparty is not fundamental to the transaction,[40] the principal can procure the contract by concealing itself behind undisclosed agency. Agency law thereby reflects the general objective immateriality of identity in commercial matters,[41] a broad policy that personal scruples should not outweigh efficient business,[42] and the inability to prevent a genuinely independent counterparty from subsequently retransferring the received consideration to the disliked prin-cipal or from assigning the benefit of most contracts to an assignee of its unfet-tered choice.[43] Indeed, such is the commitment of agency law to the doctrine of the undisclosed principal that it is not excluded even where a contract by its nature cannot be assigned[44] or contains a non-assignment clause precluding any transfer of the benefit of the third party's performance obligations.[45]

9.23   Secondly, the undisclosed principal doctrine enables a principal to avoid paying a premium price where the contractual subject-matter possesses an especial value to the principal, for example where the third party owns the final item required

---

[36] See S Stoljar, *Law of Agency* (London, Sweet & Maxwell, 1961), pp 204–11.

[37] *Teheran Europe Co Ltd v ST Belton (Tractors) Ltd* [1968] 2 QB 545, 555; *Siu Yin Kwan v Eastern Insurance Co Ltd* [1994] AC 199, 207. And see Tan Cheng-Han, 'Undisclosed Principals and Contract' (2004) 120 LQR 480, 481–86.

[38] *Keighley, Maxsted & Co v Durant* [1901] AC 240, 261.

[39] Albeit that non-disclosure of the existence of a principal may result in limited rights as against the third party: below, para 9.32 et seq. For a case in point, see *Re Henley* (1876) 4 Ch D 133.

[40] Where identity is so fundamental, an undisclosed principal is excluded from any engagement with the contract: see below, para 9.26.

[41] *Keighley, Maxsted & Co v Durant* [1901] AC 240, 261.

[42] *Sotiros Shipping Inc v Sameiet Solholt (The Solholt)* [1983] 1 Lloyd's Rep 605 (unreasonable for victim of breach to decline to conclude substitute contract with contract-breaker by way of mitigation of loss).

[43] *Dyster v Randall & Sons* [1926] Ch 932, 938.

[44] *Siu Yin Kwan v Eastern Insurance Co Ltd* [1994] AC 199, 210.

[45] *Browning v Provincial Insurance Co of Canada* (1873) LR 5 PC 263, 273.

to complete a collection or a plot of land required to enable a larger property development project to progress. While agency law may appear to deny the third party a legitimate market advantage, it is consistent with the general tolerance of non-disclosure of objectively material information in contractual negotiations.

9.24 The doctrine of the undisclosed principal, nevertheless, requires a modification of orthodox contract law theory, although it remains unclear whether the relevant modification is to the foundation concept of consent or to the effective range of a contract as delineated by the doctrine of contractual privity. General contract law considers a contract as based upon a manifestation of consent, objectively construed, to a legally binding agreement. In the case of an agent acting on behalf of an undisclosed principal, both agent and third party, viewed objectively, manifest their consent to a contract between themselves as principals. To that contract, the undisclosed principal is a stranger and engages with it, without increasing the burden on the third party, only by way of exception to the privity of contract doctrine with respect to both rights and liabilities.[46] An alternative analysis is that agency law tempers the general principles of contract formation to generate a contract concluded between principal and third party by deeming, subject to clear contrary intention, the third party to consent with either the apparent counterparty or, if that person is in fact acting as an agent, the principal on whose behalf that person is acting.[47] The fundamental principle of consent objectively construed is, nevertheless, recognised by acknowledging rights and liabilities on the part of the agent as if it were a contracting party and ensuring that the third party's liabilities on the contract with the principal are no greater than they would have been on the contract with the agent to which it consented.[48]

Exclusion of Undisclosed Agency

9.25 The applicability of the doctrine of the undisclosed principle is subject to exclusion on the true interpretation of the contract.[49] The courts have warned, however, that adopting an approach to interpretation that readily produces the conclusion that the doctrine is excluded will jeopardise the commercial convenience on which the doctrine is founded and which it promotes.[50]

---

[46] *Keighley, Maxsted & Co v Durant* [1901] AC 240, 256; *Siu Yin Kwan v Eastern Insurance Co Ltd* [1994] AC 199, 207. See also *Smith & Snipes Hall Farm Ltd v River Douglas Catchment Board* [1949] 2 KB 500, 514–15. And see A Goodhart and C Hamson, 'Undisclosed Principals in Contract' (1932) 4 *Cambridge Law Journal* 320. It is perhaps noteworthy that the undisclosed principal doctrine was established before contract law fully espoused the privity doctrine.

[47] *Teheran-Europe Co Ltd v ST Belton (Tractors) Ltd* [1968] 2 QB 545, 555. For detailed analysis favouring the undisclosed principal as a full party to the contract, see Tan Cheng-Han, 'Undisclosed Principals and Contract' (2004) 120 *Law Quarterly Review* 480.

[48] See below, para 9.32 et seq.

[49] See A Goodhart and C Hamson, 'Undisclosed Principals in Contract' (1932) 4 *Cambridge Law Journal* 320, 338–45.

[50] *Siu Yin Kwan v Eastern Insurance Co Ltd* [1994] AC 199, 208–09.

9.26   The contract may exclude undisclosed agency in two ways. First, the nature of some contracts dictates that a party's identity is critical to any decision whether to contract. Such contracts are said to be 'personal'. In some instances, the identity of the counterparty defines the contractual subject-matter such that the contract is intrinsically and inextricably connected to the identified counterparty to the exclusion of all others, and performance by any other person would constitute a repudiation of the contract.[51] The most obvious example is a contract for the painting of a portrait by a celebrated artist: the identity of the artist defines the contract and substitution of performance by another is incompatible with the contractual bargain. Alternatively, under other contracts, identity does not serve to define performance, but the object of the contract is such that the opportunity to participate may fairly be regarded as by way of personal invitation,[52] or, albeit commercial, is such as to require knowledge of identity in order to decide suitability for participation. Accordingly, undisclosed agency was held excluded where an assessment of financial credibility that required revelation of identity was critical to a decision to contract.[53]

9.27   Where a contract is not by its nature personal in this sense, the undisclosed principal doctrine is not excluded by the fact that the third party would have refused to enter into the contract had it known the apparent counterparty was in fact acting instead for the now revealed principal, and irrespective of the fact that the principal knew the third party would have refused and adopted the strategy of undisclosed agency in order to obtain the contract.[54]

9.28   Secondly, undisclosed agency may be excluded as a matter of the true interpretation of the contract. The contractual counterparty may be described as acting in a capacity incompatible with agency, but such a description is rare. The terms 'owner' and 'proprietor' have been held to be so incompatible, on the basis that it is not possible, as a matter of property law, to have such status on behalf of another.[55] However, designation as assuming the rights and liabilities of a contracting party is not interpreted as a statement that the party so designated is the sole and exclusive party entitled to enjoy for the purposes of the contract the status attached to that designation.[56] Provided, therefore, the description in context is essentially a synonym for 'contracting party', it will be interpreted, subject to contrary intention, as denoting only an assumption of the contractual rights and liabilities attaching to a party of that description and not as speaking to the question of the capacity in which the designated party is acting.[57] It may, therefore, be

---

[51]   ibid, 210.
[52]   *Said v Butt* [1920] 3 KB 497, 503 (McCardie J) (admission to the first night of a theatre production: 'the personal element was strikingly present').
[53]   *Collins v Associated Greyhound Racecourses* [1930] 1 Ch 1 (acceptance of sub-underwriters of public share offering and allotment of shares).
[54]   *Dyster v Randall & Sons* [1926] Ch 932.
[55]   *Humble v Hunter* (1848) 12 QB 310; *Formby Bros v Formby* (1910) 102 LT 116.
[56]   *Fred Drughorn Ltd v Rederiaktiebolaget Transatlantic* [1919] AC 203.
[57]   *Danziger v Thompson* [1944] KB 654.

suggested that even the terms 'owner' and 'proprietor' are open to the interpretation that the identified party either has the designated status or, if not, accepts liability as if it has that status, without prejudice to the possibility of agency for the party that in truth has that status.[58] All other descriptions tested in the courts have been held compatible with agency.[59]

9.29   Occasionally, the terms of the contract as a whole may, on their true interpretation, exclude undisclosed agency. In one case,[60] the articles of association of a mutual insurance association provided that every person accepted for insurance whether contracting personally or on another's behalf became a member of the association, and the association undertook liability for losses incurred by members, but only to the extent of contributions collected from members, and only members were liable for contributions, such that in financial reality members' finances were pledged to cover members' losses: 'membership and mutuality are the essence and vitality of the concern.'[61] And the individual policy issued to members did not detract from this conclusion. It was held that undisclosed agency was excluded so that the association could not enforce liability for unpaid contributions against the undisclosed principal of an insolvent member.[62]

Insurance Contracts and Undisclosed Agency

9.30   The example just given of a contract excluding undisclosed agency on its terms happens to be a form of insurance. Are there, however, inherent incidents of insurance that may militate against undisclosed agency?[63] Contracts of insurance are not personal by nature,[64] but an insurer under a commercial policy is entitled to pre-formation disclosure of all material circumstances and may avoid

---

[58] In *Epps v Rothnie* [1945] KB 562, 565, Scott LJ obiter expressed doubt regarding *Humble* and *Formby Bros*, albeit on the mistaken basis of disapproval in *Fred Drughorn Ltd v Rederiaktiebolaget Transatlantic* [1919] AC 203, whereas members of the House of Lords in that case either considered the decisions uncontroversial (ibid, 207) or expressed no view (ibid, 209, 210).

[59] 'Charterer': *Fred Drughorn Ltd v Rederiaktiebolaget Transatlantic* [1919] AC 203; 'tenant': *Danziger v Thompson* [1944] KB 654; 'disponent owner': *O/Y Wasa SS Co v Newspaper Pulp Wood Export Ltd* (1949) 82 LlLR 936; 'proposer' and 'insured': *Siu Yin Kwan v Eastern Insurance Co Ltd* [1994] AC 199; 'employer': *Ferryways NV v Associated British Ports* [2008] EWHC 225 (Comm), [2008] 1 Lloyd's Rep 639. Cf *Asty Maritime Co Ltd v Rocco Giuseppe & Figli SNC (The Astyanax)* [1985] 2 Lloyd's Rep 109, in which extrinsic evidence established a common intention that a party described in the contract as 'disponent owner' was acting as principal.

[60] *United Kingdom Mutual Steamship Assurance Association Ltd v Nevill* (1887) 19 QBD 110.

[61] ibid, 122 (Lopes LJ).

[62] cf *Great Britain 100 A1 Steamship Insurance Association v Wyllie* (1889) 22 QBD 710, in which an association's differently worded policy admitted of liability for contributions beyond members.

[63] For extended discussion, see H Bennett, 'The Doctrine of the Undisclosed Principal and Contracts of Insurance', in DR Thomas (ed), *The Modern Law of Marine Insurance*, Vol III (London, Informa, 2009), ch 3.

[64] *Browning v Provincial Insurance Co of Canada* (1873) LR 5 CP 263, 272–73; *Siu Yin Kwan v Eastern Insurance Co Ltd* [1994] AC 199.

the policy if induced into the contract by material non-disclosure.[65] Consequently, where the identity of the assured would alert a prudent insurer to a circumstance that is relevant to the assessment of the proposed risk,[66] non-disclosure of the assured's identity will entitle the insurer to avoid the policy provided disclosure would have resulted in the risk being declined or accepted on different terms.[67] If, however, disclosure of the relevant circumstance as relating to the party to be insured is duly made, the fact that the party named in the proposal is not the party to be insured but an agent acting for that party is not of itself a material circumstance and need not be disclosed.[68] Moreover, the insurer's disclosure entitlements constrain the doctrine of undisclosed agency as a matter of practice rather than principle: while insurance law's disclosure rules may encourage revelation of the principal's identity, there is no reason why non-disclosure of the identity of the assured even where material should preclude the normal intervention rights of an undisclosed principal, subject always to the insurer's right of avoidance. Should the insurer elect not to exercise, or otherwise lose, the right to avoid, the principal's position would solidify.

9.31   Where an insurer pays a claim arising out of a loss caused by the actionable fault of another party, the doctrine of subrogation permits the insurer to exercise the assured's legal rights against the culpable party in order to recoup the money paid to the assured. On the basis that subrogation rights are impliedly waived against parties entitled to benefit from the insurance contract, it has been held that the true interpretation of a policy will preclude the doctrine of the undisclosed principal from operating in favour of a potential subrogation defendant.[69] However, a circumstance that impairs recourse against a likely defendant to a subrogation claim will satisfy the definition of materiality and require disclosure.[70] Moreover, any implied waiver of subrogation rights might be restricted to co-assureds identified in the policy, and not benefit an undisclosed principal. It is suggested, therefore, that the protection of the insurer's legitimate expectations by way of subrogation rights does not require any denial of undisclosed agency.

---

[65]   Marine Insurance Act 1906, s 18(1) (articulating for the purposes of marine insurance a doctrine of general insurance contract law). For implication into s 18(1) of the requirement of inducement, see *Pan Atlantic Insurance Co Ltd v Pine Top Insurance Co Ltd* [1995] 1 AC 501. The insurer's disclosure entitlement was, however, abolished for consumer insurance by the Consumer Insurance (Disclosure and Representations) Act 2012. For the definition of consumer insurance, see ibid, s 1. Accordingly, the argument advanced in this section regarding the relationship between the disclosure rules of insurance law and undisclosed agency is inapplicable to consumer insurance.

[66]   For the definition of materiality, see Marine Insurance Act 1906, s 18(2), as considered by the House of Lords in *Pan Atlantic Insurance Co Ltd v Pine Top Insurance Co Ltd* [1995] 1 AC 501.

[67]   For the definition of inducement, see *Assicurazioni Generali SpA v Arab Insurance Group (BSC)* [2002] EWCA Civ 1642, [2003] Lloyd's Rep IR 131, [62].

[68]   *Siu Yin Kwan v Eastern Insurance Co Ltd* [1994] AC 199.

[69]   *Talbot Underwriting Ltd v Nausch, Hogan & Murray Inc (The Jascon 5)* [2006] EWCA Civ 889, [2006] 2 Lloyd's Rep 195.

[70]   *Tate & Sons v Hyslop* (1885) 15 QBD 368.

Protection of the Third Party

9.32 In return for according contractual standing to the undisclosed principal, the law requires and ensures that the third party is not prejudiced by the revelation that the counterparty apparently acting on its own behalf was in fact acting as an agent. The third party can, therefore, oppose against the undisclosed principal, once revealed, all defences and rights of set-off arising out of, or pertaining to, the contract by reason of the agent's conduct before revelation of the principal's existence.[71] The third party can, therefore, rescind the contract for misrepresentation by the agent, treat the contract as discharged by reason of repudiatory breach of contract committed by the agent, and hold the principal liable in damages for breach of contract committed by the agent. Once the existence of the principal is revealed, however, whether wrongdoing of the agent binds the principal depends upon the normal principles of attribution.

9.33 In principle, moreover, the third party should be entitled also to oppose against the principal all rights of set-off established against the apparent counterparty independently of the contract before the third party acquired actual notice of its status as agent.[72] The third party may be induced to contract with, as it believes, an apparent counterparty by reason of a pre-existing debt owed to it by the counterparty in order to obtain discharge of that debt through set-off against the consideration payable by the third party under the contract. The third party's legitimate expectations should not be frustrated by non-disclosure of the counterparty's true status. There is, however, a problematic case directly in point.

9.34 In *Greer v Downs Supply Co*,[73] the third party contracted for the purchase of goods in reliance on a fraudulent misrepresentation by the apparent counterparty, one Godwin, that Godwin was acting on his own behalf. Godwin owed the defendant money on a previous transaction, and the contract was concluded on the basis of part payment by set-off of the outstanding debt. In fact, Godwin procured delivery by his employer, which subsequently claimed the full contract price of the goods. The claim failed. A majority of the Court of Appeal seems to have held that the claimant was precluded from intervening in the contract at all because the set-off rendered the contract personal to Godwin.

---

[71] *Siu Yin Kwan v Eastern Insurance Co Ltd* [1994] 2 AC 199, 207. Similarly, all variations to the contract agreed before revelation of the agent's true status are binding on the principal: *Blackburn v Scholes* (1810) 2 Camp 341.

[72] *Rabone v Williams* (1785) 7 TR 360n; *George v Claggett* (1797) Peake Add Cas 131; *Browning v Provincial Insurance Co of Canada* (1873) LR 5 PC 263, 272. See also Restatement, § 6.06(2). In this respect, the position of an undisclosed principal is directly analogous to that of an assignee of the benefit of a contractual promise, although the analogy is far from complete: an assignee cannot incur liability on the contract, and see above, para 9.22.

[73] *Greer v Downs Supply Co* [1927] 2 KB 28.

9.35 Such reasoning, it is suggested, is questionable. The concept of the personal contract serves to protect the third party against being compelled to accept performance that is fundamentally incompatible with its legitimate expectations.[74] Extending the personal contract concept to set-off cases, however, serves only to frustrate the third party's intentions of obtaining the promised performance in return for payment in whole or in part through set-off of a pre-existing debt. Upholding the contract but subject to the set-off, as advocated by the third member of the Court of Appeal and supported by older authorities,[75] would afford the third party full satisfaction of its expectations.

9.36 Alternatively, it might be argued that Godwin had no actual authority to contract on behalf of his employer on terms of part-payment by set-off of a debt owed by Godwin personally, and an undisclosed principal cannot ratify.[76] And, indeed, the Divisional Court in *Greer v Downs* upheld the employer's claim on the basis of an absence of authority.[77] It is suggested, however, that authority is simply irrelevant. Orthodox principles of general contract law recognise a contract between third party and apparent counterparty. The issue is the price the undisclosed principal must pay as a matter of agency law for the adaptation of those principles for its accommodation.[78]

9.37 It may also be noted that equity will not assist an undisclosed principal by granting a decree of specific performance of an otherwise specifically enforceable contract where the third party has been induced to contract on the basis of a misrepresentation by the principal's agent that it was contracting on its own behalf.[79] Other remedies may, however, be available. Continued voluntary acceptance of the benefit of the contract after disclosure of the existence of the principal could provide the foundation for an implied contract directly between principal and third party. Moreover, the third party may incur strict liability in the tort of conversion by acting in respect of a chattel inconsistently with the rights of the principal as true owner.[80] There are, nevertheless, certain instances in which property rights in chattels can be defeated by dispositions other than by duly authorised agents.[81]

---

[74] See above, para 9.26.
[75] See above, n 72.
[76] See above, para 5.10.
[77] *Greer v Downs Supply Co* [1927] 2 KB 28, 30.
[78] Restatement, § 6.06, Comment C.
[79] *Archer v Stone* (1898) 78 LT 34.
[80] It is unclear whether the full facts of *Greer v Downs Supply Co* would have supported either of these claims. Neither was pleaded.
[81] Notably, the 'mercantile agent' provision in s 2(1) Factors Act 1889. See also the doctrine of apparent ownership: above, para 4.34.

Discharge of Payment Obligations

9.38　A payment obligation incurred by a third party on a contract concluded by an agent acting on behalf of a disclosed principal is owed to the principal as contracting party and cannot, in principle, be discharged by payment to any other party. Consequently, payment by way of discharge can be made to the agent only where the agent has authority, actual or apparent, to receive such payment. Receipt of payment in the absence of actual or apparent authority will effect discharge only if ratified by the principal.

9.39　Likewise, a payment obligation incurred by a disclosed principal on a contract concluded on its behalf by an agent cannot be discharged by settlement between principal and agent. The obligation is owed by the principal to the third party. If the principal transfers funds to the agent with the intention that the agent employs those funds to pay the third party, but the agent, by reason of fraud or insolvency, fails to do so, the third party is entitled to call upon the principal to find the funds a second time to make effective payment.[82] Exceptionally, however, the third party may represent to the principal either that it has received payment from the agent in discharge of the relevant obligation,[83] or that it has elected to look for payment to the agent to the exclusion of the principal.[84] Where, in such a case, the principal alters its position in reliance on the representation,[85] normally by transferring funds to the agent in purported reimbursement of payment already made or in order to enable future payment to be made, the third party will forfeit, through estoppel, any right to payment from the principal.[86]

9.40　In the case of an undisclosed principal, prior to revelation of the principal's existence, the third party may – indeed can only – discharge any payment obligation it owes on the contract by tendering payment to the agent.[87] Once the third party has actual notice (supported, presumably, by reasonable proof) of a principal's existence, the ability of receipt by an agent to effect a discharge of the third party's obligation depends upon the authority of the agent in the same manner as if the principal had been originally disclosed.[88]

---

[82]　*Irvine & Co v Watson & Sons* (1880) 5 QBD 414.

[83]　*Horsfall v Fauntleroy* (1830) 10 B & C 755 (third party contracted to sell goods on terms of delivery against payment but delivered without receiving payment).

[84]　*Smith v Ferrand* (1827) 7 B & C 19.

[85]　*Wyatt v Marquis of Hereford* (1802) 3 East 147 (although no reliance on the facts).

[86]　*Heald v Kenworthy* (1855) 10 Ex 739.

[87]　And it may do so in any manner as if the agent were indeed the contracting party it appears to be. The third party may, accordingly, avail itself of rights of set-off that it cannot oppose against the principal once revealed: see above, para 9.33 et seq.

[88]　Disclosure of the fact of agency may, of course, leave the principal unidentified. The Restatement, which considers the agent for an unidentified principal liable on the contract (above, para 9.16), entitles the third party to demand reasonable proof of both the alleged agency and the principal's identity and entitles the third party to obtain a good discharge by payment to the agent until receipt of such proof:

9.41 With respect to obligations owed to the third party under a contract concluded by undisclosed agency, discharge of liability requires performance in accordance with the terms of the contract. In principle, therefore, an obligation to pay money should require payment to the third party, or authorised payee.[89] It has, however, been held that settlement between undisclosed principal and agent while the existence of the principal remains unknown to the third party, so that the third party continues to rely on the credit of the agent alone, serves to discharge the principal as against the third party.[90] It is unclear whether this discharge rule is confined to payment obligations. Assume a contract of sale of goods under which the third party is the buyer. If one applies the same approach, supplying the agent, while the principal's existence remains undisclosed, with goods for delivery to the third party in satisfaction of the contract will discharge the principal's contractual liability for delivery. A liberty for the principal to settle payment obligations with the agent may, therefore, illustrate a general rule or it may constitute an anomalous, isolated exception. Its justification appears to be that it would be unfair to the principal to compel it to pay twice when it has paid the agent at a time when, the agency remaining undisclosed, the third party looked exclusively to the agent for satisfaction of the payment obligation.[91] Any unfairness is, however, the result of the principal's own election to operate through undisclosed agency; a convincing justification for affording an undisclosed principal discharge privileges not enjoyed by a principal that reveals the full contractual picture to the third party at the outset is elusive. On the contrary, since the principal enjoys a latent privilege of personally suing the third party that it can activate whenever it wishes by revealing its existence, reciprocity would suggest the third party (disabled by lack of knowledge from any election to trigger direct liability) should automatically enjoy an entitlement to the tendering of payment directly to itself.[92]

9.42 Applying to undisclosed principals the same approach adopted to disclosed principals would still admit of the possibility of acts of the third party inducing settlement between the principal and undisclosed agent so as to discharge the principal's payment liability. Where, for example, the third party provides a document that erroneously evidences payment by the agent and is not expressed to be confidential, payment to the agent induced by such document could serve to discharge the principal's liability. The non-confidential nature of the document

---

§ 6.07(3)(c). And see D de Mott, 'Statutory Ingredients in Common Law Change: Issues in the Development of Agency Doctrine' in S Worthington (ed) *Commercial Law & Commercial Practice* (Oxford, Hart Publishing, 2003), ch 3, pp 73–75.

[89] This is the reasoning and the approach of the Restatement: see § 6.07, Comment (d).

[90] *Armstrong v Stokes* (1872) LR 7 QB 598.

[91] 'Intolerable hardship' ibid, 610 (Blackburn J). And see F Reynolds, 'Practical Problems of the Undisclosed Principal Doctrine' [1983] *Current Legal Problems* 119, 133–35.

[92] In *Irvine & Co v Watson & Sons* (1880) 5 QBD 414, the Court of Appeal either doubted the validity of separate rules for disclosed and undisclosed principal regarding settlement with the agent as held in *Armstrong v Stokes*, or suggested that the latter case might turn on a local trade custom.

would permit interpretation as containing representations to the world, capable of founding an estoppel against the third party.[93]

Alternative Liability

9.43   In those circumstances where both agent and principal are liable on the contract, namely in cases of disclosed agency where the agent manifests a personal engagement with the contract additional to that of the principal and in cases of undisclosed agency, the established default position of English law is of alternative liability.[94] Subject to contrary intention of joint liability,[95] the third party is entitled to enforce its claims against either agent or principal but not against both. Controversially, if the third party pursues a claim against either agent or disclosed principal to judgment, it cannot thereafter pursue a claim in respect of the same loss against the other if the judgment obtained proves incapable of enforcement so as to satisfy the claim.[96] Even more controversially, the same principle applies in cases of undisclosed agency, so that the third party can lose its rights against the principal before it discovers the existence of the alternative defendant and despite the fact that the judgment obtained against the agent remains unsatisfied.[97]

9.44   Where the third party is aware of the existence of two potential defendants, a doctrine of election may explain why pursuit of rights against one party liable imports forfeiture of rights against a known other. Absence of knowledge of material circumstances, however, precludes election from explaining forfeiture of rights against a still undisclosed principal. Instead, the main underlying principle appears to be 'merger of liability': although both principal and agent are liable to be sued, there is only one contract and only one liability.[98] Once pursued to judgment, that liability is exhausted: the liability is considered to merge into the judgment.[99] The third party will, therefore, forfeit rights against one potential defendant if it either pursues a claim to judgment against the alternative or otherwise makes an informed, unequivocal election to hold one of two known potential defendants liable, to the exclusion of the other.[100]

---

[93] Such generosity of interpretation would be consistent with the commercial convenience underpinning undisclosed agency generally.

[94] *Marel Bros & Co Ltd v Earl of Westmorland* [1994] AC 11; [1903] 1 KB 64, affd [1904] AC 11 (rejecting an argument for joint liability).

[95] See, eg, *Middle East Tankers & Freighters Bunker Services SA v Abu Dhabi Container Lines PJSC* [2002] 2 Lloyd's Rep 643. Where joint liability is established, the recovery of judgment against one debtor does not release the other: Civil Liability (Contribution) Act 1978, s 3.

[96] *Marel Bros & Co Ltd v Earl of Westmorland* [1904] AC 11; *RMKRM (a firm) v MRMVL (a firm)* [1926] AC 761.

[97] *Priestly v Fernie* (1863) 3 H & C 977; *Kendall v Hamilton* (1879) 4 App Cas 504, 514.

[98] *Barrington v Lee* [1972] 1 QB 326, 348.

[99] *Moore v Flanagan* [1920] 1 KB 919.

[100] The prospects of establishing such an election are, however, remote.

9.45   The merits of this approach are, however, elusive. It is simply not credible to consider, in the absence of an explicit release, that the third party truly elects to relinquish rights against the alternative defendant unless and until judgment is not only obtained against the other but also satisfied so as to discharge the underlying debt. Moreover, the doctrine of merger of liability, it is suggested, is merely a circular, technical explanation, devoid of convincing justification.[101] Concerns about proper measures of recovery, which may underpin it,[102] are misplaced: where, for example, an assured has suffered an insured loss by reason of a legal wrong, rights of indemnification under the insurance policy and of suit against the culpable party subsist independently of either other, and enforcement of one does not discharge the other. Issues of double recovery are addressed by the doctrine of subrogation. The Restatement duly rejects any forfeiture of rights in the absence of a representation that the third party will look exclusively to one party for satisfaction of liability on which the other party relies to its detriment, giving rise to an estoppel.[103]

An Agent's Warranty of Authority

9.46   A third party that deals with an agent for a disclosed principal will naturally assume that the agent is acting within the scope of its actual authority and may arrange its affairs in reliance on the creation of legally binding rights against the principal. Where the agent has in fact acted without actual authority, the third party may be able to invoke apparent authority against the principal, or the principal may elect to ratify. Otherwise, and assuming the agent has not accepted personal liability on the contract, the third party's reliance may result in the incurring of loss. The loss arising from the absence of rights on the supposed contract, the third party must seek redress against the agent outside the purported transaction.

9.47   The third party may be able to avail itself of a tort claim, but usually elects to invoke a collateral contract. An agent acting for a disclosed principal is considered impliedly both to represent and to warrant that it acts within the scope of its actual authority. In appropriate circumstances, the third party can invoke the implied representation as the basis for a tort action in deceit or negligent misstatement. An absence of authority may, however, arise without the commission of a tort, and the law of agency imposes the risk of an absence of authority upon the agent rather than the third party, irrespective of whether the agent is considered a wrongdoer under the law of tort. An agent acting for a disclosed principal

---

[101]   *Moore v Flanagan* [1920] 1 KB 919, 925 (Scrutton LJ), but *cf* ibid, 927 (Atkin LJ).
[102]   *Kendall v Hamilton* (1879) 4 App Cas 504, 514–15; *RMKRM (a firm) v MRMVL (a firm)* [1926] AC 761, 770–71.
[103]   Restatement, § 6.09. For the estoppel exception, see Comment (d).

is, therefore, considered to warrant that it is acting within the scope of its actual authority, the warranty giving rise to a collateral contract on which the agent incurs strict liability for any loss caused to the third party should the agent in fact lack authority.[104]

9.48 Liability for breach of the warranty of authority being strict, an agent will incur liability even if it has neither knowledge nor the means of knowledge that its authority has terminated. Solicitors who commenced authorised proceedings have, accordingly, been held personally liable for all costs incurred by the defendants after their client, unknown to them, became insane, the onset of insanity terminating their actual authority.[105]

9.49 Damages for breach of the warranty of authority compensate the third party for loss it sustains by reason of the absence of authority. Causation between breach and loss must be proved. Where the third party can hold the principal to the unauthorised contract through the doctrine of apparent authority or where the principal elects to ratify the transaction, the breach of warranty occasions no loss.[106] Where and to the extent that the principal could not or would not have performed the contract in any event, the loss caused by the breach of warranty and the damages payable for that breach are extinguished or commensurately reduced. Moreover, the agent is entitled to invoke any defence available to the principal if the contract had been authorised. Where, for example, the third party fails or would have failed to perform the unauthorised contract so as to obtain the contemplated benefit, the agent incurs no liability since the non-performance negates any causal link between the absence of authority and the loss accruing to the principal.[107]

9.50 In respect of recoverable losses, the warranty protects the third party's expectation interest: the measure of damages recoverable against the agent is equivalent to that recoverable by the third party against the principal if the agent's acts had been authorised and the principal had then failed to perform the contract. The damages are quantified by calculating the benefit that would have accrued to the third party had the agent had the warranted authority and then crediting any benefit that has accrued to the third party despite the absence of authority.[108]

---

[104] *Collen v Wright* (1857) 8 E & B 647; (1857) 7 E & B 301. See generally, F Reynolds, 'Breach of Warranty of Authority in Modern Times' [2012] *Lloyd's Maritime and Commercial Law Quarterly* 189.

[105] *Yonge v Toynbee* [1910] 1 KB 215. Such unwitting incurral of liability would be avoided by a different approach to the termination of actual authority. Restatement, § 3.08(1) provides for termination of actual authority by the onset of mental incapacity of a principal who is a natural person only when the agent has notice thereof. See generally, below, para 11.15.

[106] DCFR, art II-6:107(1), (2).

[107] *Singh v Sardar Investments Ltd* [2002] EWCA 1706, [2002] NPC 134.

[108] *Firbank's Executors v Humphreys* (1886) 18 QBD 54, 60, 62–63. Likewise, PECL, art 3:204(2); PICC, art 2.2.6(1); DCFR, art II-6:107(2); Restatement, § 6.10.

9.51   The warranty is not confined to the third party: the agent incurs liability to any party to whom on the facts authority is warranted and who sustains loss through reliance on the existence of the warranted authority. It is not a condition of being able to invoke the warranty against the agent that the claimant contracts with the principal in reliance on the warranted authority.[109] In order to generate collateral contractual liability, consideration must be given by the promisee in return for the promise, but contracting with another party will suffice.[110] Accordingly, a warranty of authority to make statements included in a negotiable bill of lading (a commercial document designed to facilitate successive sales of the cargo represented by the bill and to be transferable down a chain of purchasers) is made to, and breach is actionable by, any subsequent holder of the bill of lading who purchased the cargo represented by the bill in reliance on the authority of the signatory of the bill to make the statements in the bill on behalf of the carrier.[111]

9.52   The warranty is merely as to the fact of authority, as to which the agent has actual knowledge. An agent does not warrant the good character or financial reliability, or indeed any other attribute, of its principal, as to which no assumption of knowledge on the part of an agent can be made so as to justify the imposition of strict liability.[112] No warranty, therefore, is generally implied as to the principal's identity: identity is usually not material of itself but serves rather as an indication of character or solvency. Moreover, even in a case where identity is material of itself, it cannot be assumed that the agent will have, or at least ought to have, accurate knowledge of the principal's true identity.[113] And in cases of an inaccuracy in the correct styling of the principal's identity, as opposed to wrong identification, no loss is likely to result that justifies a general extension of strict liability to the principal's identity, correctly styled.[114]

9.53   A warranty of authority is not presumed as a matter of law but inferred as a proposition of fact.[115] Accordingly, no action for breach of warranty can lie where in truth the agent makes no promise of authority, whether as a matter of the true interpretation of the contract[116] or by reason of the terms of the inter-

---

[109]   *Penn v Bristol & West Building Society* [1997] 1 WLR 1356 (lender financing purchase of house by third party in return for security right nullified by reason of breach of warranty).

[110]   ibid, 1363.

[111]   *Rasnoimport V/O v Guthrie & Co Ltd* [1966] 1 Lloyd's Rep 1.

[112]   Accordingly, solicitors issuing proceedings do not warrant that their client has a good cause of action, or is solvent and, therefore, able to pay the other party's costs if the action is unsuccessful: *Nelson v Nelson* [1997] 1 WLR 233.

[113]   *SEB Trygg Liv Holding AB v Manches* [2005] EWCA Civ 1237, [2006] 1 WLR 2276 (solicitors do not warrant that the name in which proceedings are issued is their client's true name). Nothing, of course, precludes a third party contracting with the agent for an express warranty of the principal's identity.

[114]   *Knight Frank LLP v Du Haney* [2011] EWCA Civ 404.

[115]   *Halbot v Lens* [1901] 1 Ch 344, 351.

[116]   *Lilly, Wilson & Co v Smales, Eeles & Co* [1892] 1 QB 456.

action between agent and claimant outside the contract.[117] Even where a promise of authority does exist, moreover, there can be no reliance on the promise as required for an action for breach of warranty where the claimant knows of the agent's lack of authority,[118] or does not in fact rely upon the agent's statement of authority but seeks independent verification.[119]

[117] *Halbot v Lens* [1901] 1 Ch 344, 350–51; *Yonge v Toynbee* [1910] 1 KB 215, 227. Although an agent could give an undertaking to obtain authority or to exercise reasonable endeavours in seeking authority: *Halbot v Lens* [1901] 1 Ch 344, 351.

[118] Subjective awareness is required, consistently with the approach to reliance in the context of apparent authority (see above, para 4.12). Likewise PECL, art 3:204(2); Restatement, § 6.10(3). *Cf* PICC, art 2.2.6(2); DCFR, art II-6:107(3), which deny liability where the third party should have known the agent lacked authority.

[119] See the example given in *Beattie v Lord Ebury* (1872) LR 7 Ch App 777, 800–01 (although the point in issue was the since overruled distinction between misrepresentations of fact and law).

10

Agency and Tort

10.1 The interaction of agency with the law of tort raises questions not only of personal liability on the part of the agent and the principal for torts committed directly by themselves, but also of a principal's vicarious liability for the torts of its agent.

An Agent's Liability in Tort

10.2 An agent incurs tortious liability to the third party in accordance with ordinary principles of tort law: that an agent's tortious conduct occurs in the course of agency affords the agent no defence. Accordingly, the managing director (M) of a trading company who collaborated in the production of fraudulently backdated bills of lading that the company then presented to a bank under a letter of credit[1] along with a written assurance of compliance with the terms of the credit signed by M, despite his knowledge of its falsity, incurred personal liability to the bank in the tort of deceit. That M was at all material times acting on behalf of the trading company detracted in no way from his responsibility in the law of tort for his own actions.[2]

10.3 Personal liability in tort does, however, require personal commission of the tort. Thus, a negligent misstatement by an agent in the course of representing its principal will engender personal liability of the agent only where the third party can establish a duty of care owed to it by the agent through an assumption of personal responsibility for the statement. Even where the agent has authority to evince an assumption of responsibility on the part of the principal, it does not

---

[1] A letter of credit is a banking transaction commonly employed in international trade whereby a bank undertakes an obligation independent of the underlying sale contract to pay a seller on presentation of specified documents. The seller thereby avoids the risk of non-payment by a buyer in a foreign jurisdiction, while the specified documents will have been chosen to provide evidence of performance by the seller of its obligations under the sale contract.
[2] *Standard Chartered Bank v Pakistan National Shipping Corp (Nos 2 & 4)* [2002] UKHL 43, [2003] 1 AC 959. See also *Lewis v Yeeles* [2010] EWCA Civ 326 (company director personally liable for inducing breach of contract).

follow that the agent thereby undertakes personal liability.[3] The terms of engagement between agent and third party may also explicitly deny any assumption of responsibility or exclude or limit liability subject to the statutory controls on exemption clauses.[4]

A Principal's Personal Liability in Tort

10.4   A principal will incur personal liability in tort to the third party where its own conduct either directly or through the agent as an instrument fulfils the requirements of the law of tort. Conduct of the agent will engender personal tortious liability of the principal where either mandated by the terms of the agent's actual authority or initially unauthorised but subsequently ratified.[5] With respect to torts of strict liability, no further gloss is necessary. An authorised act of the agent that constitutes a tortious interference with a chattel of the third party renders the principal personally liable to the third party in conversion. Where, however, the tort requires an element of direct, personal engagement, this must be proved on the part of the principal. The prime example is provided by the tort of deceit.

10.5   Liability in deceit requires conscious wrongdoing in that the representation must be made with knowledge of its falsity, without belief in its truth, or carelessly, aware of the possibility of its falseness but made nonetheless without reservation.[6] Accordingly, the principal cannot incur personal liability in the tort of deceit through a false statement on the part of the agent unless the principal is complicit in one of the following ways: (a) authorising the agent to make the statement, the principal being possessed of the requisite knowledge or suspicion of the statement's falsity, or (b) standing by without reservation and thereby deceitfully condoning the making of a statement that the principal knows or suspects is false, or (c) deceitfully procuring a false representation by, for example, supplying information to the agent that the principal knows or suspects is false with the aim that the agent incorporates that information in a misstatement to the third party. It follows that a division of the elements for deceit can result in neither principal nor agent incurring liability to a misled third party. Assume that the agent makes a false statement but has neither knowledge nor suspicion of its falsity. Assume further that the principal knows or suspects the truth such that any statement by itself would constitute deceit but that it has not acted deceitfully

---

[3]   *Williams v Natural Life Health Foods Ltd* [1998] 1 WLR 830. Tort law must be careful not to undermine the principle of the independence of the liability of a company from its directors, servants, other agents, or investors: ibid, 834–35.

[4]   *Overbrooke Estates Ltd v Glencombe Properties Ltd* [1974] 1 WLR 1335; *Avrora Fine Arts Investment Ltd v Christie, Manson & Woods Ltd* [2012] EWHC 2198 (Ch), [2012] PNLR 35.

[5]   On ratification of tortious conduct, see above, para 5.16.

[6]   *Derry v Peek* (1889) 14 App Cas 337.

by authorising, condoning, or procuring the making of a statement known or suspected to be false. Neither the agent nor the principal has committed the tort of deceit. Both are innocent, and the innocence of the one cannot be added to the innocence of the other to produce liability in deceit.[7]

10.6   Liability in negligence depends upon establishing a duty of care owed by the defendant to the claimant. A principal cannot incur liability on the basis of an authorised, condoned or procured act of negligence on the part of the agent unless the principal itself owes the third party a duty of care.[8]

10.7   In addition, as with the tort of deceit, complicity of the principal is required for personal liability in negligence. In *Anderson (WB) & Sons Ltd v Rhodes (Liverpool) Ltd,*[9] for example, the defendant company operated in the potato market sometimes on its own account and sometimes as intermediary. Having contracted with a buyer on its own account over a period of time, it elected to act henceforth as an intermediary. Its agent for introducing potential contracting parties (R) introduced the claimant seller to the buyer and gave the seller an assurance as to the creditworthiness of the buyer. Knowing that its principal had been content to deal with the buyer, R was not negligent. However, its principal should have known, but through a failure to maintain and monitor financial records properly did not know, and, therefore, did not inform R as it should have done that the buyer habitually incurred levels of indebtedness generally considered unacceptable in the market. Consequently, having negligently caused R to make a material misrepresentation that induced the claimant to contract with the buyer, the principal was held liable in negligence for loss ensuing when the buyer became insolvent.

10.8   Where a misrepresentation induces entry into a contract with the representor, liability may arise under section 2(1) of the Misrepresentation Act 1967. Although the misrepresentation may be made by an agent, liability under the statute can be incurred only by a contracting party, which in most instances will be the principal, so that the agent will not be liable to the misrepresentee.[10] Liability arises prima facie simply by virtue of the fact of a misrepresentation that induces a contract resulting in loss, but the representor is excused if it proves a reasonable and honest belief in the truth of the facts represented continuing from the time of the representation to the time of conclusion of the contract. Since liability under the statute may only be incurred by the principal, the defence will be established by reference only to the honesty and absence of negligence of the principal even

---

[7] *Cornfoot v Fowke* (1840) 6 M & W 358; *Armstrong v Strain* [1952] 1 KB 232. And see P Devlin, 'Fraudulent Misrepresentation: Division of Responsibility Between Principal and Agent' (1937) 53 *Law Quarterly Review* 344.

[8] *Anderson (WB) & Sons Ltd v Rhodes (Liverpool) Ltd* [1967] 2 All ER 850, 856–62; *Skandinaviska Enskilda Banken AB v Asia Pacific Breweries (Singapore) Pte Ltd* [2011] SGCA 22, [2011] SLR 540.

[9] *Anderson (WB) & Sons Ltd v Rhodes (Liverpool) Ltd* [1967] 2 All ER 850.

[10] *Resolute Maritime Inc v Nippon Kaiji Kyokai (The Skopas)* [1983] 1 WLR 857.

where the representation was made by an agent.[11] Where the principal is a legal person, it will be necessary to identify the person whose mind is to be equated with the principal for the purposes of section 2(1) of the 1967 Act, who may or may not be the person who made the representation.[12]

Liability of a Principal for the Torts of an Agent

Vicarious Liability

10.9   The doctrine of vicarious liability imposes strict liability on an innocent superior for the tortious conduct of a subordinate. The doctrine is informed by the basic idea that a party that pursues its own interests in a manner that necessarily generates a risk of rendering another the victim of a tort should bear the loss if that risk duly materialises. Consequently, where pursuit of the superior's enterprise involves entrusting subordinates with inherently risk-bearing activities, fairness requires the superior to assume responsibility for the conduct of its subordinates in carrying out their duties. In practice, moreover, such imposition of liability may serve both to maximise the satisfaction of liabilities in that the superior will often be in a better position to meet claims or to insure against liabilities,[13] and also to prevent harm from occurring by incentivising the superior, against whom the establishing of any personal liability may be extremely challenging, to select, train, and monitor its subordinates more diligently.[14]

10.10   Risk-generating pursuit of interest may inform and justify vicarious liability, but it does not constitute a test for its imposition. Two requirements must be satisfied, namely an appropriate relationship between superior and subordinate, and an appropriate connection between that relationship and the conduct of the subordinate.[15]

---

[11] *MCI Worldcom International Inc v Primus Telecommunications Inc* [2003] EWHC 2182 (Comm), [2004] 1 All ER (Comm) 138, [57]–[59], revd on other grounds [2004] EWCA Civ 957, [2004] 2 All ER (Comm) 833.

[12] [2003] EWHC 2182 (Comm), [58]–[60]. In *Howard Marine & Dredging Co Ltd v A Ogden & Sons (Excavations) Ltd* [1978] QB 574, the representor was the ultimate decision-maker of the company and, therefore, the relevant person by reference to whose mind the applicability of the defence was to be determined.

[13] Although the doctrine is not to be applied simply to effect distributive justice on what the court perceives to be the factual merits: *Jacobi v Griffiths* [1999] 2 SCR 570, (1999) 174 DLR (4th) 71, [29].

[14] *Bazley v Curry* [1999] 2 SCR 534, (1999) 174 DLR (4th) 45, [26]–[34]; *Lister v Hesley Hall Ltd* [2001] UKHL 22, [2002] 1 AC 215, [65]; *Dubai Aluminium Co Ltd v Salaam* [2002] UKHL 48, [2003] 2 AC 366, [75]; *Viasystems (Tyneside) v Thermal Transfer (Northern) Ltd* [2005] EWCA Civ 1151, [2006] QB 510, [55]; *Catholic Church Welfare Society v Various Claimants* [2012] UKSC 56, [2012] 3 WLR 1319, [34], [84]–[87].

[15] *Catholic Church Welfare Society v Various Claimants* [2012] UKSC 56, [2012] 3 WLR 1319, [21].

10.11   Apparently reflecting a general assumption of the extent to which an employer can control and monitor the conduct of an employee, as opposed to that of an independent contractor engaged to undertake duties but with discretion as to the manner of discharge of those duties,[16] the doctrine of vicarious liability has traditionally been restricted to the relationship of employer and employee. A recognition, however, that the rationale for imposing vicarious liability is not coterminous with the limits of the employment relationship has led in turn to recognition of the possibility of vicarious liability in the context of relationships 'akin to employment'.[17] A number of related factors are relevant in determining whether the relationship between the parties possesses the requisite kinship:[18] first, the extent to which the defendant enjoys control over the tortfeasor in the sense of a power of direction over the role and work to be undertaken by the subordinate;[19] secondly, the degree of centrality of the work to the activities of the defendant; thirdly, the extent to which the carrying out of the activity is integrated into the defendant's organisational structures; and, fourthly, the extent to which the tortfeasor is truly operating in a commercially independent manner, assuming risks and benefiting from profits. Accordingly, in cases of transferred employment – where a contracting party supplies personnel it employs to work under the direction, and for all relevant intents and purposes as if also employed by, its contractual counterparty – not only the true employer but also the counterparty may be vicariously liable.[20]

10.12   The mere fact of an appropriate relationship does not, however, suffice for the imposition of vicarious liability. Even an employer cannot have liability imposed in respect of all torts committed by employees irrespective of the circumstances: a connection is required between the conduct of the employee that constitutes a tort and the duties assumed under the employment appropriate for the imposition of liability on an otherwise innocent employer. Traditionally and generally, this is expressed by saying that the tortious conduct must occur 'in the course of the employment', a concept sometimes sought to be explained through a distinction between unauthorised acts, for which an employer is not liable, and the performance of authorised acts in an unauthorised manner, for which an employer is vicariously liable. This distinction, which can be easier to state than to apply, has been said should be applied to favour the third party victim of a tort the

---

[16]   See Restatement, § 7.07(3)(a).

[17]   *JGE v Trustees of the Portsmouth Roman Catholic Diocesan Trust* [2012] EWCA Civ 938, [2012] 4 All ER 1152; *Catholic Church Welfare Society v Various Claimants* [2012] UKSC 56, [2012] 3 WLR 1319, [47].

[18]   *JGE v Trustees of the Portsmouth Roman Catholic Diocesan Trust* [2012] EWCA Civ 938, [2012] 4 All ER 1152, [72], [131].

[19]   The evolving expertise of individual workers has transformed the question of control: the enquiry cannot any longer relate to how the relevant work is to be done but only to what work is to be undertaken. Tortfeasor autonomy as to the methods of achieving the goal for which it has been retained is, therefore, not inconsistent with vicarious liability: *Catholic Church Welfare Society v Various Claimants* [2012] UKSC 56, [2012] 3 WLR 1319, [36].

[20]   *Viasystems (Tyneside) v Thermal Transfer (Northern) Ltd* [2005] EWCA Civ 1511, [2006] QB 510.

commission of which arises out of the pursuit of the employer's business.[21] Accordingly, an employer has been held liable for fire damage where an employed lorry driver negligently lit and discarded a cigarette during transfer of petrol from the lorry to a tank,[22] but not liable when a bus conductor stepped outside his duties of collecting fares and negligently drove a bus, running over the claimant.[23]

10.13   The language of the traditional approach is, however, ill-suited to intentional torts. Instead, a broad and flexible approach has to be adopted to the degree of closeness between the employment and the tortious conduct in order to determine whether it is fair and just in all the circumstances to impose vicarious liability on the employer. In particular, employers should be vicariously liable in respect of risks inherent to the nature of the employee's duties.[24] Thus, while the deliberate sexual abuse of pupils in a boarding school or the violent assault of persons seeking entry to a night club can hardly be described as simply an unauthorised way of performing the duties of the warden of a boarding house or of a night club doorman respectively, the risk of such assaults is inherent in such employment and such assaults have accordingly engendered vicarious liability.[25] Liability would not, however, attach in respect of a sexual assault on another member of staff or an armed assault on a passer-by not seeking entry to the club as such assaults would lack the requisite close connection with the employee's duties. Likewise, an employer was held liable when an employee stole part of the contents of a shipping container he was employed to fumigate: the performance of his duties both afforded knowledge of the contents and necessarily involved access to them, rendering theft an inherent risk of the employment,[26] although theft by an employee whose duties did not involve contact with the stolen property would engender no liability in the employer.[27]

10.14   It is important to note, however, that nothing about the intentional nature of a tort demands a different level of preparedness of the law to the recognition of vicarious liability. Developments in respect of intentional torts are intended not to apply fundamentally different criteria but rather to address problems in the factual application of traditional formulations of the test.[28] Indeed, the formulation developed to accommodate intentional torts is likely to gain general applicability to torts both intentional and non-intentional.

---

[21] *Kay v ITW Ltd* [1968] 1 QB 140, 156.

[22] *Century Insurance Co Ltd v Northern Ireland Road Transport Board* [1942] AC 509.

[23] *Beard v London General Omnibus Co* [1900] 2 QB 530.

[24] *Lister v Lesley Hall Ltd* [2001] UKHL 22, [2002] 1 AC 215; *Dubai Aluminium Co Ltd v Salaam* [2002] UKHL 48, [2003] 2 AC 366, [23]; *Bernard v Attorney-General of Jamaica* [2004] UKPC 47, [2005] IRLR 398, [18].

[25] *Lister v Lesley Hall Ltd* [2001] UKHL 22, [2002] 1 AC 215; *Mattis v Pollock* [2003] EWCA Civ 887, [2003] 1 WLR 2158.

[26] *Brink's Global Services Inc v Igrox Ltd* [2010] EWCA Civ 1207, [2011] IRLR 343.

[27] *Lister v Hesley Hall Ltd* [2001] UKHL 22, [2002] 1 AC 215, [79].

[28] Although they may connote a slight expansion in the scope of vicarious liability: *Brink's Global Services Inc v Igrox Ltd* [2010] EWCA Civ 1207, [2011] IRLR 343, [31], [34]–[37].

Vicarious Liability for Torts of Misstatement

10.15   A different approach is adopted with respect to vicarious liability for the tort of deceit: the tort law concept of course of employment is tied to, and effectively replaced by, the agency doctrine of apparent authority. Under that doctrine, the principal will be bound by any act of the agent appearing to fall within the agent's actual authority, notwithstanding that it is perpetrated in pursuance of a fraud and irrespective of whether the victim of the fraud is the principal or a third party.[29] The justice of imposing vicarious liability on an innocent employer for an employee's fraudulent misstatement is established by the employer's words or conduct that induce the third party to believe that the employee is acting in the course of employment, here meaning in the scope of its authority, in making the statement.[30] This narrows the scope of liability. The course of employment usually extends to all acts closely connected to the carrying out of the engaged duties. Apparent authority is confined to those acts that a reasonable person in the position of the third party would believe fell within the scope of the duties of the agent in question. A sexual assault may fall within the course of employment, as that concept is generally conceived, but it is inconceivable that it could fall within apparent authority. With respect to representations, however, the essence of the tort is being misled: the victim is induced voluntarily to walk into the injury rather than having the injury visited upon him. The law is prepared to impose liability upon the employer for injury caused to the involuntary victim even though it may be obvious that the tortious conduct was unauthorised. In the context of representations, however, where the statement falls outside the employee's apparent authority, a third party that voluntarily elects to proceed in reliance upon the statement reposes faith exclusively in the employee and is not entitled to look to the employer in the event of resulting loss.[31]

10.16   On the basis that the critical factor behind the resort to agency reasoning is the reliance element of the tort, the same approach should apply to vicarious liability for all torts of misrepresentation, whether at common law in deceit or negligence or under the Misrepresentation Act 1967. And indeed, the Privy Council held a valuation company not vicariously liable for a negligent valuation

---

[29]   *Lloyd v Grace, Smith & Co* [1912] AC 716; *Briess v Woolley* [1954] AC 333.

[30]   *Armagas Ltd v Mundogas SA (The Ocean Frost)* [1986] AC 717, 782–83.

[31]   [1986] AC 717, 739–40 (CA), 783 (HL). It follows also that an undisclosed principal cannot incur vicarious liability for deceit, except perhaps where the principal is estopped from disputing the statement: see above, para 4.33. In Singapore, the close connection test has been held to extend to deceit as more readily admitting considerations of fairness: *Skandinaviska Enskilda Banken AB v Asia Pacific Breweries (Singapore) Pte Ltd* [2011] SGCA 22, [2011] 3 SLR 540. On the facts, however, there was neither the requisite representation to establish apparent authority nor vicarious liability on the close connection test, and the circumstances that rendered the imposition of vicarious liability unfair would, it is suggested, have denied reasonable reliance on any representation of authority: ibid, [93]–[94].

in the absence of apparent authority.[32] A more recent rejection of agency reasoning by the Court of Appeal in favour of the general test of close connection to employment (obiter, since on the facts the employer was not liable irrespective of the test to be applied) is, with respect, unconvincing, the analysis being confined to noting the generality with which the close connection test has been expressed together with the deceit-specific language of the cases adopting agency reasoning.[33] None of the authorities cited, however, were concerned specifically with torts of misstatement, no reference was made to the Privy Council decision, and the Court of Appeal failed entirely to identify and address the underlying reasoning behind the agency analysis adopted in the deceit cases.[34]

10.17   The critical nature of reliance leads also to the conclusion that agency reasoning is inapplicable to vicarious liability for fraud in the context of bribery. Consequently, the principal will be vicariously liable in damages for loss caused by fraud where the principal's agent bribes the third party's agent in order to procure a contract between principal and third party. The principal has no defence based on an absence of authority to offer a bribe since the cause of action does not invoke a fraudulent misrepresentation inducing reliance but rather the secret corruption of the recipient of the bribe.[35]

Independent Contractors

10.18   The fundamental distinction drawn in the law of vicarious liability between employees (and subordinates akin to employees) and independent contractors is too deeply embedded to be extracted,[36] and, as already noted, dictates that the pursuit of interest through the engagement of another to undertake duties inherently subject to the risk of tortious conduct is not, of itself, sufficient to engage vicarious liability.[37] In an era, however, where the mode of pursuit of business activities is increasingly regarded not as inherent in the nature of the business but as facultative according to regulatory, fiscal, and efficiency concerns, it may be considered increasingly unsatisfactory for the rights of a third party tort victim to depend upon the happenstance of the organisation of a business and the extent to which interaction with third party customers and other activities are outsourced to independent contractors. Thus, whether a sales representative is

---

[32] *Kooragang Investments Pty Ltd v Richardson & Wrench Ltd* [1982] AC 462. For confirmation of the apparent authority basis of *Kooragang*, see *Dubai Aluminium Co Ltd v Salaam* [2002] UKHL 48, [2003] 2 AC 366, [127].

[33] *So v HSBC Bank plc* [2009] EWCA Civ 296, [2009] 1 CLC 503, [53]–[63].

[34] For an extended discussion critical of *So v HSBC Bank plc*, see P Watts, 'Principals' Tortious Liability for Agents' Negligent Statements – Is "Authority" Necessary?' (2012) 128 *Law Quarterly Review* 260.

[35] *Petrotrade Inc v Smith* [2000] CLC 916, [19]. On the nature of the claim as distinct from the tort of deceit, see also above, para 6.45.

[36] *Sweeney v Boylan Nominees Pty Ltd* [2006] HCA 19, (2006) 226 CLR 161, [33].

[37] ibid, [13].

retained on an employed or self-employed basis may be driven by factors ranging from an unscrupulous attitude to child support obligations[38] to a more principled – or at least strategic – consideration of financial rights under the Commercial Agents Regulations. It is questionable, however, whether either matter should impact upon the remedies available to a third party victim of a tort committed by the representative, and there are, indeed, two doctrines under which the conduct of an independent contractor can result in liability of its principal.[39]

Non-Delegable Obligations

10.19   Certain obligations are considered by law to import a warranty of due performance. The obligee is permitted to delegate performance of the obligation to an independent contractor, but cannot delegate responsibility for non-performance. Should the contractor fail to fulfil such a 'non-delegable' obligation, its principal (the obligee) will incur personal and strict liability.

10.20   Characterisation of an obligation as non-delegable generates, therefore, an end result parallel to the imposition of vicarious liability, albeit that the principal's liability is primary. Since widespread recognition of non-delegable obligations would undermine the non-applicability of vicarious liability to independent contractors, it is unsurprising that only a minority of obligations have non-delegable status. An underlying rationale for their characterisation has yet to be authoritatively articulated, although a likelihood of harm to others in the event of non-performance is a common theme.[40] Accordingly, for example, under the Hague-Visby Rules a carrier is obliged to ensure that due diligence is exercised with respect to the seaworthiness of a ship and is, therefore, liable where independent ship repairers negligently survey a ship, thereby failing to identify a defect rendering it unseaworthy in a manner that subsequently damages cargo,[41] and a landowner undertakes that a contractor engaged to clear bushes by fire will take all reasonable precautions to prevent the spread of fire to neighbouring properties.[42]

'Representative Agency'

10.21   A principal's liability may also be engaged through the concept of 'representative agency', recognised in Australian jurisprudence as a basis for vicarious liability, and attaching to actions of independent contractors performed not just

[38] Above, para 2.20.
[39] It is possible, moreover, that increased recognition of vicarious liability as underpinned by enterprise liability may herald a fundamental reorientation of the scope of vicarious liability away from the formal legal relationship between principal and representative towards the commercial relationship between the principal's enterprise and the services provided by the representative. See D Brodie, 'Enterprise Liability: Justifying Vicarious Liability' (2007) 27 *Oxford Journal of Legal Studies* 493.
[40] Restatement, § 7.06 attaches non-delegability to obligations 'required by contract or otherwise by law to protect another'. See also *Bower v Peate* (1876) 1 QBD 321, 326, 328–29.
[41] *Riverstone Meat Co Pty Ltd v Lancashire Shipping Co Ltd (The Muncaster Castle)* [1961] AC 807.
[42] *Black v Christchurch Finance Co* [1894] AC 48.

at the behest of but *on behalf of* the principal. Such contractors do not just supply services to the principal but act in the capacity of the principal. Accordingly, vicarious liability in defamation has been recognised in respect of an independent contractor engaged to canvass customers for an insurance company and who, contrary to the express terms of his engagement, falsely impugned the solvency of another insurance company in doing so.[43] While recognising that an independent contractor normally performs its duties as a principal rather than as a representative, the position was different where 'the function entrusted [to the contractor] is that of representing the person who requests its performance in a transaction with others, so that the very service to be performed consists in standing in his place and assuming to act in his right and not in an independent capacity.'[44] The independent contractor must, therefore, be engaged to speak or act on behalf of the principal in its relations with third parties and commit the tort in the course, and for the purpose, of executing its commission.[45] Accordingly, representative agency includes, for example, commercial agents, estate agents, and solicitors in their relations with third parties, when their duty is to act as the voice of the principal, but excludes, for example, carriers, couriers, and building contractors, who in the performance of their functions act on their own behalf in supplying services to the principal.

10.22   The Restatement also adopts the principle of representative agency, extending vicarious liability to 'a tort committed by an agent in dealing or communicating with a third party on or purportedly on behalf of the principal when actions taken by the agent with apparent authority constitute the tort or enable the tort to be committed.'[46] This formulation accommodates not only the making of statements on behalf of the principal in the negotiation of transactions but also, for example, the tortious abuse of legal process by a solicitor on behalf of a client and the tortious levying of distress by a bailiff on behalf of a landlord.[47]

10.23   English law has yet formally to recognise a general principle of representative agency as a basis for vicarious liability, although in one case Pollock CB acknowledged, albeit without further clarification, a 'great distinction' between a solicitor representing a client and a building contractor.[48] Authority, moreover, recognises isolated instances of agency-based vicarious liability for independent contractors with respect, notably, to solicitors giving instructions as to enforcement of judgment[49] and bailiffs levying distress.[50] A future recognition of a general

---

[43] *Colonial Mutual Life Assurance Society Ltd v Producers & Citizens Co-operative Assurance Co of Australia* [1931] HCA 53, (1931) 46 CLR 41.
[44] ibid, 48–49 (Dixon J).
[45] *Sweeney v Boylan Nominees Pty Ltd* [2006] HCA 19, (2006) 226 CLR 161, [22].
[46] Restatement, § 7.08.
[47] ibid, Comment (a).
[48] *Collett v Foster* (1857) 2 H & N 356, 359–60.
[49] *Jarmain v Hooper* (1843) 6 M & G 827; *Collett v Foster* (1857) 2 H & N 356.
[50] *Perring & Co v Emerson* [1906] 1 KB 1.

principle has, therefore, support in existing authority and would, it is suggested, be welcome.

Primary vs Vicarious Liability

10.24   From the third party's point of view, whether a principal's liability is primary or vicarious is irrelevant, unless an exemption clause draws a distinction between the two forms of liability. From the principal's perspective, however, the distinction may be material to its prospects of recouping the damages it has paid to the third party.

10.25   First, a principal is likely to seek recoupment through an insurance policy covering wrongdoing by its agents. Such a policy is apt to cover vicarious liability but not the principal's own primary liability engendered by acts of an agent attributed to the principal.[51] Secondly, a principal that is the victim of wrongdoing by its own agent cannot hold a third party liable for failing to warn the principal where the wrongdoing is attributed to the principal, so that the claim against the third party requires the principal to rely on its own wrongdoing.[52] Accordingly, a company that is the victim of fraud by its own controlling director cannot hold the company's auditors liable for failure to alert the company to the fraud.[53] Thirdly, a principal held vicariously liable for the tortious conduct of its agent is entitled to a complete indemnity from the agent. Conversely, where the conduct of an agent generates personal tortious liability on the part of both principal and agent, the third party may hold either or both liable as joint tortfeasors.[54] Where, in such a case, the third party subsequently recovers from either principal or agent in excess of that person's proportionate liability, such excess will be recoverable from the other by way of contribution[55] unless the claimant's illegal conduct is inimical to seeking legal recourse.

---

[51] *KR v Royal & Sun Alliance plc* [2006] EWCA Civ 1454, [2007] Lloyd's Rep IR 368.
[52] A principle expressed through the maxim *ex turpi causa non oritur actio.*
[53] *Stone & Rolls Ltd v Moore Stephens* [2009] UKHL 39, [2009] 1 AC 1391.
[54] *Jones v Manchester Corp* [1952] 2 QB 852, 869.
[55] Under the Civil Liability (Contribution) Act 1978.

11

Termination of Authority

11.1 This final chapter is concerned with the circumstances in which authority may be terminated, and the consequences of such termination. In the latter context especially, commercial agents benefit from significant mandatory rights not available at common law.

Termination of Actual Authority

11.2 Subject to the possibility of irrevocable authority, discussed below, actual authority may terminate in accordance with the terms of the agreement or by operation of law. It is worth noting immediately, however, that the third party may nevertheless remain able to invoke apparent authority.[1]

Termination in Accordance with the Agency Agreement

11.3 The duration of actual authority depends inevitably upon the interpretation of the agency agreement. Where the agreement addresses duration of authority explicitly, the issue of duration resolves into interpretation – or, assuming an absence of controversy as to meaning, simple application – of the relevant terms. In the absence of such express consideration, authority to accomplish a specific purpose will expire by obvious inference upon the accomplishment of that purpose[2] or, in the absence of success, upon the lapse of a reasonable time. Otherwise,[3] duration of authority involves a more holistic consideration of the agreement and its context in order to determine whether the authority is terminable at will, automatically upon the expiry of a reasonable time, at any time but upon giving

---

[1] See below, paras 11.26–11.28.

[2] *Blackburn v Scholes* (1810) 2 Camp 341 (broker employed to sell goods is devoid of office once the contract has been concluded and has no authority subsequently to vary the terms of the contract).

[3] Including where an agency is originally for a predetermined fixed term but after the expiry of that term is then tacitly prolonged by conduct for an indefinite period.

reasonable notice, or by (reasonable but shorter) notice but only after a reasonable duration for the agency.[4]

11.4   An agency will be terminable at will where by its nature it is more transient and does not call for dedicated initial investment of capital and expenditure. Estate agency and the relationship of solicitor and client constitute two examples.[5] Automatic termination at the end of the day of conferral was upheld on the basis of custom in respect of authority to sell goods in a certain market, the custom reflecting the high price-volatility of the market. A sale concluded two days later was, therefore, unauthorised.[6]

11.5   An agency where the agent is prohibited from acting for any competitors, that predictably accounts for a very high proportion of the agent's overall business, and that involves considerable initial investment of time and effort by the agent but without the promise of real reward for some time, naturally imports an entitlement to a reasonably lengthy minimum exploitation time. This has been achieved by implying a requirement of a lengthy notice period, on the facts of 12 months,[7] although an alternative analysis of an implied term of reasonable duration of the agency before (a shorter) notice of termination can be given has also been posited.[8] In contrast, however, in *Alpha Lettings Ltd v Neptune Research & Development Inc*,[9] a case involving an informal sole agency for the United Kingdom for a manufacturer of specialist valves used in medical and scientific equipment, the Court of Appeal held that a period of 12 months fell outside the range a trial judge could legitimately consider to be reasonable. On the facts, the range was between three and six months, with the Court of Appeal substituting a specific period of four months. The Court reasoned as follows.[10] First, a lengthy notice period was more consistent with a more formal agreement, which might in any event be expected to address duration of authority expressly. An informal relationship was innately less congruent with extended commitment. Secondly, the agent remained free to represent competitors of the principal, whereas a more formal agreement containing an express notice period might be expected to prohibit the agent from representing products that competed with those of the principal. Thirdly, the agency constituted only 20 per cent of the agent's overall turnover. Fourthly, in general, the length of the agency relationship (on the facts, 15 years) and normal, recurrent expenses are not especially relevant since the risk

---

[4] DCFR, art IV.D-6:102(1) applies a uniform principle of termination on reasonable notice to all cases of agency of indefinite duration and extends it also to cases of authority to accomplish a particular task on the basis that uncertainty of accomplishment can otherwise equate to indefinite duration (see Comment A).

[5] *Luxor (Eastbourne) Ltd v Cooper* [1941] AC 108; *Court v Berlin* [1897] 2 QB 396, 400–01.

[6] *Dickenson v Lilwall* (1815) 4 Camp 279.

[7] *Martin-Baker Aircraft Co Ltd v Canadian Flight Equipment Ltd* [1955] 2 QB 556. See also *Decro-Wall v Practitioners in Marketing Ltd* [1971] 1 WLR 361.

[8] *Alpha Lettings Ltd v Neptune Research & Development Inc* [2003] EWCA Civ 704, [36]–[37].

[9] [2003] EWCA Civ 704.

[10] ibid, [31]–[34], [38].

of termination is an ordinary business risk. However, the extent to which the agency requires an initial investment of capital and incurring of expenditure in the legitimate expectation of future return is relevant. Fifthly, the circumstances and nature of the termination on the facts are irrelevant to the interpretation of the contract: an otherwise reasonable notice period will not be rendered unreasonable by a malicious termination. However, practical difficulties in continuing to operate the agency relationship should an acrimonious breakdown ensue must militate against implying a lengthy notice period.[11]

11.6 The Commercial Agents Regulations contemplate that the contract may provide expressly for duration by reference to a fixed period. Nothing in the Regulations, however, confers on either party a right to know by a certain date whether the other is prepared to renew beyond the contractual expiry date. Where, nevertheless, one party informs the other that it is prepared to renew, an extrapolation from the general duty of good faith suggests that a change of mind must be communicated a reasonable time before the expiry date to enable alternative arrangements to be made, with failure to inform giving rise to potential liability in damages.[12]

11.7 Where the contract is for an indefinite period, the Regulations imply a right to terminate on notice and stipulate mandatory minimum notice periods expiring, subject to contrary agreement, at the end of a calendar month: one month for the first year of the contract, two months once the second year has commenced, and three months for an agency that exceeds two complete years.[13] A contract of initially fixed duration that continues to be performed after its expiry date is considered to be transformed into a contract of indefinite duration, with the initial fixed period included in the agency's duration for the purpose of determining the minimum mandatory notice period.[14] Accordingly, in the case of an agreement for an initial period of six months, renewable for further periods of six months, two months' notice of termination would be required if given at any time during the third or fourth period of six months, and three months' notice if given at any time after the fifth period had commenced.

11.8 There is no implied right to terminate fixed-term commercial agency agreements on notice. Nothing, however, in the Directive or the Regulations prohibits

---

[11] For a further example of determining what constitutes reasonable notice on the particular facts, taking into account the factors identified in *Alpha Lettings*, see *Jackson Distribution Ltd v Tum Yeto Inc* [2009] EWHC 982 (QB).

[12] See DCFR, art IV.E-2:301, which provides not only for an obligation to inform of a change of mind but that breach results in renewal for an indefinite period. Under the Regulations, however, remedies for breach are for national law, and arts 3(1) and 4(1) as implied contractual terms of English law would not support the imposition of an extended contractual relationship.

[13] Commercial Agents Regulations, reg 15(1)–(2), (4). Under the Directive (art 15(3)), Member States are permitted to stipulate either mandatory or default minimum notice periods of four, five, and six months for the fourth, fifth, and sixth years respectively of an agency contract. The United Kingdom declined to do so.

[14] ibid, regs 14, 15(5).

the incorporation of express rights to terminate on notice. Indeed, the prohibition of such provisions would only militate against entering into longer-term commitments, contrary to the spirit of enduring cooperation that the Directive encourages as manifested by the mutual duty of good faith.

Discharge of Agency Contract

11.9   Actual authority is terminated where the contract under which it is conferred is frustrated or rendered illegal in performance.[15] Authority will also be terminated by repudiatory breach on the part of either principal or agent if and when the breach is accepted by the other party.[16] These principles are unaffected by the Commercial Agents Regulations. By virtue of regulation 16, the Regulations do not affect 'any enactment or rule of law which provides for the immediate termination of the agency contract' on the basis of either total or partial non-performance of its contractual obligations by principal or agent, or the occurrence of exceptional circumstances. This qualification contemplates any provision of the applicable law justifying immediate termination of the contract independently of its terms. Accordingly, the otherwise mandatory minimum notice periods discussed above[17] are subject to the doctrines of repudiatory breach and frustration, but not to contractual termination rights or force majeure clauses.[18]

11.10   At common law, a party is permitted to justify an otherwise wrongful contractual termination on the basis of a repudiatory breach of which that party had been unaware, and which that party had therefore not invoked, at the time of the act of termination.[19] As a principle of termination for non-performance, it falls within regulation 16, which is not confined to termination rules based on known non-performance. On the contrary, the whole purpose of regulation 16 is to leave entirely to national law the circumstances in which a commercial agency contract shall be discharged by reason of breach or exceptional circumstances.

11.11   It is arguable that the spirit of joint enterprise and mutual commitment that underpins commercial agency is incompatible with contractual rights to terminate in the absence of an occurrence considered sufficient to sustain discharge at common law.[20] However, nothing in the Regulations expressly invalidates such a provision, and the remedies for breach of the mutual duty of good faith, as

---

[15] *Sovfracht (V/O) v Van Udens Scheepvaart en Agentuur Maatschappij (NV Gebr)* [1943] AC 203 (solicitor's authority to act for a client terminates immediately upon outbreak of war rendering the client an enemy alien).

[16] *Atlantic Underwriting Agencies Ltd v Compagnia di Assicurazione di Milano SpA* [1979] 2 Lloyd's Rep 240, 246-7. And see *Geys v Société Générale* [2012] UKSC 63, [2013] 2 WLR 50 (elective theory applicable to employment contracts).

[17] See para 11.7.

[18] *Crane v Sky In-Home Service Ltd* [2007] EWHC 66 (Ch), [2007] 1 CLC 389, [84].

[19] *Boston Deep Sea Fishing & Ice Co Ltd v Ansell* (1888) LR 39 Ch D 339.

[20] See DCFR, art IV.E-2:304.

granted by English law, may extend to compensation for the improper exercise of a contractual discretion but cannot extend to invalidating the existence or exercise of any such discretion entirely.

Revocation and Renunciation of Authority

11.12 As a conferral of actual authority empowering the agent to act on behalf of the principal in relations with third parties, agency may be considered as an alienation of a fundamental aspect of the principal's legal personality. Such loss of autonomy – and the concomitant investing of trust and confidence, reflected in the fiduciary nature of agency – demands unilateral revocability at will by the principal.[21] Revocation is effective on communication to the agent in such terms as to make its import clear,[22] albeit that its efficacy is qualified by the possibility of continued apparent authority.[23]

11.13 Revocation may not be lawful. It may constitute a repudiatory breach of contract by the principal, but it is nonetheless effective to terminate the relationship of principal and agent. The principal, therefore, enjoys a *power* of unilateral termination, even if, on the true construction of the contract, there is no such *right*. Revocability, therefore, precludes specific performance of the agency as a remedy for revocation in breach of contract. The principal is liable to compensate the agent for any remuneration lost by reason of an unlawful termination and to indemnify the agent for any liability thereby incurred by the agent to a third party.[24] By way of exception, moreover, where an agent acts pursuant to actual authority and thereby incurs a personal undertaking, the principal cannot deny the agent's authority to fulfil its undertaking, even upon terms that the principal will indemnify the agent against the consequences.[25]

11.14 Reciprocity might suggest a power of unilateral renunciation of authority by the agent,[26] but agency imports no loss of agent autonomy that would require it. It follows, therefore, that a renunciation must be accepted by the principal, subsuming lawful renunciation into rescission by mutual agreement.

---

[21] Restatement, § 3.10, Comment (b); *Temple Legal Protection Ltd v QBE Insurance (Europe) Ltd* [2009] EWCA Civ 453, [2009] 1 CLC 553, [49]. The consent basis of actual authority fails to explain why authority lacks the enduring binding power of contract: Restatement, ibid.

[22] *Heatons Transport (St Helens) Ltd v Transport & General Workers' Union* [1973] AC 15, 110.

[23] See below, paras 11.26-11.28.

[24] *Warlow v Harrison* (1859) 1 E & E 309, 317.

[25] *Chappell v Bray* (1860) 6 H & N 145; *Read v Anderson* (1884) 13 QBD 779; *Kuwait Petroleum Corp v I & D Oil Carriers Ltd (The Houda)* [1994] 2 Lloyd's Rep 541 at 558–59. The inhibition is properly analysed not as an irrevocable form of authority, but as a general principle that arises wherever one party (whether or not an agent) acts on the instructions of another: *The Houda*, 559.

[26] Restatement, § 3.10(1); DCFR, art IV.E-6.101(1).

Termination by Operation of Law

11.15   The demise of the principal, whether the death of a natural person or winding up of a company, terminates the actual authority of any agents of the principal.[27] Accordingly, a tenant's statutory notice of repairs served after the landlord's death was invalid when served on the person who acted as the landlord's agent prior to the latter's demise.[28] Similarly determinative at common law is the onset of mental incapacity of the principal.[29] In each case, actual authority terminates irrespective of whether the agent is aware of the terminating event. Consequently, any act subsequent to the terminating event within the erstwhile mandate and performed in the genuine and reasonable, but mistaken, belief of continuing authority is in truth unauthorised, engenders no entitlement to remuneration,[30] and renders the agent liable for breach of warranty of authority.[31]

11.16   The personal nature of agency, reflected in its fiduciary character and the principal's power of revocation of authority at will, imports that the demise of the agent also terminates actual authority.[32] Agency cannot, therefore, be the subject of inheritance. Actual authority will terminate similarly with the onset of mental incapacity in the agent.

Lasting Powers of Attorney

11.17   Faced with the challenges of infirmity or illness, individuals may choose to authorise a trusted person to exercise certain power on their behalf. Such a conferral of authority may be formalised in a power of attorney, but the execution of such an instrument does not alter the nature of the authority conferred, which remains subject to the common law principles governing termination. At some stage, therefore, progressive mental deterioration of the principal will frustrate the delegation of power since the incapacity of the principal will simultaneously terminate the delegate's authority. The introduction of a statutory form of agency, regulated now by the Mental Health Act 2005,[33] that can survive the onset of the

---

[27]   *Farrow v Wilson* (1869) LR 4 CP 744.

[28]   *Lodgepower Ltd v Taylor* [2004] EWCA Civ 1367, [2005] 1 EGLR 1.

[29]   *Drew v Nunn* (1879) LR 4 QBD 661.

[30]   *Campanari v Woodburn* (1854) 15 CB 400 (although, on the facts, expenses recoverable in unjust enrichment).

[31]   *Yonge v Toynbee* [1910] 1 KB 215. The Restatement rejects the imposition of liability in such circumstances on agents of principals who are natural people, providing that actual authority is terminated by the demise or onset of mental incapacity of such a principal only when the agent has notice thereof: §§ 3.07(2), 3.08(1). And see DCFR, art IV.D-7:102, providing that the principal's death does not itself terminate an agency relationship but rather permits either the principal's successors or the agent to terminate the agency by notice.

[32]   Restatement, § 3.07(1), (3). Likewise DCFR, art IV.D-7:103 (although a default rule only), which appears at odds with the broad acceptance in the Draft CFR of delegation.

[33]   Replacing the previous system of 'enduring powers of attorney' created under the Enduring Powers of Attorney Act 1985.

principal's mental incapacity serves to answer three concerns. First, through choice of delegate the principal remains able to exercise a measure of autonomy notwithstanding loss of capacity. Secondly, it facilitates efficient decision-making on behalf of a principal lacking capacity without the time and expense otherwise involved in drawing upon the finite resources of the Court of Protection. Thirdly, it avoids the difficulties faced by the agent of a principal of uncertain or variable capacity in knowing whether authority endures.

11.18   Under the 2005 Act, a principal can create a 'lasting power of attorney', expressly granting the donee of the power authority to act or take decisions on the principal's behalf once the principal succumbs to mental incapacity. The power may extend to either the principal's health and personal welfare or the principal's property and financial affairs, and may be general, restricted to specified matters, or contain specific exceptions to an otherwise general scope.[34] It must be created in the proper form and in favour of an eligible donee, and duly registered.[35]

11.19   In respect of property and financial affairs, a lasting power of attorney may be created to take effect before, and will then continue beyond, the onset of incapacity. In respect of health and personal welfare, however, the authority takes effect only where at the time of the relevant act or decision the principal is, or the donee reasonably believes the principal to be, personally incapable.[36] Acts performed or decisions taken pursuant to the power must be done or taken in the principal's best interests, involving the principal so far as reasonably practicable and taking into account whether the incapacity appears permanent or temporary, the principal's previously expressed and current wishes, and all values and other factors that would have influenced the principal in acting or deciding had the principal retained capacity.[37]

11.20   To create a lasting power of attorney, the principal must have reached the age of 18 and have capacity to create it.[38] This requires the principal to be able, as at the time of the decision-making process, to comprehend, use, weigh, and retain throughout that time all information material to the decision whether to create a lasting power of attorney, including the consequences of both creating or not creating such a power. It does not require the principal to have capacity at that time to do all the acts or take all the decisions that the donee will be authorised to do

---

[34] Mental Health Act 2005, s 9(1). The separation of health and personal welfare powers from property and financial affairs powers is not stipulated by the Act but is implemented by the designated forms that must be used to create a lasting power of attorney. Consideration is being given to introducing a single hybrid form that could be used to create a power that covers both matters or is restricted to either.

[35] ibid, ss 9(2)(a), (b), 10, sch 1.

[36] ibid, s 11(7).

[37] ibid, ss 1(5), 4, 9(4).

[38] ibid, s 9(2)(c).

and take. Capacity is, therefore, both time-specific and issue-specific.[39] Once created, a lasting power of attorney may be revoked by the principal at any time when the principal has capacity to do so.[40]

Irrevocable Authority

11.21   Occasionally, actual authority is not susceptible to unilateral revocation by the principal but may be withdrawn only with the consent of the agent or in limited exceptional circumstances.[41] Such 'irrevocable authority' arises at common law only where, for good consideration, the authority is conferred for the purpose of enhancing or protecting an interest of the agent independent of the grant of authority; in this sense, irrevocable authority is a 'power coupled with an interest'. Accordingly, authority was irrevocable where granted by a creditor to its debtor to sell land and apply the proceeds to the discharge of the outstanding debt,[42] and where granted by the underwriter of a share issue to a company promoter to subscribe shares in the company being launched.[43] The agents in each case had an interest independent of the authority conferred: the discharge of the debt, and the floating of the company. Authority is not, however, irrevocable where the only benefit to the agent lies in remuneration for its exercise; even a contractual right to earn remuneration generates no interest denying the principal the power to curtail the agent's opportunity to exercise that right.[44]

11.22   The grant of authority must be intended to benefit an interest of the agent.[45] A factual coincidence of authority and interest does not suffice, nor does the incurring of liability by the agent in response to the conferral of authority if the conferral was not made in contemplation thereof.[46] Assuming the authority is irrevocable, however, it follows from the intention to benefit the agent that the usual fiduciary duties attendant upon the conventional agency relationship do not apply. An irrevocable authority must, nevertheless, be performed in accordance with its own terms. It may, therefore, be withdrawn in the event of a repudiatory breach of the terms of its conferral or, where the irrevocable authority serves an ongoing relationship, a repudiatory breach of that relationship by the agent.[47]

---

[39]   ibid, s 3(1), (4). And see *Re Collis* (Court of Protection, 27 October 2010). Capacity is assumed unless the contrary is proved: ibid, s 1(2).

[40]   ibid, s 13(2).

[41]   See F Reynolds, 'When is an Agent's Authority Irrevocable?' in R Cranston (ed) *Making Commercial Law* (Oxford, Oxford University Press, 1997), ch 10.

[42]   *Gaussen v Morton* (1830) 10 B & C 731.

[43]   *Re Hannan's Empress Gold Mining & Development Co (Carmichael's Case)* [1896] 2 Ch 643.

[44]   *Temple Legal Protection Ltd v QBE Insurance (Europe) Ltd* [2009] EWCA Civ 453, [2009] 1 CLC 553, [50]–[52].

[45]   *Schindler v Brie* [2003] EWHC 1804 (Ch).

[46]   *Smart v Sandars* (1848) 5 CB 895, 917–18; *Frith v Frith* [1906] AC 254.

[47]   The suggested exceptions to irrevocability are derived from DCFR, art IV.D-1:105(2)(a).

11.23   At common law, authority is not rendered irrevocable merely by a statement to that effect. Absent the requisite interest, authority is revocable irrespective of the terms of conferral. Assuming the requisite interest is present, an express statement of irrevocability may confirm the necessary connection between authority and interest, but no such formal confirmation is required.

11.24   Irrevocable authority may also be conferred pursuant to section 4(1) of the Powers of Attorney Act 1971. The instrument must be given to secure either '(a) a proprietary interest of the donee of the power; or (b) the performance of an obligation owed to the donee'. These terms appear to reflect the extent of agent interest as recognised as capable of supporting irrevocable authority at common law.[48] However, the instrument must also be executed as a deed by the principal[49] and expressly state the conferred power to be irrevocable.[50] For so long as the interest or obligation remains undischarged, the power is then immune from revocation by the unilateral act of the principal and by the principal's death[51] or onset of mental incapacity.

11.25   Authority irrevocable at common law likewise survives any attempt at unilateral revocation. The impact of death or incapacity of the principal has yet to be considered but is likely to reflect, and may indeed be influenced by, the 1971 Act.[52]

Termination of Apparent Authority

11.26   The termination of actual authority does not necessarily also terminate apparent authority: it is important to distinguish the internal and external aspects of agency. An event that, as between principal and agent, ends the consent upon which is based an agent's actual authority may, as between principal and third party, leave uncontradicted the representation of authority upon which is based the agent's apparent authority.[53] Accordingly, a principal will be bound by a sales manager's continuing general apparent authority, notwithstanding a reduction in actual authority through the introduction of a requirement of the principal's prior approval for sales of the type in question.[54] Similarly, where actual authority is conferred and apparent authority created by appointment to a representational

---

[48] Although the statute requires identity of donee of power and person with requisite interest, while the common law probably does not (P Watts and F Reynolds (eds), *Bowstead and Reynolds on Agency*, 19th edn (London, Sweet& Maxwell, 2010) para 10-007).

[49] Powers of Attorney Act 1971, s 1(1).

[50] ibid, s 4(1); *Schindler v Brie* [2003] EWHC 1804 (Ch), [22].

[51] Or winding-up or dissolution in the case of a corporate principal.

[52] Similarly Restatement, § 3.13(2).

[53] A principle adopted also by the Powers of Attorney Act 1971: see s 5(2).

[54] *Rockland Industries Inc v Amerada Minerals Corp of Canada Ltd* (1980) 108 DLR (3d) 513.

position, the complete cessation of actual authority through departure, enforced or voluntary, of the agent from that position does not prejudice continuing apparent authority with respect to a third party unaware of that departure.[55]

11.27   Apparent authority may survive likewise where actual authority is terminated through the onset of mental incapacity in the principal,[56] and logically also in the case of the principal's demise, with apparent authority binding the principal's estate.[57]

11.28   Apparent authority will clearly be terminated by notice to the third party. Where authority is terminated by operation of law, it suffices to have knowledge of the event that triggers termination even if the third party is unaware of the consequence in law.[58] Where, however, apparent authority is based upon a representation to a wide audience, notification to all representees may be impractical. Consequently, the representation upon which apparent authority is based may be withdrawn by the taking of reasonable steps to publicise its revocation. The reluctance of the English courts to import constructive notice into apparent authority is confined to the question of reliance upon a representation[59] and does not extend to the objectively assessed question of whether a representation has been made in the first place or remains in place. Accordingly, apparent authority may be terminated – or, indeed, limited in time or scope – by a communication that parallels in all material respects the original representation.[60]

Financial Reparation on Termination of Authority (1): at Common Law

11.29   Where the principal revokes authority unlawfully, the agent's remedies lie in damages for breach of contract; a contract of agency is not specifically enforceable,[61] nor, where a principal fails to provide adequate notice of termination in accordance with regulation 15, is the contract automatically continued until the earliest lawful termination date.[62] The measure of damages is assessed, in

---

[55] *Summers v Salomon* (1857) 7 E & B 879; *SEB Trygg Liv Holding AB v Manches* [2005] EWCA Civ 1237, [2006] 1 WLR 2276.

[56] *Drew v Nunn* (1879) 4 QBD 661. 'Insanity is not a privilege, but a misfortune which must not be allowed to injure innocent persons': ibid 668 (Bramwell LJ).

[57] ibid, 668; Restatement, § 3.11, Comment (b).

[58] Powers of Attorney Act 1971, s 5(5).

[59] See above, para 4.12.

[60] Compare *Shuey v US* 92 US 73 (1875) (revocation of offer to the world at large). In this sense, it suffices that the third party knows or ought to know of the termination or limitation of the represented authority: PECL, art 3.209(1); PICC, art 2.2.10(1); DCFR, art II-6:112(1); Restatement, § 3.11(2).

[61] See above, para 11.13.

[62] *Roy v MR Pearlman Ltd* [1999] 2 CMLR 1155, [23].

accordance with general contract law, by reference to the loss sustained by reason of the breach.[63] In particular, it must be asked whether the agent had any right to remuneration and, if so, for how long. On the first point, agents often have opportunities to earn remuneration but not contractual rights to do so.[64] With respect to duration, the agent will be entitled to compensation, if any, only on the basis of the shortest period for which the principal was legally obliged to maintain the agency.

Financial Reparation on Termination of Authority (2): Under the Commercial Agents Regulations

11.30 The joint enterprise model of commercial agency imports that, upon termination of the agency, the agent is entitled to financial acknowledgment of its contribution towards the business asset created or enhanced. Termination of the agency may unjustly expropriate in favour of the principal the benefit of the agent's endeavours, simultaneously forfeiting the agent's opportunity to reap its due rewards and amortise its expenses. The legislation is designed to ensure fair recompense to the agent for loss of the agency:

> The overall purpose of the Council Directive was not only to achieve harmonisation of the legal relationship of commercial agents and principals throughout the Community but also to remedy the perceived vulnerability and insecurity of commercial agents vis-à-vis their principals particularly on termination. It might take years for an agency to be developed to a state of profitability. If then terminated the commercial agent loses his livelihood. The resources and effort he has put into the development of a profitable agency are lost to him whereas the principal gains a valuable asset.[65]

Commercial Agents' Entitlement to Compensation or Indemnity

11.31 By virtue of regulation 17(1), a commercial agent is entitled to either 'compensation' in accordance with regulation 17(6)–(7) or an 'indemnity' in accordance with regulation 17(3)–(5). The alternatives of compensation and indemnity reflect the differing approaches of civil law systems. Compensation represents the traditional French approach, while the indemnity option reflects German law. Unless the agency contract provides otherwise, the agent's entitlement is to compensation

---

[63] See, for example, *Bell Electric Ltd v Aweco Appliance Systems GmbH & Co* [2002] EWHC 872 (QB).

[64] See above, para 8.17 et seq.

[65] *Ingmar GB Ltd v Eaton Leonard Inc* [2001] CLC 1825, [33] (Morland J). Likewise *Tigana v Decoro Ltd* [2003] EWHC 23 (QB), [2003] ECC 23, [77]; *Lonsdale v Howard & Hallam* [2007] UKHL 32, [2007] 1 WLR 2055, [9].

rather than an indemnity.[66] If the contract purports to exclude both compensation and indemnity (an exclusion that would be invalid[67]), it does not 'otherwise provide' so that compensation is payable.[68]

11.32   The compensation or indemnity is always payable except in the circumstances stipulated in regulation 18,[69] or unless the agent fails to notify the principal within one year of termination of the agency of an intention to pursue the financial entitlement.[70] In the absence of a formal termination notice stipulating a clear termination date, the question is when on the facts the agent ceased to have authority not just to negotiate or negotiate and conclude contracts on behalf of the principal but also to liaise with customers on behalf of the principal in connection with orders.[71]

11.33   Regulations 17 and 18 are mandatory in nature; the parties cannot derogate therefrom to the detriment of the commercial agent before the agency contract expires.[72] However, an express term that affords the principal the right to reduce the agent's territory or range of potential customers is not invalid as a prohibited derogation.[73] Detriment is judged at the time the derogation is agreed. Derogation is permissible only if there is no possibility that the derogation will prove detrimental to the agent at the end of the contract: the agreed scheme must always, under any circumstances, produce a figure at least equal to that produced under the Regulations. A derogation that might produce a lower figure is invalid unless it provides for the Regulations to continue to apply if they favour the agent.[74]

'Termination of the Agency Contract'

11.34   The right to compensation or an indemnity is triggered by 'termination of the agency contract'.[75] This does not connote unlawful termination. The purpose of the Regulations is not to compensate the agent for loss caused by a wrongful act of the principal. Nothing in the Regulations supports such a qualification; on the

---

[66] Commercial Agents Regulations, reg 17(2).

[67] Below, para 11.33.

[68] *Crane v Sky In-Home Service Ltd* [2007] EWHC 66 (Ch), [2007] 1 CLC 389, [93].

[69] See below, para 11.47 et seq.

[70] Commercial Agents Regulations, reg 17(9). No particular formality requirements are imposed. It suffices that the communication 'conveys to the objectively reasonable reader that the agent intends to pursue claims under reg 17': *Hackett v Advanced Medical Computer Systems Ltd* [1999] CLC 160, 163 (HHJ McGonigal). There is no requirement for the communication to state that the entitlement is in fact being pursued or specify whether the claimed entitlement is to an indemnity or compensation: ibid.

[71] *Claramoda Ltd v Zoomphase Ltd* [2009] EWHC 2857 (Comm), [2010] ECC 1, [43].

[72] Commercial Agents Regulations, reg 19. And see the discussion of *Ingmar GB Ltd v Eaton Leonard Technologies Inc* [2000] ECR I-9305, above, para 2.10 et seq.

[73] *Vick v Vogle-Gapes* [2006] EWHC 1665 (TCC), [95].

[74] Case C-465/04 *Honyvem Informazioni Commerciali Srl v Mariella De Zotti* [2006] ECR I-02789.

[75] Commercial Agents Regulations, reg 17(1).

contrary, compensation or an indemnity is expressly payable in the event of termination because of the commercial agent's demise.[76] The purpose of the Regulations is to compensate the agent simply for the fact of loss of the agency in the light of the agent's contribution towards its value. 'Termination', accordingly, carries a broad meaning, including expiry of the agency in accordance with its own express terms as to duration.[77] It also includes closure by the principal of a healthy business, even if unaccompanied by any formal termination of the agency.[78]

11.35   What must be terminated, according to the wording of the Regulations, is 'the agency contract'. This, however, must be understood as referring to the agency relationship rather than the contract that happens to be in force between principal and agent at the date of termination. Accordingly, where an agent is engaged on a series of contracts, one following immediately on the other, regulation 17 is triggered not by the expiry of each agency contract but by the fact that the overall agency ultimately comes to an end, and, when it does, account should be taken of the agent's contribution throughout the entirety of the agency and not just during the final contract.[79]

Indemnity

11.36   The calculation of an indemnity is a three-stage process.[80] First, relevant benefits accruing to the principal must be quantified. These are the substantial benefits the principal continues to derive from new customers introduced by the agent and any significant increase in business of pre-existing customers in respect of which the agent's intervention was at least instrumental.[81] The valuation will reflect any diminution in business following the departure of the agent. There is no time limit to the ongoing benefits to be taken into account. Secondly, the valuation must then be moderated to produce a figure that is equitable in all the circumstances. Particular consideration should be given to the commission the agent would have earned had the agency continued,[82] taking into account both expenses that would have been incurred to earn the commission and the fact that the indemnity may produce accelerated receipt.[83] The concept of mitigation is,

---

[76] ibid, reg 17(8).

[77] *Tigana v Decoro Ltd* [2003] EWHC 23 (QB), [2003] ECC 23; approved obiter *Light v Ty Europe Ltd* [2003] EWCA Civ 1238, [31]–[36], [46]; [2004] 1 Lloyd's Rep 693.

[78] *King v T Tunnock Ltd* [2000] EuLR 531 (Court of Session, Inner House).

[79] *Moore v Piretta PTA Ltd* [1999] 1 All ER 174, 180.

[80] Case C-348/07 *Semen v Deutsche Tamoil GmbH* [2009] 3 CMLR 12 [19]; *Moore v Piretta PTA Ltd* [1999] 1 All ER 174.

[81] Commercial Agents Regulations, reg 17(3)(a); *Moore v Piretta PTA Ltd* [1999] 1 All ER 174, 180. Where the principal is a member of a corporate group, benefits accruing to other group members are disregarded: Case C-348/07 *Semen v Deutsche Tamoil GmbH* [2009] 3 CMLR 12.

[82] Although care must be taken to avoid double recovery resulting from factoring into quantification of an indemnity under reg 17 commission on post-termination transactions recoverable under reg 8 (discussed above, para 8.38 et seq).

[83] Commercial Agents Regulations, reg 17(3)(b).

however, irrelevant. Designed to reward the agent's success in developing the goodwill in the principal's business, the indemnity affords the agent a share in the business corresponding to the contractually agreed percentage commission, unless that percentage 'is grossly disproportionate either way to the efforts of the agent so as to produce an inequitable result'.[84] Thirdly, the amount of the indemnity is subject to a ceiling figure, namely the commercial agent's average annual remuneration calculated over a five-year period or such lesser period as the contract has lasted.[85]

11.37   The European Court of Justice has accordingly held incompatible with the Directive the German method of calculation whereby the indemnity was limited to the lower of (1) the benefits continued to be derived by the principal, (2) the agent's lost commission, and (3) whatever is equitable. On the facts, the principal continued to enjoy substantial benefits in excess of the value of the agent's lost commission. The Directive, however, did not recognise the possibility of according any such element status as an arbitrary cap on the indemnity payable.[86]

11.38   Applying the three-stage approach outlined above, in one case[87] the agent's share in the two and three-quarter years following termination of the value of the business brought in by him (ie, his gross commission on the terms of the contract) was about £113,000. From that, the judge deducted (1) £5,000 representing existing customers where there was no significant increase in volume of business attributable to the agent; (2) £8,000 in respect of expenses that would have been incurred in earning commission; and (3) £8,000 for accelerated receipt. The result, after two stages, was an indemnity of £92,000. The ceiling figure was, however, £64,526.33. That was, therefore, the sum awarded.

11.39   The award of an indemnity does not prevent the agent from also suing for damages in accordance with ordinary principles to the extent that additional loss has been sustained.[88]

Compensation

11.40   Assuming the contract does not provide for payment of an indemnity, termination entitles the agent to 'compensation for the damage he suffers as a

---

[84] *Moore v Piretta PTA Ltd* [1999] 1 All ER 174, 182 (John Mitting QC).
[85] Commercial Agents Regulations, reg 17(4). The reference to remuneration comprehends the aggregate of all forms of income, not just commission.
[86] Case C-348/07 *Semen v Deutsche Tamoil GmbH* [2009] 3 CMLR 12. The Directive's guidance on calculation of an indemnity is, nevertheless, limited, affording Member States a measure of discretion, especially with respect to what is equitable: Case C-465/04 *Honeyvem Informazioni Commerciali Srl v Mariella De Zotti* [2006] ECR I-02879. For the Italian approach, see the judgment in *Honeyvem*.
[87] *Moore v Piretta PTA Ltd* [1999] 1 All ER 174.
[88] Commercial Agents Regulations, reg 17(5).

result of the termination of his relations with his principal.'[89] Some guidance is provided as to the damage contemplated by the Regulations in the form of two, non-exhaustive examples of the sort of terminations that would give rise to such damage.[90] Otherwise, however, the method of quantification of the damage sustained is not harmonised but left to the discretion of Member States. The examples are of terminations that occur in either or both of two circumstances, namely:

> circumstances which –
>
> (a) deprive the commercial agent of the commission which proper performance of the agency contract[91] would have procured for him whilst providing his principal with substantial benefits linked to the activities of the commercial agent; or
> (b) have not enabled the commercial agent to amortize the costs and expenses that he had incurred in the performance of the agency contract on the advice of his principal.[92]

11.41   These examples together with the breadth of the concept of termination make it clear that 'damage' must be understood not as loss caused by wrong but rather as loss of the benefit of the agency. An agent who has invested time and effort in developing the agency only to see the rewards fairly expected under the terms of the agency contract taken away by its termination is entitled to be bought out of the agency. The concern is both to prevent unjust enrichment of the principal and also to compensate the agent for loss of the agency. Quantification of compensation, therefore, is not to be equated with assessment of damages for breach of contract but involves assessing the value of the asset lost to the agent. Issues such as mitigation of loss by the agent are irrelevant.[93]

11.42   The reference to 'substantial benefits' in the context of compensation does not import a precondition to an entitlement to compensation that the principal has already substantially benefited from the agent's activities. That may be relevant, but it is not essential. The substantial benefits may be accrued or anticipated, or indeed both.[94]

11.43   The leading authority on the quantification of compensation in English law is *Lonsdale v Howard & Hallam*.[95] The defendant-principal's shoe manufacturing business was in serious decline when notice was given terminating the claimant's agency. The claimant sought compensation based on two years' gross commission calculated by reference to the average of the last three years of the

---

[89] ibid, reg 17(6).
[90] For confirmation of the non-exhaustive nature of the guidance, see *King v T Tunnock Ltd* [2000] EuLR 531; *Tigana Ltd v Decoro Ltd* [2003] EWHC 23 (QB), [2003] ECC 23, [96].
[91] Including the principal not illegitimately minimising the volume of business: see above, para 7.5.
[92] Commercial Agents Regulations, reg 17(7).
[93] *Lonsdale v Howard & Hallam* [2006] EWCA Civ 63, [2006] 1 WLR 1281, [28], [30].
[94] *PJ Pipe & Valve Co Ltd v Audco India Ltd* [2005] EWHC 1904 (QB), [164]. Contrast the purely prospective focus of the reference to substantial benefits in the context of an indemnity: above, para 11.36.
[95] *Lonsdale v Howard & Hallam* [2007] UKHL 32, [2007] 1 WLR 2055.

agency, in accordance with the general approach to quantification of compensation adopted in French law, from which the concept of compensation was derived. On the facts, this produced compensation of about £24,000. The claim failed.

11.44 The House of Lords held that compensation under the Regulations is for damage suffered as a result of termination of the agent's relations with the principal. The agent has lost a share in the goodwill of the business that the agent has helped to generate, and receives compensation for the loss sustained by being deprived of the opportunity to exploit that business goodwill and receive remuneration in accordance with the agency contract. That future income stream is valued by assuming a sale of the agency, ignoring any contractual restrictions on sale or continuation of the agency[96] but otherwise on the basis of the true facts, including any factors that would enhance or diminish the future prospects of the agency and thereby the price it could be expected to generate.[97]

11.45 On the facts, the trial judge[98] had described the agency as 'producing a modest and falling income in a steadily deteriorating environment'. Absent any 'evidence that anyone would have paid anything to buy it', he was 'strongly tempted to find that no damage has been established'. Since, however, that conclusion might be 'a little over rigorous given that the defendant has already made a payment', he concluded that an appropriate figure for compensation was £5,000. The House of Lords upheld this approach and assessment, and indeed would have upheld a simple dismissal of the claim.[99]

11.46 The French approach to quantification of compensation was, accordingly, rejected as a matter of English law for agencies in England. The Directive does not harmonise the method of quantification, and commercial agencies are more readily transferred in France where the standard compensation figure reflects the generally accepted market value and, therefore, the agent's true loss, absent particular circumstances, in that different market.[100]

---

[96] The contractual right of a principal to refuse consent to assignment of the agency or to truncate its duration by giving notice of termination might eradicate or severely prejudice the sale potential of the agency but would not deny the ongoing benefit to the principal of the agent's contribution to the business, and must be ignored for the purposes of calculating compensation: [2006] EWCA Civ 63, [2006] 1 WLR 1281, [48]; [2007] UKHL 32, [2007] 1 WLR 2055, [12]. Otherwise, the legislative intention to confer significant financial benefits on commercial agents could easily be frustrated by the insertion of appropriate contractual rights. This was subsequently overlooked in *McQuillan v McCormick* [2010] EWHC 1112 (QB), [2011] ECC 18, [165]–[167].

[97] *Lonsdale v Howard & Hallam* [2007] UKHL 32, [2007] 1 WLR 2055, [8]–[13]. This market price approach is supported by the fact that an agent has no entitlement to any termination recompense where it has transferred the agency to another, because recompense has already been received through the transfer price: see below, para 11.56.

[98] Ibid, [33] Judge Harris QC, quoted by Lord Hoffmann.

[99] ibid, [34].

[100] ibid, [17]–[18].

When no Entitlement to Compensation or Indemnity

11.47   Regulation 18 identifies three circumstances when regulation 17 is dis-applied so that no indemnity or compensation is payable: namely, termination by reason of agent default, termination by the agent in certain circumstances, and assignment by the commercial agent.

Agent Default

11.48   First, by virtue of regulation 18(a), no termination recompense is payable where 'the principal has terminated the agency contract because of default attribut-able to the commercial agent which would justify immediate termination of the agency contract pursuant to Regulation 16'.[101] This translates into acceptance by the principal of a repudiatory breach by the agent; termination recompense is denied since otherwise the agent would profit from the agent's own wrongdoing. This is, however, contestable in terms of substantive merits and concept. With respect to the merits, regulation 18(a) imposes a penalty of forfeiture of all termination rec-ompense without consideration of the extent of the prejudice, if any, to the benefits that the principal would otherwise have derived from agent's services. Any such prejudice, moreover, will be reflected in the quantification of the regulation 17 rec-ompense. Conceptually, regulation 18(a) identifies termination recompense as the reward for fulfilment of the principal's expectation interest in due performance of the agency contract. Regulation 17, however, is designed to indemnify or compen-sate the agent for loss of the goodwill attaching to the business that it has generated or enhanced through its endeavours and that the principal will continue to enjoy in its entirety. This benefit to the principal will ensue regardless of how the agency terminates: 'goodwill has its own value which must be differentiated from the expectation interest under the contract.'[102]

11.49   Regulation 18(a) does not apply where a fixed-term agency agreement is permitted to expire by effluxion of time. No intervention of the principal is involved; the contract expires by virtue of its own terms. Also expiry is not attrib-utable to any default of the agent. Termination recompense accordingly remains payable. Similarly, an unaccepted repudiation of itself famously has no impact upon the contract,[103] and a consequential refusal by the principal to renew the

---

[101] For discussion of reg 16, see above, paras 11.9–11.10. Strictly speaking, termination does not occur 'pursuant to', but rather 'as contemplated by' reg 16, as that provision confers no termination rights but merely leaves discharge for breach to national law: *Bell Electric Ltd v Aweco Appliance Systems GmbH & Co* [2002] EWHC 872 (QB), [54].

[102] DCFR, art IV.E-2:305, Comment A.

[103] *Howard v Pickford Tool Co Ltd* [1951] 1 KB 417, 421 (Asquith LJ: 'a thing writ in water'). A prin-cipal would obviously be well advised to accept a repudiatory breach where it has the chance: *Light v Ty Europe Ltd* [2003] EWCA Civ 1238, [2004] 1 Lloyd's Rep 693, [46].

agency is a refusal to conclude a new contract and cannot be characterised as a termination of the preceding broken contract.[104]

11.50 Should an agent commit more than one breach, termination recompense will be denied only if at least one breach constitutes a repudiation of the contract and the principal in terminating the agency relies on at least one such breach.[105]

11.51 As discussed above, the common law principle permitting justification of an otherwise wrongful contractual termination on a ground not invoked at the time of the act of termination falls within regulation 16.[106] A literal reading of regulation 18(a), however, would appear to require the act of termination to be the principal's response to a justifying default by the agent: 'terminated . . . because of default . . . which would justify immediate termination'. Nevertheless, regulation 18(b)(i), which is the counterpart to regulation 18(a) addressing termination by the agent where the principal repudiates the contract, contains no such causal requirement, and it has been held that the two provisions 'ought to be seen as the reverse sides of the same coin'.[107] It is suggested, therefore, that the scope of regulation 18(a) is controlled by the reference to regulation 16 and that the phrase 'because of' should be understood as meaning 'where as an issue of fact there exists'.[108]

Agent Termination

11.52 Secondly, by virtue of regulation 18(b), no termination recompense is payable where

> the commercial agent has himself terminated the agency contract, unless such termination is justified –
>
> (i) by circumstances attributable to the principal, or
> (ii) on grounds of age, infirmity or illness of the commercial agent in consequence of which he cannot reasonably be required to continue his activities.

11.53 Accordingly, the agent cannot trigger payment of termination recompense through the agent's own termination of the contract, even though lawful, except in two situations. As with regulation 18(a), this rule of forfeiture is contestable as potentially punitive and conceptually misconceived.[109]

11.54 Notwithstanding differences in wording, regulation 18(b)(i) is to be understood as the counterpart to regulation 18(a): termination recompense remains

---

[104] *Cooper v Pure Fishing (UK) Ltd* [2003] EWCA Civ 375, [2004] 2 Lloyd's Rep 518.
[105] *Nigel Fryer Joinery Services Ltd v Ian Firth Hardware Ltd* [2008] 2 Lloyd's Rep 108, [22].
[106] Above, para 11.10.
[107] *Bell Electric Ltd v Aweco Appliance Systems GmbH & Co* [2002] EWHC 872 (QB), [54] (Elias J).
[108] Authority is sparse: *Cureton v Mark Insulations Ltd* [2006] EWHC 2279 (Ch), [58] (obiter in favour of the common law rule applying).
[109] See above, para 11.48.

payable notwithstanding termination by the agent where the agent's termination act consists of the acceptance of a repudiatory breach by the principal. The reference to 'circumstances attributable to the principal' again relates back to regulation 16 and imports national law; there is no concept of justified termination under the Regulations distinct from the applicable national law. Accordingly, affirmation by the agent in response to a repudiatory breach by the principal will preclude reliance on regulation 18(b)(i) and incur forfeiture of the right to termination recompense under regulation 17.[110]

11.55 As regards the life circumstances exception, the references to age, infirmity, and illness of the commercial agent are to be understood disjunctively so that they can each constitute an independent factor rendering it unreasonable for the principal to oppose termination by the agent. Accordingly, reasonable termination by the agent on the sole ground of age does not disentitle the agent from claiming termination recompense, notwithstanding the absence of any age-related physically or mentally disabling wear and tear. While the precise age that renders termination reasonable is ultimately one of fact, it will usually be difficult to oppose the normal retirement age. Accordingly, a healthy and active agent in United Kingdom has been held entitled to retire and claim compensation on reaching the then usual general retirement age of 65.[111]

Agent Assignment

11.56 Thirdly, by virtue of regulation 18(c), no termination recompense is payable under regulation 17 where, with the principal's consent, the agent assigns its rights and duties under the agency contract to another. This forfeiture rule is uncontroversial: the value of the agent's share in the goodwill of the business will be reflected in the price attached to the assignment so that recompense under regulation 17 would constitute double recovery. Consistently with this rationale, there is an 'assignment' for the purposes of regulation 18(c) whenever the existing agent transfers the agency to a new agent irrespective of the characterisation of the transaction for the purposes of national law, for example as a novation.[112]

---

[110] *Bell Electric Ltd v Aweco Appliance Systems GmbH & Co* [2002] EWHC 872 (QB); *Vick v Vogle-Gapes Ltd* [2006] EWHC 1665 (TCC), [112]–[113].

[111] *Abbott v Condici* [2005] 2 Lloyd's Rep 450, [47].

[112] *Rossetti Marketing Ltd v Diamond Sofa Co Ltd* [2012] EWCA Civ 1021, [2013] 1 All ER (Comm) 308, [55].

INDEX